THE INN AT THE TOP

The delightful tale of a young couple who in the late 1970s, on impulse became the new landlords of the most remote, bleak and lonely pub – The Tan Hill Inn – located in the bleak landscape of the Yorkshire Dales. They had no experience of the licensed trade or running a pub, no knowledge of farming and a complete inability to understand the dialect of the sheep farmers who were the local customers. Eager, well-meaning, but terminally incompetent, our two heroes embark on a disaster-strewn career that somehow also turned into a lifelong love affair with the Dales.

THE INN AT THE TOP

THE INN AT THE TOP

by

Neil Hanson

Magna Large Print Books
Long Preston, North Yorkshire,
BD23 4ND, England.

British Library Cataloguing in Publication Data.

Hanson, Neil
    The inn at the top.

        A catalogue record of this book is
        available from the British Library

        ISBN   978-0-7505-3895-4

First published in Great Britain in 2013 by
Michael O'Mara Books Limited

Cover illustration by arrangement with Michael O'Mara Books Ltd.

The moral right of the author has been asserted

Published in Large Print 2014 by arrangement with
Michael O'Mara Books Ltd.

Magna Large Print is an imprint of Library Magna Books Ltd.

Printed and bound in Great Britain by
T.J. (International) Ltd., Cornwall, PL28 8RW

Contents

INTRODUCTION

by Gervase Phinn

The only country in the world that boasts the country inn is Great Britain. There are strings of Irish-themed pubs with images of garish green leprechauns and giant shamrocks, and even 'traditional' British pubs which serve fish and chips and real ale, but the only country where one can find the authentic country inn is in the United Kingdom and surely the very best are situated in 'God's own country': Yorkshire.

When we were courting back in the 1970s, my future wife Christine (a Yorkshire lass from Shipley) and I would drive up into the Dales to a small country inn which had changed little since the eighteenth century. The outside looked like a run-down private dwelling, with its bleached limestone walls, sagging roof of odd-shaped slates, many of which needed replacing, its high weathered eaves and heavy door with flaking paint. Below the door was a large, faded wooden sign that read: 'Purveyors of fine ales, liquor and porter since 1714.'

The public bar was dim and smoky; reeking of beer and tobacco, and was as hot as a sauna. There were four ancient and sticky-topped trestle-style tables, a selection of rickety, hard, wooden chairs, a dusty inglenook and a grey, flagged and heavily stained floor. The walls were bare save for a few oddments: a pair of old bellows, a tarnished warming pan, various rusty farm implements, including a vicious-looking man trap and a couple of antique shotguns. There had been no attempt to provide any kind of physical comfort for the customers. Ramblers would enter and ask if food was served, to be told bluntly by the landlord, 'No, an' close t'door on yer way out.' The other room, euphemistically called 'The Lounge', had a threadbare, red, patterned carpet and a further selection of dusty local memorabilia on the walls, a few round, plastic-topped tables, a couple of Windsor chairs and an assortment of armchairs, wing chairs and stools. It was a place of real character.

We made a nostalgic visit to the inn some years later to find it had been transformed into a modern pub in the worst sense of the word. It was bright, brash and noisy with game machines, karaoke nights and pub quizzes, and was sedulously avoided by the locals and frequented by the young.

Memories of that unique country inn that Christine and I loved so much came back to me recently when I read the manuscript of *The Inn at the Top*. The author, Neil Hanson, and his wife, Sue, on an impulse, became managers of 'the most lonely and remote pub in England', a dilapidated country inn set in 'a wild and windswept ocean of peat bog and heather moorland that stretched away unbroken as far as the eye could see'. It was an article in the newspaper that caught their attention. At first they considered it a preposterous idea but they applied and a week later they found themselves driving up an endless ribbon of a road that twisted through bleak fells for the interview. Three weeks later they were ensconced behind the bar.

This massively readable account of how they tried to make this cold, wet, windy, rat-infested ruin habitable, win over the regulars and attract new custom is full of rich anecdote, wry and often touching observations, amusing characters, witty dialogue and fascinating information. It is said that nothing is ever achieved in this life unless there is some element of risk, that the person who risks nothing does nothing. Neil and Sue certainly took a great risk in taking on the management of the 'Inn at the Top'. The journey they took was well worth making and Neil Hanson's account is well worth reading.

AUTHOR'S NOTE

The Inn at the Top is based on my experiences over the course of a year while running a pub in 'the back of beyond' in the Yorkshire Dales in the late 1970s. Although all the stories and characters featured in the book have their roots in my time at the inn, all the names, places, occupations, locations and other identifying features have been changed to protect the innocent – and the guilty alike!

Neil Hanson

CHAPTER 1

Even Heathcliff Wouldn't Live Up Here

Once upon a time, not so long ago and not so far away, a young man and his wife were living in a state of contented idleness in a tiny Yorkshire hill village on the northern fringes of the Peak District; I know because I was that young man. In that year of our Lord 1978, the 'Winter of Discontent' was just a lowering cloud on the horizon, Jim Callaghan was prime minister, the Yorkshire Ripper was still at large, and the leader of the opposition was the 'Grantham Ripper', Margaret Thatcher, also known as 'the Iron Lady' and 'Attila the Hen'.

It was a time when pub licensing laws were strict and strictly enforced, shops shut on Saturday lunchtime and didn't reopen until Monday morning, olive oil was only obtainable from chemists and was used not for culinary purposes but for dissolving earwax, and the only spices in general use were salt and pepper. Even when served in cafes and coffee bars, coffee was almost always instant. Made with a teaspoonful of brown powder from a catering-size tin behind the counter, it neither smelt nor tasted – or indeed looked – remotely like the real thing. If you were doubly unlucky, you might be offered Camp Coffee instead, which, disappointingly, had nothing to do with flamboyant costumes and effete behaviour, but rather was a brand name for a particularly disgusting thick brown liquid made from chicory, vast quantities of sugar and a trace element of 'coffee essence'.

If you wanted to go out for a meal and didn't live in London, the chances are that you'd either be eating in a Wimpy Bar – the first British burger chain, eventually to be swept away by a tide of Big Macs – or a hotel dining room (to call them restaurants would be to give them a kudos they usually didn't deserve). Dinner, often still announced by the beating of a gong in the hallway, would start at 6.30 or 7p.m. and the last diners would probably be seated no later than 8.

If you were offered wine it would probably be Mateus Rosé or Blue Nun, and your gourmet meal out would almost invariably consist of soup, roast meat and overcooked vegetables – I still wake up screaming at the thought of the Brussels sprouts I was once served that were so overcooked the waiter had to shake the serving spoon to dislodge them – followed by ice cream or a steamed pudding with custard. If you were really sophisticated you might opt instead for a Berni Inn, where you could feast on prawn cocktail, steak and chips, and Black Forest gateau, followed by coffee (see previous comments) and After Eight mints.

In those far-off days, mobile phones had just been invented and were a hernia-inducing combination of a normal telephone handset on top of a battery the size and weight of a car battery, and the most sophisticated computer game on the market was Space Invaders. Even that would have seemed like science fiction to many of the inhabitants of 'The Dale': the most beautiful, remote and self-contained of all the Yorkshire Dales. It was a place where the pace of life had altered little in centuries. Men still ruled the roost while women did most of the work and sheep outnumbered both of them by a factor of ten. The Dale was strong on tradition, hard work and self-reliance, and largely indifferent to the fads and fashions of the world beyond the towering valley walls.

Near the head of the Dale, a sharp right turn led to a steep, twisting side road that passed through a narrow valley and then climbed the fell-sides. It levelled off briefly in the midst of the wild moorland around the watershed, before beginning the plunge down into the next valley. On the top of that desolate, windswept plateau stood a solitary building – the Inn at the Top – the highest and most isolated pub in the country.

Our decision to take over as landlords of the Inn at the Top was a typically impulsive and quixotic one. My wife, Sue, and I were living at the time in the Village Institute of a place so small it barely qualified for the description 'village'. The only shop was the dairy farmer's front parlour, and though the village did have a pub, it relied largely on passing trade, because the local population was only about fifty strong and many of them were Methodist teetotallers. Our accommodation was spartan: the caretaker's wing of a draughty, stone-built Victorian edifice, comprising a stone-flagged living room, a bedroom, a subterranean kitchen in the cellar at the bottom of a precipitous flight of stone steps, and a bathroom, shared with

17

the Institute's patrons and reached through a large room containing the village's pride and joy: a full-sized snooker table. Upstairs, as well as the bathroom, was another large room with a table-tennis table. Our duties as live-in caretakers were less than onerous; all we had to do was keep the central heating boiler in the cellar stoked and sweep out the snooker room once a week and the less well-used upstairs room once a month. Our only other obligation was to pay the scarcely extortionate rent of £1 a week.

We were both in our late twenties. Sue had a job some fifteen miles away down the valley, while I was in the early stages of my career as a freelance writer, which meant that I spent every morning making myself endless cups of coffee and reading three daily newspapers from cover to cover, including the small advertisements, the court circulars and the births, marriages and deaths. Just when I had finally managed to force myself to think seriously about settling down at my desk, our dog would place her chin trustingly on my knee, our dark brown eyes would meet and I would decide to 'just take the dog for a quick walk, before really getting down to work'.

Three hours later, the pair of us would return muddy and tired but exhilarated from a ramble over the moors, leaving me just enough time to towel the dog clean of incriminating mud and peat, crumple a dozen or so sheets of paper and scatter them around my desk and sit down at my typewriter – personal computers had not been invented then, or if they had, the news had so far failed to reach Yorkshire – before Sue returned from her genuinely hard labours, with a solicitous enquiry: 'Had a tough day?'

'Hellish,' I'd reply, getting up to make yet another pot of coffee and happily abandoning any further attempts at work for the day.

One early spring morning, however, while completing my customary leisurely perusal of the papers, I came across an article with the promising title of 'The Loneliness of the Long Distance Landlord'. It was about the most remote and lonely pub in England and its owners' search for a new manager. I read the piece with mounting incredulity. Continuing his raid on the kitchen sink school of 1950s English literature, the writer of the article noted that there was 'Room at the Top' for a new landlord of the highest inn in England. It was a wild, windswept inn, set alone in an ocean of peat bog and heather moorland that stretched away, unbroken, as far as the eye could see. There were only sheep and grouse for company; the pub's next-door neighbour was four miles away and the nearest town – and even then it was a very small one – was twelve miles off, as one writer in the interwar years had noted with grim satisfaction, 'and those some of the stiffest miles in the North'.

The wind was so ferocious –'strong enough to blow the horns off a tup [ram]', in the words of one former landlord of the inn – that it would frequently rip car doors from their hinges and force would-be customers to enter the pub on their hands and knees; for reasons entirely unconnected with the wind and weather, there has never been a shortage of customers leaving a pub by that method. The winters were so long and hard that the pub was regularly cut off by snowdrifts for weeks on end. The annual rainfall was over eighty inches and it rained 250 days of the year; the other 115 it was probably just drizzling. There were also 132 days of frost a year to contend with, winter temperatures could drop south of minus twenty Celsius and the winds blew at more than fifty miles an hour ... unless there was a storm brewing, when things might get a whole lot worse.

The inn had already had a chequered history after changing hands for just £2,500 ten years earlier. The then owner, George Carter, described it as 'the smartest little pub you could find in a day's march', although, as another newspaper correspondent sourly noted, 'it did, after all, take a whole day's march to get there'. Once you arrived, there were no mains services of any sort, just a radio telephone for communications with the outside world, a septic tank for drainage, a Calor gas cooker, a geriatric diesel generator for electricity and an arthritic ram-pump – a pump placed in a spring or stream and powered by the force of the water passing through it – to supply water, sited in a stream 400 yards from the inn. The only exception to this enforced self-sufficiency in all life's necessities was in refuse disposal; a council wagon called once a week to empty the bins, always providing the roads weren't blocked by snow. Perhaps unsurprisingly, the inn had racked up four changes of landlord in the previous three years. Now yet another one was being sought. The owners, the article said, were 'prepared to consider an inexperienced couple if they are prepared to work hard'.

'What a preposterous idea. Only a pair of complete idiots would want to run a place like that,' I thought, as I dialled directory enquiries. By the time Sue came home that night, I'd already arranged an interview. Seven days later, having already climbed more mountains and crossed more dales than Julie Andrews ever managed in *The Sound of Music*, we found ourselves driving up an apparently endless road, cloud down around our ears, rain and wind lashing the surrounding bleak and barren fells.

'We must have missed it,' I said. 'Even Heathcliff wouldn't live up here. Let's turn round.'

Since the road was barely wide enough for two cars to pass, with glutinous peat bog to either side, we were forced to carry on, and, right at the top of the hill, we found the building we were seeking.

On first impressions, it was hard to disagree with the judgement of the nineteenth-century writer who had remarked of the inn that, 'whether you judge by maps or intuition, it must strike you as the loneliest habitation in the land'. It was also one of the ugliest. The building was covered in cracked and collapsing rendering, painted a hideous mustard-yellow. A couple of the windows were cracked and the glass in the others had the sepia patina acquired though long exposure to tobacco smoke that suggested they hadn't been cleaned in quite some time. The flaking paintwork of a rotting signboard over the door confirmed that this was indeed the pub we were after. Those who can recall the Slaughtered Lamb pub from the film *An American Werewolf in London* will have a fair

21

idea of what greeted us that day, though admittedly with slightly fewer psychotic customers.

If the look of the inn itself was – to put it mildly – a disappointment, its surroundings were absolutely breathtaking. In whatever direction we looked, there was nothing but an unbroken, rolling ocean of moorland, stretching to the horizon. As one visitor in the 1930s had observed, 'Nowhere else I know are you so utterly alone in the world. There is nothing but the swelling hills and the enormous sky. Even the road dwindles into an unnoticed track, lost among these great spaces it is so hard to believe are part of England.' To a cursory glance the moors might have appeared monochrome, but as my gaze travelled over them, even at this early stage of the year, they came alive in an endless tapestry of subtle colours and textures: peat, rock, bilberry, crowberry, cloudberry, cotton grass, sphagnum moss and an astonishing array of lichens, heathers, grasses and mosses, arrayed beneath a vast cloudscape that was never the same for two seconds together. We stood there transfixed; it was love at first sight.

Turning our back on that astonishing landscape only with considerable reluctance, we opened the door and went into a porch that smelt of mildew, and then entered the inn. I was too slow to adjust my six-foot-four-inch frame to accommodate a doorway that was several inches shorter than me and, for what was to be the first of many, many times, since every doorway in the inn was the same height, I banged my head on the lintel and made my grand entrance cursing and furiously rubbing my head.

As we looked around, Sue and I exchanged a glance. From her expression, I could tell that she was sharing my sinking feeling. The walls were black with damp and the only light came from candles and storm lanterns, for the generator had broken down. A fire smouldered fitfully in the fireplace, as much smoke entering the room as escaping up the chimney, while from the next room the sound of water dripping steadily on to a sodden carpet could be heard.

When we went upstairs to look at the bedrooms, I could hear the squeaks and scratchings of rats scuttling across the ceiling.

'What's that noise?' I innocently asked Neville, one of the owners, a florid-faced Geordie wearing dark glasses, a shiny suit, a kipper tie and enough gold jewellery to finance the national debt of three banana republics.

'Oh, I think a pigeon's got trapped in the loft. I'll pop up and see if I can free it later.'

His smile was broad and friendly, but his eyes, when they could be glimpsed through his sunglasses, were cold and predatory. He was in the scrap trade and looked as straight as a sapling in a force-ten gale. As well as his official occupation, he also had his finger in several even more illicit pies, and was rumoured to be one of the main criminal 'fences' in the North East. The rumours may well have been true for, as we were later to discover, whenever he put in an appearance at the inn, he would always be bringing the week's 'Special Offers' with him.

'Fancy a new watch?' he said on one occasion.

When I looked blank, he pulled up both sleeves of his jacket to reveal half a dozen Rolex watches strapped to each forearm. 'Anything you like. Brand new. Half-price.'

It was a mantra with which I was to become very familiar. The next time it was a pocketful of gold jewellery, the time after that, car stereos.

On his home turf, Neville's preferred habitat was a cavernous club in the North East, a thieves' kitchen for the post-industrial age, where easily portable stolen property such as cigarettes, booze, perfume and jewellery was available for inspection and purchase – strictly cash, no credit cards accepted. By repute, the theft on commission of everything from cars and industrial plant to antiques and Old Master paintings could also be arranged. Stupendous sums, probably much of them ill-gotten gains, were also wagered on the outcome of winner-takes-all darts matches between the local champions, men of iron nerve and prodigious girth, who could down a pint in one and sink a dart into double top with equal rapidity and aplomb.

Neville's business partner, Stan, was another Geordie, a civil servant who seemed to have far fewer rough edges but who proved to be even less trustworthy. He wore a sober, respectable suit and his talk was sweetly reasonable, but his eyes couldn't meet mine for a second, sliding away to focus on the walls, the ceiling or the floor, whenever I tried to hold his gaze. The pair of them reminded me of middle-aged Likely Lads, two kids who had grown up in the back streets, one staying close to his roots, hustling, wheeling and dealing on the margins, while his best mate got respectable and moved to a new housing estate and a white-collar job, without ever entirely shaking himself free of his dodgy past.

The interview was a fairly cursory affair, conducted as we sat round a table in the bar, our eyes watering in the smoke from the fire. After leafing through the CV I'd prepared, in which I'd attempted the difficult task of proving that freelance journalism was not only a suitable background for a pub landlord but also practically an essential qualification, Stan and Neville asked a few less-than-penetrating questions.

'Done any bar work before?' Neville said.

'Yeah, like it says on my CV, I did a full summer season in the bar at a holiday camp in Devon.' Not only bar work but experience of the tourist trade as well – what more could they want!

Stan turned to Sue: 'And can you cook?'

'Oh yes,' she said. 'Anything from chips to cordon bleu.'

'And supposing we were to offer you the job, when could you start?'

I glanced at Sue, then shrugged.

'Next month with ease, next week at a pinch.'

They didn't seem to have any other questions.

'We've still got several other couples to interview,' Stan said. 'So we'll be making a decision after we've seen them. We'll be in touch in a day or two to let you know.'

'And our expenses?' I asked – you can take the man out of journalism, but you can't take journalism out of the man.

'We're not paying expenses,' Neville said, with

almost indecent haste. 'It wouldn't be fair on the others.'

'The others?'

'The ones who don't ask for expenses.'

Sue and I exchanged another meaningful glance. After a last look around the bar and a rather longer look over the landscape outside, we set off back down the hill. On the long journey home to the Village Institute, we considered the advantages and disadvantages of accepting the job, if it were offered.

'We'd be giving up a pretty near idyllic existence,' Sue said. 'We'll never get another house for a pound a week.'

'Least of all one with a full-sized snooker table.'

'And we're already living in a beautiful place,' she said, ignoring the interruption. 'It's got moors, hills, lakes, peace and quiet, and nice people. I've got a good job and you're just beginning to make a success of freelancing.'

'The local pub isn't bad, either,' I said, helpfully.

'So we've got everything we need where we are. We'd have to be mad to want to swap all that for a cold, wet, windy, rat-infested ruin in the middle of nowhere, working for two of the sleaziest people I've ever met.'

'So that settles it, then,' I said. 'If they offer it, we'll take it.'

We heard nothing from Stan and Neville at all, however, and assuming – correctly, as it turned out – that the job had been offered to someone else, we went back to the village, the Institute and the full-sized snooker table, and got on with our normal lives.

On an April Monday morning, three weeks later, the phone rang.

'It's Neville.'

'Neville?'

'From the Inn at the Top.'

'Oh, right. I wasn't expecting to hear from you again. We assumed you'd got someone else.'

'We did.'

There was a pause.

'So, what can I do for you now?' I said at last, having waited in vain for Neville to get to the point.

'Well, the other couple haven't worked out,' he said. 'We're going to have to let them go. Are you still interested?'

'I don't know,' I said. 'We might be. I'll have to ask Sue when she gets home from work. Do I take it the job's ours if we want it?'

'If you can start next week, yes.'

'Fair enough. I'll let you know this evening.'

In the event my impatience got the better of me and I phoned Sue at work.

'What do you think?' I said, when I'd relayed the gist of Neville's call. 'Do you still want to do it?'

'What do you think?' she said, returning service. 'Although, erm ... I think we'll always be curious about it if we don't.'

'Then I suppose we'd better do it, hadn't we?'

The result of this *folie à deux* was that, six frantic days later, Sue and I found ourselves ensconced behind the bar of the Inn at the Top. The latest in a series of moves we had made to

27

ever more inaccessible areas, it was the logical – if that's really the word – culmination of a process begun several years earlier.

We had spent the first years of our relationship in a small town on the edge of the Yorkshire Dales but had then moved in incremental steps, by way of a narrowboat on the Leeds–Liverpool Canal, to a village in the foothills of the Pennines, and then the tiny hamlet on their upper slopes. By this process of *reductio ad absurdum*, a move to a solitary dwelling on the very top of the Pennines was an impeccably logical choice. Whether we were getting away from it all or just running away from it all was a little harder to discern – we tended to move house every three years whether we needed to or not. However, we did share a love of the Yorkshire Dales, from the gentle, intimate landscapes of the valley floors to the wild and bleak 'tops', where one dale merged into the next and the sheep and the grouse browsing among the heather were likely to be our only companions.

Our flippancy about our motives for wanting to move to the inn also concealed a real desire to become a genuine part of a rural community, living in it, working in it, giving to it as well as taking from it. Such was my own enthusiasm for the idea that – perhaps as a result of too many Yogi Bear cartoons in my youth – I'd recently applied and been shortlisted for a job as a 'Mr Ranger': a Park Warden with the Yorkshire Dales National Park. I admit I would have been a wild-card selection, basing my application largely on my skills as a communicator and my professed ability to bridge the gap – often a yawning chasm – between the

28

public on one side and the Dales farmers on the other, with the National Park holding an uneasy position in the middle ground. Having failed to appreciate the exact nature of the interview process, I turned up at the National Park offices wearing a shirt and tie, a purple suit – well, it was the seventies – and my best shoes, to find that the other five shortlisted candidates were all dressed in the regulation Dales uniform of tweed jacket, Viyella shirt, moleskin trousers and brogues. I then discovered that we would be spending a large part of a sweltering July day walking the fields and woods around Grassington and supplying solutions to problems posed by assorted wardens role-playing as irate farmers, bewildered ramblers and so on. By the time I'd completed the circuit, I was dripping with sweat and my face was almost as purple as my suit. Unsurprisingly I didn't get the job, but my ambition of finding work in the heart of the Dales remained undimmed.

Although Sue and I had been living in rural areas for some time, we felt almost like parasites on those communities, living there but working elsewhere, doing work that was close to incomprehensible to the people we lived among. 'We get calluses on our hands, you get blisters on your backside,' as one farmer put it to me, not entirely in jest.

We wanted, quixotically, no doubt, to take up work that would involve us in a Dales community and have a perceived value to our peers there. The Inn at the Top seemed to fulfil those criteria admirably. It conferred community benefits, particularly those of late or occasionally all-night opening, and, perhaps just as important to a rural community, it was demonstrably hard work, involving long hours, some strenuous physical effort carting barrels and crates around, and a measure of hardship in living on those exposed 'tops'. After we'd moved up to the inn, I swelled with pride whenever a local confided to me, 'You wouldn't catch me living up there.'

Sue and I were a dangerous combination, however: both incurable romantics, prone to impulsive decisions and positively allergic to thinking anything through before committing to a course of action; if we'd ever got around to adopting a family motto, it would probably have been 'Leap Before You Look'. Yet, although we both had those qualities in spades, there is no denying that I was playing the leading role in this Shakespearian tragedy in the making. If I'd expressed even a scintilla of doubt about the wisdom of dropping everything and disappearing into the back of beyond without a route map, let alone a paddle for the barbed wire canoe, I'm sure – with the benefit of hindsight – that Sue would have professed her disappointment but privately uttered a sigh of relief. No such doubts were expressed and, in the grip of something as powerful and as illogical as the lemming's desire to see what's over the next clifftop, we packed our bags and sold or gave away what bits of our furniture could not be squashed into our cramped accommodation at the inn.

In retrospect, it might have been wiser to have given away our washing machine as well, or, better still, left it in the cellar as a farewell gift for the next caretakers of the Village Institute. But since there was no washing machine at the Inn at the Top – best not to dwell on how, or indeed whether, the glass cloths, drip towels and the bed linen from the guest rooms there had ever got washed – we had decided to take ours with us.

No doubt a pair of seasoned removal men would have had the machine out of the cellar and onto their truck with no more than a few grunts and the odd muffled curse, but Sue and I, though we could grunt and curse with the best of them, were rather less adept when it came to the actual moving of large heavy objects. We manoeuvred the washer to the foot of the cellar steps easily enough, but now came the tricky part. We began to ascend the stone steps, me at the bottom, bearing most of the weight, while Sue navigated from in front, taking what part of the load she could.

Sweating and gasping with the effort, we had almost reached the top step of the stairs when I felt the weight suddenly begin to increase, just as my strength was starting to give out. The machine, vertical a moment before, was now beginning to lean towards me, slowly at first but rapidly accelerating. At the same moment I heard Sue's strangulated cry from the far side of the washer and her by now superfluous comment, 'I can't hold it! Look out!'

Precariously balanced with my right foot half-way between one step and the next, I discovered that the washing machine was now beginning the return journey to the cellar whence it had come and, left to my own devices, I couldn't hold it either. The washer was obeying the laws of gravity as inexorably as the piano in that old Laurel and

Hardy movie *The Music Box* and I was squarely in its path. There was only one honourable course of action left open to me: to beat a hasty retreat. Descending a steep stone staircase backwards is tricky enough at the best of times, without the added complication of being pursued down it by a two- or three-hundredweight washing machine. Our two-step – me and the washer in perfect harmony – began in four-four time and accelerated rapidly. Well before the bottom step I had lost the race and I ended up flat on my back with a twisted ankle beneath me and the washing machine on top of me.

Although our dog and the washing machine were going with us – with the aid of a couple of farmers' lads from the village, we completed the job at the second attempt without any further mishaps – there was no room at the inn for our cat, which a friend was adopting. Pet dogs were not exactly flavour of the month among the farmers of the Dale, who regarded them all as potential sheep-worriers, but the dog was soft as butter and too timid to chase sheep, plus there were things like dog leads to make sure there were no ugly incidents. A cat was another matter.

'Why can't we take him?' Sue said. 'He's hardly going to start chasing sheep.'

'No, but he'll kill the moorland birds, and especially grouse chicks, and then we'll be lynched by the gamekeepers.'

That was a bit over the top, I know, but we'd seen *Straw Dogs* a few weeks earlier and my dreams were still haunted by images of shotgun-toting psychotic yokels.

Sue was heartbroken about having to leave the cat behind, but I confess my own feelings were rather more ambivalent. Every night between about ten and eleven o'clock, the cat would take up position on the doormat and then start scratching at the door and miaowing piteously, at ever-increasing volume, until we let him out. He would disappear into the darkness to go and strut his stuff around the neighbourhood and we would see nothing more of him until the early hours when he would reappear on the windowsill outside our bedroom – it was on the ground floor – and start howling and banging on the window with his paws.

The windows didn't open so the only options were to ignore the cat – difficult to do, since he made such an unholy noise – or drag myself out of bed and go and open the front door. Unfortunately, even if I shouted myself hoarse once there, the cat, while intelligent enough to have worked out which was our bedroom, was not intelligent enough to come round to the door – or perhaps he just took a sadistic pleasure in forcing me to go stumbling and shivering out into the field behind the building in my pyjamas. After enduring that tiresome routine almost every night for months, it's perhaps not surprising that I was able to take the news that we would have to part company in my stride.

Having said a tearful – in Sue's case, at least – farewell to the cat, which, true to its species, completely ignored us both, we took a last wistful look round the Village Institute and the full-sized snooker table that we were leaving behind. Then we set off to meet our destiny in a two-vehicle convoy, with Sue blazing the trail at the wheel of our ancient Morris 1000, while I lagged behind, shrouded in a fog of burning oil and exhaust fumes, at the wheel of a hired and even more elderly Ford Transit.

Our arrival at the Inn At The Top proved to be a little uncomfortable, to say the least. It turned out that Neville and Stan had not actually mentioned to the previous managers that they were being sacked until the last possible moment – and that was when we turned up. When, incredulous, I asked Neville why they hadn't given their managers notice after they'd hired us to replace them, he countered, 'They'd only have been trying to nick stuff. That's why we've sacked them.'

So, while we waited in the bar with Neville, Stan was upstairs watching the understandably disgruntled former managers pack their things. When they came downstairs to leave, Neville ushered us through to the back bar, out of the way, presumably to stop the departing managers airing their views on exactly what sort of people we had just agreed to work for. There was a burst of shouting and swearing from the main bar and Neville went and hovered by the connecting door, in case Stan had to call for back-up, but a couple of minutes later the front door slammed shut with a thud that echoed through the pub and the unhappy couple were gone.

We went upstairs to clean the room the departing duo had just vacated, so that we could move our stuff into it, and then Neville and Stan gave us a quick Americans-tour-of-Europe guide to running a pub and talked us through all the ins and outs of the building and the equipment. This included a pretty superfluous lecture on pulling a pint and tapping a barrel – I'd worked behind enough bars in the past to have those sorted – and an eye-opening run-through of all the cheap tricks and petty scams they wanted us to practise. These ranged from watering down everything that an inspector from the Weights and Measures Department wouldn't check, including all the bottles of squash and cordial and even a bottle of Advocaat used to make 'Snowballs', to decanting cheap whisky into the empty bottles of more expensive brands on the optics behind the bar.

'The punters'll never notice,' Neville said.

It was hard to know which was more pathetic, the lengths to which Stan and Neville were willing to go to achieve no more than a few extra quid of profit, or their obvious expectation that we'd be impressed by these tricks of the trade. Sue and I exchanged a meaningful glance; whatever Neville and Stan might want, they were cheap tricks we were going to do without. Rather more usefully, not to say legally, Neville – Stan didn't like to get his hands dirty – also showed me how to start and stop the generator, how to use the radio telephone and how to prime the ram-pump that supplied the pub's water. It seemed remarkably straight-forward, although in that, as in so much else in life, appearances could be deceptive.

After completing their layman's guide to the pub and its quirks and foibles, Stan and Neville sat us down for one final briefing. Stan cleared his throat, looking even more shifty than usual.

'Now, don't get too friendly with the locals,' he said. 'They're just a bunch of shit-stirrers. They'll be telling you all sorts of stories about us, given half a chance, and they're not worth having as customers. All they do is complain about the prices and nurse a half-pint for two or three hours. So don't worry about them; the tourists are the priority – they're the ones who pay all our wages.'

I could see why the locals might be complaining about the prices. They were set eye-wateringly high – on a par with the West End of London, which made them about fifty per cent higher than the prices in any other pub in the area. When I queried this, Stan shrugged.

'Eighty per cent of the customers here are tourists,' he said. 'And most of them only come here once, just so they can say they've had a drink in the highest pub in Britain, so we need to make as much out of them as we can while they're here. They won't be coming back this way, anyway, or at least not for another year, so if they have to pay a few pence a pint more than they do anywhere else, it isn't going to be a problem.'

'Just a thought,' Sue said, 'but if they got good food and drink, and good value for money, maybe they might come more than once.'

There was a glacial silence, while Stan directed a look of withering contempt in her direction.

'Like I said, just a thought,' she repeated, giving me the ghost of a wink.

Having sorted out the eighty per cent of our potential customers who were tourists, we turned our attention to the other twenty per cent: local farmers, the most price-conscious individuals on earth. If, as the old joke says, Yorkshiremen are Scotsmen without the generosity, Yorkshire farmers were even more parsimonious than that. Despite Stan and Neville's contempt for them, we wanted the locals to come to the pub and we knew that if we tried to charge them these prices they'd be out of the door before you could say 'rip off'. Faced with the prospect of having no local trade whatsoever, we launched into a free and frank discussion and eventually managed to persuade Stan and Neville to accept a compromise: prices for the visitors would have to stay at those astronomical levels, but locals would be given discount rates. Clearly this would create its own problems when serving a tourist and a local side by side at the bar, but we would just have to find a way to avoid any ugly confrontations.

Not without a few anxious backward glances, Stan and Neville finally left us to it, promising that they would be back on the following Saturday to trouser the week's takings and give us the night off. We just had time to conduct a more leisurely exploration of our happy new hovel and take the dog for a short walk up on the moor before it was time to open the doors and take our first small step as landlord and landlady. Whether it would prove to be a giant leap for Dale-kind only time would tell.

We weren't entirely without expertise in pubs; Sue was a skilled cook and had worked in a bar as a student, while I'd had a close personal relationship with bars, both as a consumer and producer, since my teens. The road to my personal ruin had begun early. I was very tall for my age with a deep bass voice that enabled me to pass for much older than my actual years, and I was a regular at my local pub well before reaching the legal drinking age. That came to an abrupt end when our local paper published a photograph of the village's championship-winning Under-Sixteen cricket team, including its over-tall fast bowler. The next time I went into the pub, the photograph was pinned up behind the bar. The landlord glanced at me, pointed to the picture, winked and said, 'Well, see you in a couple of years, then.' Fortunately there were other pubs in the area whose landlords took a less active interest in the local junior-sports scene, and the profits from my paper round were soon passing across someone else's bar counter instead.

Perhaps it was those formative experiences and the fond, if understandably sometimes hazy; memories of happy nights in pubs that persuaded me to spend most of my gap year before university in 1967 working as a barman at a Pontins holiday camp in Devon – the experience that I was now naively assuming would be all the preparation I'd need before taking on the running of a pub. Pontins was, of course, entirely different from Butlins – the blazers were blue instead of red – and the fondly remembered BBC TV programme *Hi-de-Hi!* does not even begin to convey the full awfulness of the British holiday camp experience in that era.

Most of the camps, including the one in which I worked, were sited in redundant army barracks or converted prisoner-of-war camps, and, in keeping with their origins, they provided a standard of food and accommodation that would have provoked riots in many jails. Yet people flocked to them. Those who did so seemed to combine two of the worst British traits of that era – mindless obedience to authority and complete indifference to appalling food – and therefore enjoyed themselves enormously. For reasons that continue to baffle sociologists to this day, they and thousands of other apparently sane British people were happy to pay large amounts of money in order to spend their annual summer holidays in voluntary incarceration in these camps, being harangued and harassed from dawn to dusk via screeching tannoys that could not even be turned off in the bedrooms. In our off-duty moments, we used to amuse ourselves by imagining the tannoy dictators taking over every aspect of the campers' lives: 'All right, campers, it's Friday night and we know what that means, don't we? It's time for sexual intercourse! Chalet 76, that's more than enough foreplay. Get on with it, man, for heaven's sake. Chalet 14, missionary position only, please; where do you think you are – France? Chalet 22, I was talking to the married campers. Stop that at once. All right, campers, two minutes is up. What do you mean, you haven't finished, Chalet 7? You'll just have to learn to be quicker next time, won't you? Now then, campers, lights out, night-night, sleep tight and don't let the bedbugs bite.'

The reality was only slightly less bizarre than that fantasy. Shocked awake by the tannoy at seven every morning, the campers' days were filled with a heady mix of physical jerks, crazy golf, bingo, and 'Junior Talent', 'Glamorous Granny' and 'Knobbly Knees' competitions. One of my fellow detainees – sorry, employees – Mick, had been a singer with a pop group who'd had an enormous Top Ten hit with their debut record. On the strength of that, the group's manager had persuaded Mick to have all his rather uneven teeth extracted and replaced with a gleaming set of pearly white false teeth, in anticipation of the long and successful show business career that awaited him. Sadly, the group then proved to be the archetypal one-hit wonders and their fall was as meteoric as their rise. Within eighteen months the closest Mick could get to showbiz stardom was working as a Pontins Bluecoat and leading the campers in a rousing chorus of *Roll Out the Barrel* in the bar on Saturday nights.

However, his investment in cosmetic dentistry wasn't entirely wasted because every Thursday morning the campers would be frog-marched down to the camp swimming pool for the weekly Pontins Swimming Gala. Once all the happy campers had been cajoled – or pushed – into the pool to take their turn in the swimming races, and the hugely popular 'Best Belly-flop' competition had been decided, a hush would descend on the crowded arena as the members of the camp enter-tainments staff went through their ritual weekly humiliation. After a few of the junior members had been pelted with wet sponges, thrown fully clothed into the pool or subjected to a trial by ordeal involving an updated version of the medi-eval ducking-stool, Mick made his grand entrance

40

to a tinny tape recorded fanfare from the camp's PA system. Every eye was focused upon him as, resplendent in his Pontins uniform, he circled the swimming pool twice and then began to climb the steps of the diving boards. Up and up he went, past the springboard and the middle board, until finally he reached the top board. An expectant hush fell as Mick advanced, inch by inch, to the very tip of the top board, fifty feet above the water below. There was a dramatic pause and a drum-roll on the PA, then Mick opened his mouth, took out his false teeth and dropped them in the deep end. While he descended the steps again, the campers had a diving competition to retrieve his teeth, with a cash prize for the lucky winner. They just don't make entertainment like that any more...

Fortunately for me, unlike Mick, my job description didn't require me to take part in the compulsory entertainment, if that isn't too strong a word for it, but I did have to earn my keep through my own wage slavery – £10 a week plus free board and lodgings, in return for a six-day, seventy-two-hour week working in the bar. We did at least keep licensing hours – 11a.m. to 3p.m and then 5.30p.m. to 11p.m. – but the bar was packed from the moment it opened until the moment it closed, with the campers intent on throwing down the maximum possible number of drinks in the time available. It was while working there that I first learned to serve three customers at once – serving one customer while taking the money from and issuing change to the previous one and taking the order from the next – but even working at top speed, by the time we'd finished clearing up after the lunchtime session and restocked the shelves for the evening, my two and a half hours' time off had shrunk to a maximum of sixty minutes.

There were compensations for the long hours and meagre pay, however. The holiday camps were like poor men's cruise liners, if only in the sense that they were enclosed worlds where people tended to leave their normal inhibitions at the gates, and there was clearly something about a man in uniform – even one as naff as a blue nylon Pontins blazer – that acted as a powerful aphrodisiac on the unattached, and even sometimes the attached, female campers.

It was the celebrated 'Summer of Love' and in keeping with the times, like my fellow workers, I had many a torrid love affair with the campers, though no matter how intense, given the constraints of holiday bookings, none lasted longer than a fortnight. Every Saturday morning a stream of moist-eyed beauties from the Yorkshire wool mills, the Lancashire cotton mills, the West Midlands car factories, or whichever industrial region was just finishing its two-week annual holiday, would depart as the callous blue-coated staff tried to look suitably broken-hearted. Two hours later the entire staff was back in position to run the rule over the next batch of campers – fresh meat – as they began arriving. By the following day or even the same night, new affairs would have begun.

The camp staff were a motley crew. The manager bore an uncanny resemblance to Arthur Lowe when in character as Captain Mainwaring in *Dad's Army*, but his employees were, on the

42

whole, rather less respectable. The chef, an East End thug with dyed blond hair, was a Cockney Gordon Ramsay as far as the swearing went, though sadly not in the culinary arts. Many of his kitchen porters appeared to be on the run from police warrants or unpaid alimony, because every time a police car came through the front gate it seemed half of them disappeared over the back wall, never to return. Most of those who remained were not the most savoury of specimens, either, and the food they prepared was a good match for them. Since I worked split shifts and the camp was sited three miles outside Brixham at the top of a steep hill, there was no alternative to eating in the camp cafeteria and it was very far from a gourmet experience. 'Chips with Everything' just about summed it up, and in the entire summer season I never once glimpsed a piece of fresh fruit, a salad or a vegetable that hadn't been boiled to a grey, gelatinous pulp. The bland menu also concealed even worse horrors. On my first day there I ordered soup but was immediately dissuaded by one of my fellow bar staff.

'I wouldn't eat the soup, if I were you,' he said. 'It... Well, it just isn't very nice.'

He would offer no further explanation than that, but I took his advice and avoided it from then on, though the only visible problem was the way the soup gradually changed colour over the course of the week, darkening steadily from Saturday's watery off-white leek and potato, by way of minestrone and tomato, to the full dark-tan Brown Windsor the following Friday. It was only several weeks later that I learned the other

43

reason for avoiding the soup – sensitive readers, look away now – was that some of the kitchen porters reputedly took revenge for the perceived indignities that the campers had inflicted on them by urinating in the soup tureen. Nice.

The state of the kitchens reflected the incompetence and indifference of everyone who worked in them. They would have been shut down in seconds by a modern health inspector but instead they survived untouched for several weeks until Sir Fred Pontin made one of his unannounced inspections of his camps. He arrived in his trademark helicopter, hovering over the camp for five minutes and waving to the overexcited campers' kids who'd turned out to stare in wonder at his craft, and then landed on the lawn in front of the offices. After greeting the manager, Sir Fred strode magnificently through the cafeteria, dispensing regal waves right and left while his retinue ran to keep up with him. But as he entered the kitchens his foot slipped on a patch of grease and he finished up flat on his back. As he lay on the floor his eyes roved over the filthy stoves and work surfaces, the grease-stained walls and the almost equally grease-stained kitchen staff and then, still lying there, he began barking, 'You're fired! You're fired! You're fired!' at every kitchen employee in turn, including the psychotic Cockney chef. Sir Fred then staggered to his feet and limped painfully out on the rest of his tour of inspection.

Staff were hastily bussed in from every other camp in the region, the kitchen was spring-cleaned overnight and normal service was resumed the next day, though within a few weeks it had become a festering grease trap once more. Given that there was no alternative, I continued to eat the food in the camp cafeteria – still avoiding the soup, of course – and after five months dining exclusively 'chez Pontin', I went home at the end of the summer with my gums turning purple and my teeth loose in my head. When I went to see my dentist, he was so delighted at what he found when he peered into my mouth that he called in his partners and the dental nurses to take a look as well. Apart from illustrations in dental textbooks and magazines, it was the first case of scurvy that any of them had ever seen.

CHAPTER 2

Dost Tha Ken Swardle Yows?

Our first evening as the new landlord and landlady of the Inn at the Top was a Sunday towards the end of April, the same weekend that Nottingham Forest, under their shy, unassuming manager, Brian Clough, were crowned First Division (as it then was) champions for the first time in their history. Before throwing open the doors to the public, we strolled around the inside and outside of the pub on a brief tour of inspection. At the front of the pub, facing due south and projecting a few yards from the building, was the squat, stone entrance porch, which, during opening hours, was usually packed wall to wall with massed cagoules, rucksacks and peat-encrusted hiking boots. Outside the door was a crazy-paved terrace and a wooden bench, sheltered from the prevailing westerly winds by the porch. It would prove to be a favourite spot for us to sit on sunny mornings on the rare occasions when we could take five minutes for a cup of coffee and a chat before the first customers of the day started appearing.

A row of miners' cottages had once stood beyond the west wall of the inn, in the teeth of the prevailing winds, but they had been demolished some years earlier and all that remained was a pile of rubble that was slowly reverting to nature. At the other end of the terrace, the car park, on the eastern side of the pub, was an expanse of gravel just wide enough for two rows of parked cars and the access route between them. Beyond the far edge, a steep slope ran down to the banks of a small stream issuing from the hillside; it would have been a potential source of drinking water had it not been in such close proximity to the outflow from the inn's septic tank, buried beneath the car park. As we later learned, the car park had once been much narrower, but one of Neville's many scams had been to bribe the driver of the council's road-sweeping truck to dump the contents of his vehicle over the edge of it every time he passed the inn. As a result it was slowly advancing across the fell, though the stability or instability of its outer limits remained an open question.

Neville had also made use of the steep slope beyond the edge of the car park as a handy dumping ground for builders' rubble, bits of scrap metal and even an old caravan, presumably the forerunner of the ugly mobile home that now stood in the inn's back yard. Sadly the council's accumulated road sweepings had not yet been sufficient to bury this unsightly rubbish, and in any event Neville kept adding to it, maintaining it as Britain's highest eyesore. Later that year I persuaded one of the local farmers to bury it under a few trailer-loads of rock and peat, giving it a rather more pleasing and natural look.

At the far end of the car park, a gate led into the backyard to the north of the inn, a bleak and unlovely patch of grass and mud, criss-crossed by tyre tracks. A Calor gas bulk tank stood at one side, close to the rear wall of the inn, and facing the generator shed and the adjoining coal shed on the other side, while the aforementioned mobile home stood at the far side of the yard from the inn, close against a rock face. It was another of Neville's innovations, providing weekend accommodation for him and Stan and their wives, so that they needn't occupy guest bedrooms that could more profitably be let to passing walkers or tourists. It was in the most sheltered site that could be found, in the lee of the rock outcrop, and the drystone walls on either side of the yard gave it some additional protection from the wind, though not quite enough, as Stan and Neville were to discover one gale-wracked autumn night when the strength of the wind seemed to be rocking even the inn's stone walls.

Hurrying across the yard to the inn, one or both of Stan and Neville had neglected to check that they had closed the door of the mobile home. The door duly swung open and, needing no second invitation, the wind went in and made itself at home to such an extent that within a few minutes we heard the squeal of tortured metal and burst out of the back door just in time to see the twenty-four-by-twelve-foot roof of the mobile home lifting off and sailing away downwind before jack-knifing into the moor a hundred yards or so away. Left unprotected, its walls soon followed suit and in due course, together with the chassis and the ravaged fixtures and fittings, they were retrieved and joined the wreckage of the earlier caravan as the latest additions to Neville's car park extension scheme. Our pleasure at the total destruction of this hideous eyesore was only increased by the ferocious argument that ensued between Stan and Neville as each tried to pin the blame for this mishap on the other, aided and abetted by their furious wives, whose clothes, carefully placed in the wardrobes, had also been picked up by the gale and scattered for several miles downwind.

Sadly that other eyesore, the flat-roofed modern extension housing the games room, was rather less easy to dispose of. On the side of the inn facing the car park, it was a curious sight from outside. Its flat roof, already an open invitation to leaks in this region of high winds and torrential rain, was pierced at intervals by truncated steel rods, as if an original intention to build a two-storey extension had been abandoned, either because the owners had run out of money or, according to local rumours, because the foundations had not been made deep and strong enough to bear the additional load.

The lovely Neville and Stan had bought the pub and presided over its rebuilding after it was destroyed by fire in 1973, and they were not the sort of men to spend four pence where two pence would do. Every material they had used was the cheapest and nastiest they could lay their hands on. Rather than using the traditional heavy sandstone slates, the roof had been retiled with cheap concrete slates, which were fragile and prone to cracking and breaking in the extreme weather conditions that governed the Inn at the Top. The exterior of the building had been clumsily rendered and painted – presumably there was a cheap deal available on mustard-yellow, because only the blind would have picked it out otherwise – and the ugly flat-roofed, single-storeyed, breeze-block extension had been added at one side. The door- and window-frames were filled with a ramshackle assortment of cheap or second-hand installations; we counted no less than nine different styles of window around the building ... and all of them leaked.

When you entered the pub you passed through the cramped porch, which opened onto the main bar. A brown hair-cord carpet, bearing ample evidence of the heavy traffic it had seen, covered the concrete floor. The walls were bare stone and the ceiling was plasterboard, with steel RSJs clad in dark-stained plywood in a desperate and wholly unsuccessful attempt to make them look like oak beams. The 'olde worlde' theme also extended to the tables, which had wrought iron legs and roughhewn pine tops bearing an assortment of ersatz adze marks. The chairs were the sort of

49

spindle-backed, wobbly-legged ones you could pick up – cheap – in any downmarket furniture store and were regularly repaired and as regularly broken again, while the half-dozen tall bar stools ranged along the front of the bar were master-pieces of instability to which only the brave or foolhardy would have entrusted their full weight. A rather more attractive – and solid – job-lot of church pews salvaged from some sale room stretched right round the walls.

The bar itself had a wood and formica top, and was stone-fronted, with the stones punctuated by green, brown and clear wine-bottle ends in which Stan or Neville had placed fairy lights that must once have winked and twinkled but which were all by now defunct. By some considerable distance the nicest feature of the room was the stone inglenook fireplace filling the wall next to the bar from floor to ceiling. The fire burned continuously – the only times we ever extinguished it were during a very occasional summer heatwave and on the day the chimneysweep paid his annual visit – and the benches to either side of the fireplace were never empty of customers for more than a few seconds.

The fire still smoked quite badly and one of the first things we did was have the chimney swept. One of our locals, Fred, obligingly offered to clean it for nothing more than the price of a couple of pints, but fortunately one of our other regulars warned us about Fred's recipe for no-frills chimney-sweeping. It involved placing a bowl of petrol in the fireplace, retiring for a beer while the fumes drifted up the chimney and then tossing a match into the bowl. Fred had tried this method on his own chimney first. The resultant explosion had sent a tongue of flame fifty feet in the air and, while it certainly cleaned his chimney very effectively, it had also necessitated several hundred pounds of building work to repair the chimney stack. Fred swore that he had now refined his method to remove any possibility of those unpleasant side effects but, just in case, we decided to stick with the traditional sweep's brushes instead and called a proper chimneysweep in to do the job.

Fred and his fireplace were clearly accident-prone, because a few months later he was poking the fire during a thunderstorm when a lightning bolt struck the field at the back of his house. Since the fire had a cast-iron back boiler and the poker was touching it when the lightning struck, Fred became his very own lightning rod and was blown right across the room. When he came to his senses he was sprawled against the far wall, but apart from a burn to his hand and a buzzing in his ears he was unharmed, and he was certainly in sparkling form – quite literally – in the pub that night.

At the other end of the bar from the inglenook, a doorless doorway led to the kitchen and the stairs to the upper floor, and a doorway at one end of the bar opened on to what, for no visible reason, was known as the dining room. At the opposite end of the bar, another door led to the games room, which, in justification of its name, contained a pool table, a jukebox and a fruit machine, as well as giving access to the loos. The Ladies contained only one cubicle, leading to lengthy and frequently irate queues at busy times.

Neville and Stan had also done the rewiring themselves, with the result that stray electric cables trailed here and there across the upstairs walls and ceilings and, interestingly, two of the power sockets were live when they appeared to be switched off. However, their *pièce de résistance* was the new toilet block, opening off the dining room. Once all the concrete had set, they discovered that they'd managed to lay the drainage channels so that any liquids would overflow back into the room rather than emptying into the drains. Since they couldn't be bothered to do the job again, they'd continued using the old loos and converted the toilet block into a bottle store, leaving the unusable toilet fittings *in situ* in case they ever got around to finishing the original job, with the result that we had to negotiate our way around dusty urinals and toilet bowls when getting the crates in and out.

The kitchen, at the back of the pub and looking out over its drab and muddy backyard, was a white-painted rectangular box with a quarry-tiled floor and pitiless fluorescent lighting. Beyond it was the beer cellar, actually a flat-roofed garage built onto the back of the games room. It was almost perfectly inappropriate as a beer store, being too hot in summer and by some distance too cold in winter, but it was all there was; the original cellars had been filled with rubble and debris and then concreted over after the pub had burned down in the 1970s and no one now knew where the entrance to them had been.

The stairs to the first floor went up behind the

bar, opening onto a landing from which two corridors led respectively to the quaintly named and little-used residents' lounge and, in the other direction, in succession, to the bathroom, our bedroom and then four guest bedrooms. There were no locks or bars separating the upstairs rooms from the bar area and no shutters to isolate the bar itself from the rest of the pub, so it seemed wisest for the managers to take the room nearest the head of the stairs, in the hope of intercepting any overnight guests who fancied helping themselves to a few free nightcaps once everyone else had gone to bed for the night.

The upstairs floors had been laid with the cheapest and flimsiest grade of chipboard. Rather than plaster, the walls of the stairway and landing had been rendered with Artex – hideous stuff that never set and clung like clay if you tried to scrape it off, or even brushed against it – and then painted magnolia. Some sort of bizarre hardboard 'panelling' had been used in the bedrooms, and the hardboard sheets on which parallel grooves had been made in crude imitation of planks of wood had not only been nailed on the walls but also used instead of plasterboard on the ceilings, and the carpets, curtains and bed linen were everything we had already come to expect from Stan and Neville: cheap, garish and made of nylon.

More than a little subdued, we returned downstairs, drew the bolts on the front door and declared ourselves well and truly open for business. Our initiation as landlord and landlady that first night was short, sharp and not entirely sweet. It turned out that Sunday was the night when, along with a few hikers and early-season tourists, a lot of the local farmers liked to meet at the pub for a drink. The news that yet another gullible young couple had arrived to try their luck at running the inn was already circulating on the Dale's gossip and rumour mill, and many other locals had also turned up, partly out of curiosity, to cast an eye over the new couple, and partly – as we later discovered – to place bets on how long we would last. Although the summer season had barely begun, we were already the second set of new managers to appear that year, and in recent years none had lasted longer than a few months.

As we soon discovered, there were four or five distinct local groupings. There were the transients – the hikers and tourists – who tended to keep separate from each other and from the Dale's permanent inhabitants. Some of the hikers were sociable enough, even if only when comparing notes – and blisters – with their peers, but others were solitary types, staying in the inn only long enough to purchase a drink and some food and then sitting in the furthest corner of the bar or on the terrace outside, communing with nature and scrutinizing their maps as if the meaning of life, or at the very least, the solution to the Da Vinci Code, were concealed there.

The tourists were usually more sociable. They were on their holidays, had chosen to come to this area rather than just hike through it on their way somewhere else and were often eager to find out more about the inn and the Dale it served. Some of the farmers were happy enough to chat to them and answer their questions, though others regarded the visitors with disinterest and a few with disdain.

With a few exceptions, the weekenders and second-homeowners who were more regular visitors to the Dale than the tourists usually had little to do with the permanent population and largely seemed to socialize with each other, bemoaning the impossibility of obtaining extra virgin olive oil from the village shop and the *mañana* attitude of the local builders, carpenters, plumbers, electricians, painters and decorators they hired to do up the houses they'd bought.

Most of them were perfectly nice people but were widely regarded in the Dale (at least behind their backs) as parasites, contributing little to the local economy, other than the builders and allied trades presumably, arriving with a stack of groceries purchased from some distant Sainsbury's or Waitrose store in the city where they lived, and disappearing again at the end of the weekend, leaving as transitory an imprint on the Dale as the black-bagged rubbish they left out for the bin men.

Other 'offcomers' had taken up permanent residence in the Dale, occupying a sometimes uneasy middle ground between the natives and the weekenders. In the eyes of some of the older Dale diehards, merely living in the Dale was not enough to qualify someone for resident status. Even being born there was not necessarily enough to grant full citizenship rights; only those whose fathers and fathers' fathers had had their roots in the Dale

55

could truly claim to be of it as well as in it. The rest, even if they had merely made the short journey over the tops from the neighbouring Dale were, always and forever, 'offcomers'. Among these semi-pariahs were some who would become our most loyal customers and best friends – if nothing else we at least had our offcomer status in common – but on this opening night everyone was a stranger to us, and in the event it was one of the local farmers who was first to break the ice, though it proved to be a very temporary thaw.

I was busily polishing a glass behind the bar and trying desperately to look like 'mine genial host', when one of the farmers approached the bar, cap pulled low over his eyes, lower lip jutting out like the prow of a destroyer.

'You're the new 'uns then?' he said. 'Last lot didn't stop so long, did they? Any road, let's see if you can pull a pint, shall we?' He watched me fill his glass and then paid his money, showing no reaction to the locals' discount I gave him, then paused and gave me an appraising look. 'Nah then, lad, dost tha ken Swardle yows?'

'Pardon?' I asked.

'Thought so,' he said, stumping off to announce to a group of his peers in the corner that some offcomer with 'plums in his gob' and a total ignorance of the Dale's trademark breed of sheep had taken over the pub.

In 1978 pub licensing laws had yet to be liberalized and, by kind permission of the licensing magistrates, we were only allowed to serve alcohol between 11a.m. and 3p.m. and from 5.30p.m. to 10.30p.m ... or that was the theory, anyway. The

56

Inn at the Top was a place where the normal rules did not apply – at least as long as the local police weren't watching. Like most previous landlords of the inn, we were in full agreement with a visitor to the pub in 1919 who remarked that, 'should prohibition come to England, here is an irresistible case for exemption; the man who has walked to the inn has earned his tankard.'

If time did not quite stand still at the Inn at the Top, it certainly never seemed to be called, and our major contribution to community spirit was to keep the bar open to hours that would have astonished even the most vehement supporters of licensing-law reform, in defiance of fatigue, economics and common sense, although we first had to learn a salutary lesson. On that first night behind the bar, I thought I would show the locals what sort of a rough, tough, devil-may-care landlord they had acquired and tried to ingratiate myself with them by a show of remarkable generosity. The legal closing time of 10.30 came and went and I said not a word. Eleven passed, 11.30 too, and finally, round about midnight, bracing myself for their cries of gratitude and appreciation, I rang the bell and called, 'Time'.

There was a moment's stunned silence and then a thunderous roar of laughter.

'Are you closing early tonight, then?' one of the farmers asked. 'Best we all just have one for the road first.'

There was another burst of laughter and fifty pint pots were presented for refilling. I learned my lesson fast and from then on we never closed the same day we had opened.

Late opening had been a long-established tradition at the Inn at the Top, probably dating back at least as far as the time during the First World War when licensing laws were first introduced by the teetotal prime minister David Lloyd George, in an attempt to increase munitions production by imposing, if not temperance, at least moderation on the hard-drinking munitions workers. As well as restricting opening hours, Lloyd George also forced breweries to greatly reduce the alcoholic strength of their beers and introduced even more draconian restrictions in the areas where munitions works were sited, notably Carlisle and Gretna. In a bizarre attempt at social engineering, all the breweries and pubs in the area were nationalized under the Carlisle and District State Management Scheme. Many were closed down and those that remained were subjected to drastically restricted opening hours and a rigorous code of conduct. No 'loose women' were to be tolerated, no customers showing the least sign of intoxication were to be served, and no 'treating' – the buying of rounds, one of the cornerstones of British pub etiquette – was to be permitted.

More positive measures included the provision of food, newspapers and wholesome facilities for recreation, like skittle alleys and bowling greens, but this British equivalent of Prohibition was equally doomed to failure, though at least there were rather fewer gangsters in Carlisle than in Chicago. The pubs were about as appealing to the munitions workers and Carlisle's other inhabitants as kissing your granny and the only lasting effect on the problem of drunkenness among munitions workers was to make it far worse.

The men finishing the evening shift at the Gretna munitions factories would all board the last train to Carlisle, the nearest place where the pubs were still open. They immediately passed the hat round in a collection for the train driver, payable if he got the train in ahead of schedule, and the faster he went the more he was paid. Whether the co-operation of the signalmen and station-masters was also purchased is unclear, but if so it was readily given; the last train from Carlisle to Gretna was probably the only one on the entire railway network that always arrived well ahead of schedule. The train would come hurtling into Carlisle station and screech to a halt, showering the platform with sparks as the wheels locked. Then, while the driver counted his 'winnings', a torrent of thirsty munitions workers would pour out of the station and disappear into the pubs that surrounded it, where, just like a theatre bar preparing for the interval, ranks of glasses of beer and whisky were already poured and awaiting them. In the twenty or so minutes available before closing time and the ten minutes drinking-up time afterwards, the men would drink themselves close to oblivion and then spill into the streets, swearing, brawling, harassing women, vomiting and collapsing in the gutters, leaving the inhabitants of Carlisle to wonder how all of this could possibly be helping the war effort.

While some of the worst aspects of Lloyd George's state-enforced temperance movement ended with the Armistice – though the State

Management Scheme survived until Edward Heath took an axe to it during his troubled time as Prime Minister – licensing laws had come to stay … everywhere except at the Inn at the Top, where a more relaxed and traditional attitude to opening hours was maintained. Just like the management of the Windmill Theatre in the Second World War, successive landlords of the Inn at the Top could proudly boast: 'We never closed'.

Prompted by an unholy alliance of local magistrates and Methodists, the local police did their best to end or at least curtail this shocking state of affairs, and over the years many stories – some of them possibly even true – were told about the inn's landlords and customers, and their brushes with the law. Raids by the police were almost always unsuccessful, for the drinkers were often forewarned, either by the local policeman who, after all, had to live in the community themselves, or by locals further down the Dale who spotted the police cars heading up the road towards the Inn at the Top. The raiding party would then arrive to find the inn either deserted or occupied by farmers sipping cups of tea, nibbling ginger nuts and discussing the meaning of life. No sooner had the police retreated, however, than the beer glasses would reappear from under the bar, the other customers would come back from behind the hill, and the serious drinking would start again.

Even when the police did achieve a rare success with a surprise raid, an odd after-hours drinker might still escape the net. One of our customers told me the story of one night, many years earlier, when well after closing time, a tremendous pounding on the door announced that the police had finally nailed the notorious after-hours drinkers at the Inn at the Top. The offending customers were lined up and, one by one, the police took down their names and addresses. After recording the last one, the jubilant policemen departed in triumph, but no sooner had the front door closed behind them than the door of the grandfather clock swung open to reveal the hunched figure of one diminutive drinker, still clutching his pint pot.

Much ingenuity was also displayed by landlords trying to avoid a fine. One landlord in the 1960s, christened Fremont but universally known as 'Fremmy', was fined £15 by the magistrates for serving drinks at 11.50p.m. despite his excuse that 'it was a bit difficult to throw customers out if you weren't able to call the police if they got awkward'. Three months later, Fremmy's defence on a similar charge was again that: 'We have no police protection up here and it is no use me taking a customer by the neck to put him out because I might get someone jumping on my back. I like the local lads to stay back until I get the strangers away.'

Fremmy was a local lad himself, born four years before the First World War. He had left school at fourteen, and worked as a cowman and a sheep farmer, and then for many years as a miner. He had walked four miles to the mine every day, and then a further mile underground, and worked by candlelight with hammer and drill cutting chert (flint). It was so hard that Fremmy called cutting it 'the toughest work I ever did', and the stone's durability made it much in demand for road surfacing; it was said that the streets of Paris were paved with chert from the Dale. In winter Fremmy never saw the sun for months on end, for he was underground before it rose and did not re-emerge from his day's shift until after it had set.

After serving in the Army during the Second World War, Fremmy became a pub landlord, and even ran the implausibly – and inaccurately – titled Temperance Hotel in one village, before eventually moving to the Inn at the Top. When he retired, he gravitated to the village at the bottom of the moor and there became a stalwart of what was known as 'The Village Parliament': a group of pensioners, led by Fremmy as Speaker of the House, who gathered in the bus shelter on the green every morning and spent most of the day there, swapping yarns and putting the world to rights. He was still there when Sue and I ran the inn and was a great source of old tales about the place.

One Sunday night during his time at the inn, Fremmy had presided over one of the most notorious lock-ins ever staged there, interrupted by a police raid that netted the impressive total of sixty-four after-hours drinkers. It says much for our own cavalier disregard for the licensing laws that we took that figure as a challenge – a UK all-comers' record that was just begging to be broken. Although our official licensing hours remained 11 to 3 and 5.30 to 10.30, our doors were open non-stop from seven in the morning, when the hikers ate their breakfast before striding off over the moors, until two o'clock – and sometimes even later – the following morning, when the last reluctant farmer was finally propelled through the door. Although morning coffee, afternoon tea and bedtime cocoa were available for those who wanted them, we were equally happy to serve a hiker who wanted a pint of Guinness with his breakfast, or a farmer who fancied a swift double Scotch for the road seventeen or eighteen hours later.

We took pleasure in noting the looks of bewilderment and then sheer delight that flitted across the features of the more bibulous of the hordes of hikers and tourists who paused for refreshment at our lonely inn, when they realized that this really was the pub that never closed. Most, often having hastily bought themselves an extra drink just before official closing time, as they were accustomed to do in their less civilized hostelries at home, discovered that not only was no one going to stand over them, intoning 'Glasses please', 'Drink up now, please', and 'Have you got no homes to go to?', but that they could order another drink, and another after that, if they wanted.

As word spread far and wide, many customers made special pilgrimages to the pub, just for the sheer illicit pleasure of a few 'lates', a 'lock-in' or a 'stoppy-back', as it was apparently known in the North East. One such customer sidled up to me not long after we took over and, having introduced himself, confided that he and his mate were 'friends of the previous landlords. When we came up, we spent plenty on beer and they used to let us sleep on the floor of the bar. I don't suppose there's any chance...'

'Yeah, that'll be all right,' I said.

'And...' he hesitated, unsure how to phrase his

next question, then continued with much nodding and winking, 'Do you still – erm, you
know...' I'd already guessed where he was going
with this, but I let him stumble his way there
unaided. 'Do you still do lates?' he finally asked.

'It has been known, on occasions.'

He broke into a huge smile and turned to give
the thumbs-up sign to his mate.

'I hope you've got plenty of beer in, then,' he
said. 'We've a wicked thirst on us.'

'Oh, I think we should have just about enough,'
I said.

They got stuck into a few drinks and a large
meal, while the normal hubbub of a weekend
night at the pub continued around them, and
they beamed as they came up to replenish their
glasses on the far side of official closing time.
Beyond midnight they were starting to slow
down, by one o'clock their smiles were a little
wan, and by two they were looking positively
peaky. About half past two in the morning, I felt
a tug at my sleeve.

'Will you be closing soon?' the man with the
wicked thirst said. 'We're tired, and we want to
go to bed.'

'Well, why don't you tuck yourselves up under
the pool table in the taproom?' I said. 'Then the
farmers won't tread on you when they're on their
way to the Gents, and if you have a little nap,
who knows, you might be ready for another pint.'

He gave a weak smile, then disappeared into
the taproom. The two of them were still snoring
under the pool table when I got up the next
morning, and when I roused them and offered

them a breakfast pint to set them up for the day, they both turned from pale to pale green in two seconds flat and disappeared into the Gents.

CHAPTER 3

Yan, Tan, Tethera, Methera, Pip

Despite the occasional excesses of a few customers, most of our clientele heartily approved of our entirely unofficial liberalization of the licensing laws, though we did have to impose a curfew of sorts, just to stop people spending the evening at one of the other pubs in the Dale and only heading our way when everywhere else was closed and they were already full of beer.

Late opening was particularly appreciated by farmers who were often working far into the evening at lambing and hay-time, and even those who overindulged never came to any particular harm. They tended to drive home whatever state they were in, but, that said, the farmers invariably drove at ten to twenty miles an hour whether they were sober or drunk – often to the horn-blaring, steering-wheel-pounding fury of high-speed visitors trapped behind them on roads that were rarely wide enough to permit overtaking. There was no traffic coming in the other direction at that time of night, and on the open moorland, with no trees or walls to hit if they went off the road, they merely ground to a halt in a peat bog and then either slept it off in the car or walked the rest of the way home and came back with a tractor to pull their car out the next morning.

While our customers enjoyed a few lates, we found ourselves sitting up night after night, listening to our locals endlessly debating the merits of particular tups and yows (local dialect for rams and ewes). Sunday night was always the big night for the locals, with farmers coming from as much as thirty miles away to talk, drink and argue with ever-increasing noise, far into the night.

Except when discussing sheep, the Dalesman's natural discretion and reticence normally carried over into his conversation, and I found that I had to learn to decode the message underneath. Praise or optimism was sparing. 'All reet [right]' denoted complete satisfaction, and 'gare [very] good' was the highest praise possible. These Dales farmers exemplified the old joke about the Yorkshireman watching a comedian, who described the experience as 'All reet, if tha likes laughing.' Negative feelings were similarly understated. 'Fair to middling' was actually very bad.

'How's your father?' I asked one of our customers, whose father had been ill for some time.

'Oh, he's just fair,' he replied. I later discovered he'd had a heart attack the day before.

The inhabitants of the Dale all tended to display a similarly lugubrious fatalism to events great and small, as stolid and indifferent to the problems of the world outside as it had largely been to theirs. Had Orson Welles' version of *War of the Worlds* been set in the Dale and broadcast on local radio there, it is unlikely to have had quite the same impact on these phlegmatic people as it did on the population of New York.

'Sad weather, Stan.'

'Aye.'

'I see the Martians have landed, then.'

'Aye.'

'Aye. Well. Happen they'll be wanting a few yows.'

'Happen they will. Any road, best be having the one we came for, eh? Two more pints, please, Doris.'

The same stoicism also seemed to characterize the livestock. One bright, early spring morning, we watched a few cows placidly grazing in a riverside pasture, ignoring the rooks standing on their backs and pulling out beakfuls of hair to line their nests. In that same warm, wet spring, we saw sheep similarly unconcerned by grass actually growing out of their fleeces. The farmer had set up a metal hay rack in the field and, while the sheep browsed underneath it for a few stray wisps of hay, seeds dropped from the rack into their fleeces. The wet weather and the warmth of their bodies combined to germinate the seeds and for a couple of days even the sheep greened at the approach of spring, a bizarre symbol of fertility.

The centuries had also inured the human population to that other implacable scourge of the region, the weather. We soon noticed that the farmers' descriptions of the weather were always several notches below the reality. 'It's a warm 'un' meant that that rarest of natural phenomena at the Inn at the Top – a summer heatwave – was underway; 'bit draughty tonight' indicated that a hurricane-force wind was raging around the inn; 'it's rather thin out there' showed that the temperature outside was at least ten degrees below zero; and the innocuous-sounding dialect word 'damply' – used not as an adverb but an adjective, as in 'Aye, it's damply out there right enough' – told us that rain was coming down in bucketfuls.

There were many other dialect words for rain – if the Inuit supposedly had 200 words for snow, how many more could the inhabitants of the Dale not have mustered for rain? The vocabulary of the farmers and the other locals also featured a number of evocative words and phrases I hadn't encountered elsewhere, including 'slape' – slippery or icy; 'clashy' – wet and windy; 'siling down'– pouring down; 'back-endish' – autumnal; 'dowly' – dull and gloomy; 'mizzling' – misty and drizzling; 'nesh' – cold; and 'nithered' – frozen.

If the farmers of the Dale usually maintained their standard, stolid understatement about the weather and most other subjects, that certainly did not extend to their beloved partners on their journey along life's highway: their sheep. The quirks and foibles of their fellow farmers, and even the births, marriages and deaths of their friends and acquaintances, might pass with no more than a nod, a grunt or a raised eyebrow by way of commemoration, but any aspersions cast upon the quality, lineage or relative merits of yows or tups old and new could provoke an explosion. Even the most apparently innocuous remark could serve as the prelude to a ferocious pub argument about sheep, when discretion and reticence took a back seat to invective and insult.

'Now I'm going to tell you something that you may not just agree with,' said Chris one night, a big, raw-boned farmer with a habit of talking out of the side of his mouth, as if all his conversation was in confidence. Ten seconds later, having followed that mild-sounding introduction by expressing his forthright opinion about a particular tup, he had brought the place into uproar, with farmers shouting, waving walking-sticks and banging on the table, red-faced with rage.

On our first night at the inn, the heat of the argument and the strength of the language led me to believe that an all-out brawl was about to start, but ten minutes later all had quietened down again, and two old farmers who had earlier been nose to nose, puce-faced with rage and about to go out to the car park and sort it out once and for all, were soon sleeping peacefully, their heads together on the back of the old overstuffed sofa near the fire, while their peers got their breath back and revved themselves up for another argument.

I was soon taking it all in my stride.

'Aren't you going to do anything?' enquired a middle-aged tourist couple the following week, anxiously eyeing the distance to the door, as another furious argument erupted among the farmers.

'What about?' I said, sporting my newly-acquired Dale nonchalance. 'It's only a mild disagreement.'

Among the disputants was Michael, an old farmer with a bad leg and a walking stick, who lived in the tiny village at the bottom of the hill. Even though now long retired, having passed the

69

farm on to his son, he liked to keep his hand in by arguing about sheep as rancorously as the rest, brandishing his walking stick at his foes like the greatest swordsman in all France. He also needed dynamite to get him out of the pub once he was in there, but he would haul himself upright at the end of the evening, leaning heavily on his stick, and sing the local anthem, 'Beautiful Dale', like an angel, reducing even the most truculent drunk to respectful silence.

Michael and Chris were only two of the remarkable collection of characters who drank at the inn. For centuries the narrow, steep-sided Dale, with its waterfalls and fast-rushing river, had been virtually cut off from the outside world by the fells that surrounded it. As a result the inhabitants had grown up with their own special dialect and customs and often exhibited a complete indifference to those not lucky enough to have been born in 'the beautiful dale'. Although its isolation had lessened, more than a trace of that insularity still continued in the Dale – and does so even to this day.

Many of the locals had what seemed to be the archetypal farmer's look – stocky, solid, round-faced men, with a ruddy complexion derived in roughly equal measures from hard outdoor work in all weathers, substantial alcohol consumption and a cholesterol-laden diet. Their endurance and hardiness was extraordinary to soft townies like Sue and me. Even when it was well below zero with snow thick on the ground, we never saw a farmer wearing gloves.

'Do you not feel the cold?' I asked one of them,

staring at his red, raw-looking fingers.

'Aye, a little,' he said, 'but only twice a day. I feel it first thing in the morning when I first go out, but after a few minutes my fingers go numb, like, and then I don't feel them again until I finish my evening work and go inside the house. Then they sting a bit as they warm up again, like.'

That farmer and some of his peers looked to owe their lineage to the Celts who had once occupied these bleak hills and dales. They were as short, stocky and solid as bulls, with eyes so dark they were almost as black as their hair. Others had the tall, spare, long-striding figures, the fair hair and the eyes almost as translucent-blue as a clear winter sky that signalled their linear descent from the Norse, who settled the uplands a thousand years ago, displacing many of the native Celts. The names of virtually every landscape feature – fell, beck, rigg, hag, scale, scar, sike, tarn, moss (as in marsh or bog), dale, ling, foss or force (as in waterfall) – and a host of other dialect words such as 'bait' (food), 'bairn' (child), 'dollop' (lump of something soft), 'gawp' (stare), 'happen' (perhaps), 'laik' (play), 'mun' (must), 'reckon' (think), 'rive' (split) and 'skelly' (twisted, e.g. 'skelly-eyed' – cross-eyed), all derive from the Norse, as does the upland dialect, to such an extent that many words – 'gimmer' for female is one – remain almost the same in both modern Norwegian and local speech. Scandinavians could often make more sense of the dialect than British visitors, to whose ears it could sound as harsh and incomprehensible as the cawing of the rooks in the trees.

The old dialect numbers used by farmers to

count sheep – yan, tan, tethera, methera, pip; ethera, lethera, anver, danver, dic; and then beginning again with yan-a-dic, tan-a-dic, etc., grouped in fives and tens to facilitate counting on the fingers, and ending at twenty (hence 'sheep-scoring'), at which point a notch would be cut in a stick or a mark scratched on the ground, and the count resumed at yan – had long passed out of use but there was one survivor of the system, for everyone in the Dale still said 'yan' instead of 'one': 'Another pint, Dick?' 'Aye, I'll have yan'.

Many of the local farmers had not just the local dialect in common but their surnames as well; there were so many Calverts, Metcalfes and, in particular, Aldersons, in the Dale that, in order to distinguish one from another, they were either known by a name like 'Tom Jack' or 'Dick Ned', combining their own and their father's Christian names; or by linking their name with the name of their farm, like 'Dick at Greenses' or 'Bill at Thorns'; or by a nickname like 'Gurt Bill up t'steps'. That nickname identified Gurt (Big) Bill, who lived in a house up a flight of steps, a rarity among the farms of the Dale – the door usually opened straight on to the yard. When he grew old and moved to a retirement bungalow in a village further down the Dale, he was instantly rechristened 'Bungalow Bill' instead.

Although the Inn at the Top was very much dependent on visitors, it was far from being just a tourist curiosity. There was a surprisingly large local trade, or as local as it could be when the nearest inhabited building was four miles away – 'not four miles from a village or anything tame of

72

that sort', as a visitor in the 1920s wrote, 'it is four moorland miles from an inhabited house', and that one was almost as remote from any others – but despite its isolation, it was at the heart of a geographically scattered but very close-knit community. The inn was unique, perhaps the last surviving link with the days of droving and packhorse trading, and had always been a favourite meeting place for farmers, a place where men from the different dales and from east and west of the Pennine divide could meet to exchange news and talk tups far into the night. It was also a place strong on traditions. The fathers and grandfathers of our customers used to call at the inn on their way home with a cartload of fuel from the pit that once worked the seam of shaley coal that outcropped there and, although their descendants no longer bought coal there, they continued to drink at the inn.

Among them was Jed, perhaps the last man alive to have earned a living from the ancient trade of droving. When he was young, few of the farmers of the Dale took their own stock to market, and Jed and his partner would go round the farms straddling the fells of the upper Dale, buying a few wether (castrated male) lambs at a time for around eight shillings each. When they had assembled a drove of several hundred, they then drove them to market up to fifty miles away, selling them for a profit of as little as three pence a head.

Jed's face was an astonishing assemblage of pouches and folds of skin, and his stories of old times were spellbinding, though many gems were lost somewhere between his susurrating speech, the local dialect and the tobacco juice sloshing about in his cheeks. Although we did possess a Gents, Jed preferred the great outdoors and was often to be found, even on Bank Holidays, unselfconsciously relieving himself against the outside wall of the porch, as the throngs of holidaymakers milled around him.

One of his drinking buddies was Reuben, a man so dour and taciturn that 'Evenin'. Pint.' constituted a lengthy conversation. His wife was at least thirty years his junior and, according to rumour, had been acquired when she was in her teens as a result of a financial transaction between himself and her father during a marathon card game and drinking session at the inn that had gone on for three days. It showed that arranged marriages were not confined to the Muslim community, not that there was one in the Dale. Reuben looked – indeed he was – old enough to be her grandfather and, perhaps understandably in the circumstances, his wife was reputed to have a roving eye. Whatever the truth of that, they appeared to lead virtually separate lives, Reuben's main recreation being a sedate game of dominoes in the taproom with his cronies, while his wife went dancing in the Dale's one and only nightspot, though that description makes it sound rather more exciting than it actually was. Most of the young farmers in the Dale either didn't dance at all or did so only when dead drunk, and then in a style similar to that with which parents embarrass their children at family weddings.

That didn't apply to Alwyn, who was what passed for a bit of a ladies' man around the Dale and was always berating the shy farmers' boys for their failure to put the moves on the local girls. Alwyn was more than willing to demonstrate to the boys where they were going wrong, had any of the girls shown the slightest inclination to take on a man in his sixties who was completely bereft of teeth other than the two stationed like farm gateposts at either side of his mouth. In the absence of local encouragement, he was constantly sharking in on passing female tourists, smiling and winking at them, and patting his knee encouragingly as he urged them to try his lap for size. Surprisingly, one or two even obliged him, to the raucous amusement of his peers.

Alwyn's foil was Jimmy. In his fifties but as round, pink, scrubbed and shining as a newborn baby, Jimmy was a Billy Liar type and always coming out with the most wildly implausible tales in which, inevitably, he played a heroic role, but he was such good company that nobody minded in the least whether they were true or not.

The farmers' sons who came up to the inn were often pretty much chips off their fathers' blocks but with some important differences. Barry was a Jamie-Oliver-like character, rumpled, slightly chubby and cherubic-looking – in a naughty sort of way – who exuded charm and seemed equally irresistible to women of his own age and also to those of 'a certain age'. Some just felt drawn to mother him, others appeared to have a rather less maternal activity in mind. Most of them were wasting their time, however, for Barry was thoroughly smitten by a girl who lived in a market town a few miles away and whose nickname among the bar staff of the inn, at least – 'The Fox' – was by no means the result of her sly smile and sharp features.

Several of the other farmers' sons were good-looking if shy lads who, in time, would no doubt settle down with local girls, but the charms of some of the other lads were less immediately obvious to the opposite sex. A trio of hardened drinkers could pour pint after pint down without visible ill effects, but none of them were over-burdened with wit or humour, and all appeared to have had at least a nodding acquaintance with the ugly stick. As a result, their marital prospects in a Dale already suffering a serious imbalance between the sexes seemed less than good.

Farmers' sons, or at least the eldest of them, could be sure of employment on the family farm, but the Dale had very little work to offer to farmers' daughters other than bar, kitchen, cleaning or chambermaid work at the Inn at the Top or one of the Dale's other pubs or guest-houses. Most of the young women therefore commuted to office or shop jobs in the larger towns, and though some returned in time and became farmers' wives, many others found their ties with the area loosening and often eventually started living, as well as working, outside the Dale. Partly as a consequence of that, there was an increasing number of bachelor farmers whose chances of finding a life partner shrank with every passing year. That was not only bad news for them personally, but also had depressing implications for the social life of the Dale and for future demand for its schools, shops, post offices, buses and other services.

Even for those farmers' boys who were young, free and single, and with a few quid in their pockets, there were limited opportunities to meet girls other than the diminishing number who lived in the Dale. On Saturday nights there were occasional discos in a club – I use the word loosely – and a hotel in the towns at the foot of the moor on opposite side of the Pennines. However, even in an era when there was still a relatively relaxed attitude towards drinking and driving, the journey home over the moor or along the twisting road in the bottom of the Dale was long and fraught, and whatever time they staggered home, most of them would have to be up before dawn to help with the morning milking. The natural shyness and reticence of the typical farmer's boy was also a hurdle that many found hard to overcome, and even those who were gregarious and attractive to women often found it difficult to maintain relationships with girls from outside the Dale, when every date required a round trip of at least twenty miles. Many girls who had not been raised in the Dale – and even some who had – while happy to date farmers' boys, found the prospect of swapping their Jimmy Choos for Hunter wellies and enduring all the hard graft, social isolation and sheer lack of glamour of life as a farmer's wife to be less than a wholly enticing prospect.

Those boys and girls and men and women who formed relationships had to do so under the all-seeing eye of the Dale's gossips. Freedoms taken for granted in Britain as a whole were still subject to the constraints of tradition in the Dale and being seen with the wrong person at the wrong time could lead to serious trouble.

A gamekeeper who lived in a hamlet down the Dale typified that approach. He was a nasty piece of work, whose foul temper was demonstrated by the black eyes his wife sometimes tried and failed to hide with make-up. They had a teenage daughter who was forbidden by her father to date any of the boys in the Dale. When a boy from the nearby village had the temerity to be spotted kissing her one evening – there was no suggestion that anything more intimate than that had occurred – the gamekeeper and two of his sidekicks went in search of the boy and beat him to a bloody pulp. The boy's parents did not feel able to call the police, perhaps partly because of the tradition in the Dale that, like families, problems between neighbours were best solved without involving outsiders, but more probably, I suspect, because the keeper worked for the local lord of the manor, who not only owned virtually all the land in the Dale, but the houses that his tenants, farmers and other employees lived in too. To earn the displeasure of His Lordship could not only cost a man his job, but also the roof over his family's heads. Such feudalism had been eliminated from large tracts of Great Britain but it was still a powerful force in the remoteness of the Dale at the end of the 1970s.

Attitudes to extramarital affairs were similarly old-fashioned and any man 'seducing' a married woman in the Dale was apt to be visited by a bunch of her male relatives, and they would not be coming round to have a beer and watch the football. Illegitimacy was also a far stronger taboo than in the wider world outside. I knew of three or four families in the Dale whose youngest child was separated by fourteen to sixteen years from the elder siblings. In every case – or so local gossip had it – a daughter had given birth to an illegitimate child and, rather than bear the stigma, with even a shotgun marriage ruled out because of the daughter's youth, her parents had claimed it and raised it as their own, with the child's true mother reduced to the role of big sister.

Other than the distant discos, the only available social venues for the young people of the Dale were the bus shelters on the village greens, or the motley assortment of pubs, and most of those, while places in which your grandfather would have felt quite at home, were probably less than enticing to testosterone- or oestrogen-fuelled eighteen-year-olds. We at least had a jukebox in the end bar and had a disproportionate number of younger customers as a result. Every pub, including ours, also had a darts team and a pool team, if there was room for a pool table in the pub – one very cramped village inn made do with a bar billiards table instead, which, being played from only one end, was much less demanding of space.

Not all the older characters who came to the Inn at the Top were born and bred in the Dale. Among our regulars were two men who lived together in one of the most remote houses in the upper Dale. It was a mile up a rough track from the road that ran along the bottom of the valley, at the point where it began the long climb towards the dale head. One of them was over six foot tall with dark hair and brown eyes, the other five foot eight, fair-haired and blue-eyed, and their facial characteristics were just as different. Yet whenever the farmers talked about them or their house, they always referred to them as 'the two brothers who live at top o't'Dale'.

Sue and I exchanged incredulous looks when we first heard this – didn't the farmers know? Of course, we never queried the description with them, nor with the two men themselves, for that matter, largely because how they chose to describe themselves or live their lives was none of our damn business – though for anyone who could not curb their curiosity about them, though they weren't at all camp in manner, their fondness for torch singers and musical theatre might have been a bit of a clue. We were also unsure whether the farmers really did think they were brothers or if, in the tradition of the Dale, they had simply decided that what went on behind someone's front door was their affair and no one else's, and if the two men wanted to describe themselves as brothers, that was fine by the farmers. Perhaps surprisingly, given the antediluvian attitudes displayed by some residents of the Dale towards 'bra-burning women's libbers' and 'interfering, do-gooding animal-lovers', I never heard any snide comments nor detected any homophobia in local attitudes to the two men.

In our first few weeks at the inn most of the customers were the locals, whether Dale-bred farmers or exotic imports like the two 'brothers'. Winter was slow to release its grip that year and the cold and damp, and the flurries of grey, gritty snow driving through on the wind, kept most tourists well at bay. As the days lengthened, we found ourselves looking eagerly for signs of spring. Each pale sunlit morning offered hope that it might be just around the corner; each squall of rain, sleet or snow mocked that hope. The fells remained resolutely empty; save for the sheep, browsing among the peat hags for the thin gleanings left from winter, and the grouse, keeping their eternal vigils among the heather.

Yet one morning, apparently no different from those before, with cloud still clinging to the fells like a cold, grey shroud, and rain stinging the slopes, as I walked up the moor with the dog, a lapwing took to the air from a patch of rushes, in a ragged flight across the fell. It was the first of the thousands of birds returning from their winter quarters in the lowland meadows and marshes, and river estuaries to their breeding grounds high in the hills.

If the lapwings – 'teewits' in the local dialect, in mimicry of their whooping cry – signalled the end of winter, it was the haunting, liquid call of the curlew that was the confirmation that summer was at last close at hand. That magnificent call and the curlews' soaring flight counterpointed the song of the skylarks spiralling upwards into the summer skies, and at dusk, as even the sheep stilled their bleating, the last sound as night fell was often the call of a curlew gliding down the wind to land, its flight as smooth and graceful as the elegant curve of its beak.

CHAPTER 4

A Sea of Unfaithfulness

Despite our unpromising start on our first night at the pub and the continuing handicaps of my improbable Oxford tones and total inability to tell one yow – ewe – from another, the locals soon came to accept and then befriend us, and when you made a friend in the Dale, it was for life. Even in the days of mass communications and broadening horizons, the Dale's people were shy, reserved, and slow to form and voice opinions; there was no question of effusive greetings or invitations to visit on a first acquaintance. To the diehards we would forever be offcomers, but to the others, providing that you put on no airs and graces and showed yourselves willing to contribute to as well as take from life in the Dale, your reward could be a friendship and a neighbourliness that had all but disappeared from less stable communities.

Our favourite time of the day at the inn was the mid-to-late evening, when most of the tourists had gone back to their rented cottages or bed and breakfast places, and most of the bikers, weary from their exertions, had pitched their tents and gone to sleep. Then the pub really came into its own. With the dishes from the evening meals cleared away, Sue could close the kitchen and come through to the bar and we'd chat with our regulars, many of whom had soon become good friends to us. It was the best part of running a pub, our social life delivered daily to our door, and in those early days it seemed that every night was party night. Sue and I both felt a genuine respect for the place and the people who earned their living in the surrounding Dales, and we were repaid not just in money over the bar, but with their friendship, support and acceptance as members of a community in which help was willingly and readily given, without thought for thanks or reward, simply because mutual aid and mutual support were the only basis for life in such hard and unyielding conditions.

Not all our new acquaintances at the inn had been as pleasant as our locals. Along with giving the place a thorough spring clean, one other task had had to be undertaken as soon as we took over as landlords: we had to get rid of the rats that we'd heard scuttling about the ceiling during our interview several weeks earlier. We could still hear them running over the upstairs ceiling late at night, showing that whatever methods Stan and Neville had used in an attempt to eliminate them had not worked. Although there was probably not a farm in the Dale that didn't have rats in its barns, that did not mean that they would be acceptable companions in a place where people were planning to eat and drink, and I got busy at once. I first went right round the outside of the inn, pointing every gap in the masonry and every crack in the paving on the terrace so that, if the rats inside the inn could no longer get out, at least no more could get in to join them. I then set to work with a huge drum of Warfarin and a series of empty crisp packets that I'd assiduously collected and which one of our customers assured me that rats could not resist. I have no idea how he'd established this curious fact but it certainly seemed to work.

Every night and morning, I climbed up the ladder into the loft, trying without success not to picture what might happen if a big rat was sitting within an inch of my head as I appeared through the opening. I laid out fresh supplies of poison baits and removed any victims of this chemical warfare that I could find. Unfortunately most of them slunk away to die in dark corners or even inside the walls, and only when the smell became overpowering was it possible to find some of them.

Within a week our sleep was no longer being disturbed by the patter of tiny feet – and the slither of rather less tiny rattails – and I was beginning to imagine that the last one had died. But no, even after dining heartily on Warfarin, the rats had one last trick up their sleeves. The characteristic behaviour of rats in the last stages of Warfarin poisoning is, so we discovered, to wander around in a sort of drunken haze – appropriately enough, since they were living in a pub. Seemingly unaware of their surroundings, they would venture forth in broad daylight, making no attempt to evade any humans they came across. As Sue was standing at the bottom of the stairs one lunchtime, talking on the telephone to a supplier, I saw her freeze, staring horrified towards the stairs. As I watched, a large rat made its unsteady way down the stairs, walked straight over her foot and disappeared – Fawlty Towers-style – into the pub dining room, which was packed with customers eating their lunch. Not daring to venture after it, I stood rooted to the spot, holding my breath as I waited for the screams that would signal the rat's stately progress through the crowd.

Astonishingly none came, and when I plucked up the courage to go in there myself, I found no trace of the rat and the customers were all enjoying an apparently untroubled lunch. I tried to do a discreet search but, finding I was attracting too many puzzled looks, I left well enough alone and beat a hasty retreat. Somehow the rat had managed to pass undetected from one side of the dining room to the other and had finished up in the bottle store, where I found it, expired in a corner, the following morning.

We saw no more rats, living or dead, after that and confirmation that the last of them had disappeared was provided in an unexpected way one night, as Sue and I were lying in bed, about to go to sleep. As she reached out to set the alarm clock, she froze and then burst out laughing.

'There's a mouse on the shelf.'

Sure enough, a small field mouse was sitting up, quite unconcerned, next to the alarm clock and cleaning its whiskers. When it saw us staring at it, however, it began running up and down the bedside shelf in a state of some agitation before taking a running dive off the shelf and disappearing under the pillows. When we pulled the pillows off the bed and removed the cushions that were underneath them, filling the gap between the mattress and the wall, we discovered a neat and tidy field mouse's nest. The creature had not only lined the nest carefully with scraps of fabric and cotton wool purloined from the bathroom, but also laid in its food supplies: a stash of dog biscuits as big as the mouse itself, which it must have pinched one at a time from the dog bowl downstairs and carried laboriously up to the first floor. Cute as it was, it had to go, but, well aware of Sue's soft heart and watchful eye, I purchased a humane mousetrap. Having caught the culprit – it just couldn't resist those dog biscuits – I drove down into the Dale with the mousetrap on the passenger seat and then released the enterprising rodent on the far side of the river, reasoning that it would never make its way back to the inn from there. I was more than half-convinced that the hapless mouse would be eaten by a fox, owl, stoat or farm cat before I'd even driven back up the hill, but that was better – for me, if not for the mouse – than having to endure Sue's reproachful looks if I'd carried out the execution myself.

Sue and I had soon dropped into a daily routine at the inn, rattling through the jobs in the mornings to be ready for opening time – not that we ever really closed. The alarm shocked us awake and we bounced once and hit the ground running because we were so perpetually exhausted that we knew that if we even lay back for a second, we'd both be fast asleep again. We washed – usually in cold water because it was often all there was that early in the morning – then ran downstairs.

While Sue put the kettle on and got started on

her jobs, I took the dog for a quick stroll and then fired up the generator, a complicated two-handed job that involved swinging the crank-handle over a few times to get up some speed and then, still frantically cranking with one hand, flicking over the lever to start the engine with the other. Sometimes it would cough, splutter and then fire up, rumbling into its steady, thumping bass rhythm that it could keep up hour after hour, but sometimes, usually on cold mornings, it was reluctant and I'd have to crank it again and again until at last it fired. It ran on diesel, and since the tap on the bulk tank in the yard was at a lower height than the fuel tank for the generator, it had to be decanted into a five-gallon container first and then tipped into the generator tank. It took ten minutes to fill the container, so I left it running and carried on with 'bottling up' and my other jobs inside the pub ... with the inevitable consequence that every now and again I forgot about it for half an hour and found the container overflowing and toxic diesel running into the soil of the already derelict garden.

Having checked the levels in the tank of diesel and the Calor gas for the cooker, I next had to climb up the ladder to the loft to check the water levels in the four huge tanks that sat on the rafters up there. If empty – not an unknown occurrence – I'd have to sprint down the hill to the gill where the ram-pump was sited, wade up the stream, crouch under the brick and concrete housing and prime and restart the pump.

A ram-pump is a wonderfully simple piece of equipment. Place it in a spring or stream and the force of the water flowing through it will drive the pump and force a small proportion of that water a surprising height up a feed pipe. It was powerful enough not only to push the water up the hill to the inn but also to raise it to the water tanks in the roof void. To start it, I just had to bleed the water out of the chamber of the pump, then close a valve and loosen the diaphragm of the pump until it began to beat. It was a fiddly, trial-and-error process, but at last I would get it right and the pump would thump once, twice, and then settle into a steady rhythm. I had to wait for a few minutes, slowing the beat down a little, and as I listened to the steady bass thump of the pump I invariably noted with some amusement that my heart had adjusted its own beat so that both it and the pump were perfectly synchronized.

Although it needed repriming from time to time, the ram-pump never stopped and, though ancient, was very reliable – it had only one working part – but it supplied a mere trickle of water and though it was enough to fill the storage tanks overnight, it only took one coachload of tourists flushing the loos for all they were worth, or one thoughtless customer leaving a tap running, to drain all the water off again. That might explain the visceral hatred I began to feel towards coach drivers, who would inevitably phone ahead to arrange to stop at the pub, claiming that their passengers would be purchasing all manner of teas, coffees, snacks and lunches, but when they appeared, it would just as inevitably turn out that they'd already stopped for morning coffee or afternoon tea somewhere else, and all they now wanted to do was get rid of the excess fluid. Grinding our teeth, we'd watch fifty or sixty passengers pass straight through the pub, use the loo and then get back on the coach without even giving us the time of day. When we next turned on a tap we'd be greeted with a damp gurgle and would have no water for at least a couple of hours ... by which time the next avalanche of customers or specialist loo-flushers would be arriving.

It took the ram-pump at least twelve hours to replenish the water tanks, so there was also a petrol-driven pump down there that worked twenty times as fast and would give us enough water in a few minutes to see us through the morning provided no one left a tap running. I'd set the petrol pump running and then go back to the inn, leaving the pump to stop itself when it ran out of fuel.

If ever I was tempted to feel sorry for myself over the effort required to secure one of life's most basic amenities, I only had to remind myself that it could have been worse; until the installation of the ram-pump around the Second World War, all the pub's water had been carried in buckets from another spring, 400 yards from the inn. The other modern amenities of life had also come only slowly to the Dale and even more slowly – if at all – to the inn. Mains electricity did not arrive in the small town at the midpoint of the Dale until 1950; it was a long time after that before it reached the farms towards the Dale head, and it never reached the inn at all. The inn had never been lit by anything other than candles or oil lamps until one night in 1947, when a couple of dozen people from the surrounding farms sat in the bar parlour to watch a film show. The projector, powered by a borrowed generator, brought electric light to the inn for the first time in its history.

The pub's own generator was set up in the 1950s, and the radio telephone was installed a few years later, beaming its signal down from its lonely hilltop to the telephone exchange in the town twelve miles away. It was the first wireless telephone to be installed in the county and was possibly the first in the entire country. It was a primitive forerunner of today's mobile phones, though it would have taken gargantuan pockets and superhuman strength to have used it as a mobile; it took a dozen car batteries to keep it functioning, and the battery charger was as big as a fridge.

When I got back up the hill to the pub, there were the toilets to clean – always a fragrant, glamorous task – the shelves to refill and the deliveries to organize and/or put away. Sue would meanwhile have made breakfast for any overnight guests, stripped their beds, done some cleaning and begun preparing the food for lunch. We'd grab our own breakfast, almost always eaten on the hoof, and by the time we'd got through all that – and sometimes well before – the first hikers of the day would be coming over the brow of the hill. I'd take the first of a succession of cups of coffee into the bar, all of which would invariably go cold before I could get to them.

We had a little part-time help from two local women. Our main local employee, Rita, drove up from a village in the Dale every morning, cleaned the pub from top to bottom and then helped in the kitchen and dining room until the lunchtime rush was over. A one-woman pocket dynamo, she did the work of three people and the pub was always full of the sound of her laughter, often provoked by the quirks and foibles of the hikers and tourists who passed through in such torrents every day.

When she was in cleaning mode she was a whirlwind, and she could be more than a touch impatient with overnight guests who were slow to observe the official check-out time of 11a.m. One couple, who had evidently chosen the inn as the perfect place to dissipate the simmering sexual tensions of their clandestine office romance, proved particularly obdurate, and after Rita had knocked several times and got no response, she resorted to Plan B and began hoovering the carpet immediately outside the room. She carried on for five minutes non-stop, punctuating the sound of the revving hoover by banging it repeatedly against the door. Finally it was opened a few inches and a fistful of banknotes appeared round it.

'All right,' an irate male voice said. 'You win. We'll pay for another night. Now piss off!'

Rita did so at once, laughing all the way down the stairs.

We also had another part-time helper, Mary, who assisted in the kitchen at lunchtimes, the peak hours for food sales. Most tourists were daytime visitors and we served almost ten times as many lunches as we did evening meals. Like Rita, Mary was a real grafter who got stuck into any job that needed doing; we were lucky to have them and, as the inn grew steadily busier, we simply could not have managed without them.

Our first visitor of the day was usually the postman, bearing not only the mail but also a newspaper he picked up for us.

'I can get you a daily paper, if you'd like,' he'd said to me on our first morning at the inn.

'Great,' I said. 'Can you get me a *Guardian*?'

There as a pause while he furrowed his brow.

'The *Guardian*? Is that a newspaper?'

He turned up with it the next day and proudly informed me that the newsagent had had to order it specially; I was the only *Guardian* reader in the entire upper Dale and was now probably marked down as some crypto-Communist Fifth Columnist as a result.

The postman usually also brought with him our first customer of the day: Faith, a woman as old as the century, who lived in a small cottage in a nearby village with her eccentric son and nine cats. Local gossip had it that Faith's mother, the daughter of a wealthy and aristocratic family from the North East, had been exiled to the Dale after causing some unspecified disgrace to the family name. As long as she remained in the Dale and did nothing to further embarrass her relatives, a generous allowance was paid to her. Her mother was now long dead and the allowance was no longer paid, but Faith had remained in the Dale all her life.

Every morning she was carried up to the pub in the back of the Post Office van. That was strictly against regulations, but the postmen were friendly sorts and head office was a long way away. The journey from Faith's house up to the pub was about five miles door to door, as the crow flies, but probably twice that far by the time the postman had detoured to all the other houses and farms on his round. There were no passenger seats in Post Office vans, so Faith had to travel lying on a pile of mail sacks in the back, while the van bounced and bucketed up and down the steep, rutted farm tracks. When they reached the inn, Faith emerged, James Bond-style, shaken but not stirred from the rear doors of the van, and while the postman had a cup of tea she would order up one after another 'large whisky and soda, for the love of God', while chain-smoking untipped cigarettes.

Having tucked away three or four double whiskies inside half an hour, Faith would depart for home with a couple of bottles of Guinness and more cigarettes and whisky to see her through until the next day. Her face was as wrinkled as an old hiking boot, and her liver must have been the size and appearance of a pickled walnut, but her mind was razor-sharp and she kept us in fits of laughter with her invariably scurrilous tales of past misdeeds. Well-bred and well-educated, she could none the less curse like a trooper and knew every dingy taproom from Sheffield to the Scottish border.

Our affection for Faith was not always shared by the farmers' wives around the Dale. The older ones had long memories and had known Faith in her younger days, when she was a regular in all the pubs of the Dale and a very beautiful and feisty woman, if the photograph on the mantelpiece of her cottage was to be believed. There was a sizeable population of 'chapel folk' – Methodists – in the Dale, who never went near the pubs and would certainly not have approved of Faith's drinking, but many of the less devout inhabitants also harboured reservations about her. The Dale was almost a closed society when Faith was young, with few ever leaving, even temporarily, and even fewer newcomers ever arriving, and it was also even more of a man's world in those days. Except for Saturday nights when some farmers' wives might accompany their husbands and drink a sweet stout or a small sherry while their men downed their pints and whiskies, the pubs were pretty much all-male preserves, with the exception of Faith, who went where she wanted, when she wanted.

I never did discover whether there was some 'history' between her and one or two of the farmers, or whether it was just the understandable resentment of women tied to their children and their farmhouse, while Faith was free to spend time and perhaps flirt with their husbands in the pub, but there was certainly an edge to some of the women's comments about her, albeit one masked by the typical Dale mixture of discretion and understatement. It may have been my imagination, but whenever I heard one of the Dale's women say of Faith, 'Oh, yes, she's quite a character', I was sure I could detect the faint sound of grinding teeth. Further evidence was supplied when, years later, Faith died, and Sue and I were among only five people who went to her funeral – so few that I was even pressed into service as a pall-bearer.

Faith reserved her own venom for just two people. One was the farmer and Methodist lay preacher who, thirty years before, had bought the one and only pub in her village, closed it down and turned it into a house for himself and his family, with a small shop that sold food but no alcohol or tobacco. Faced with a four-mile walk to the next nearest pub, the villagers reacted with fury to this *fait accompli,* and nor was their temper improved by the new owner's statement that 'I have preached against the evils of drink, but that is not the sole reason. There is my brother and my mother and we need another house.' When it was pointed out to him that the villagers now had nowhere to go and socialize, he said, 'If the local people want somewhere to meet, there is the village hall and reading room', where they could socialize without the sinful pleasures and temptations of alcoholic drink.

There were violent scenes when he moved in, with abuse hurled and windows smashed. For months afterwards, furious villagers congregated outside the place almost every Saturday night and laid siege to it, with shouted threats and more rocks thrown, but the new owner, as stubborn as any of his peers in the Dale, remained resolute. He continued in similarly uncompromising vein for the rest of his life, even writing a letter to the local newspaper in which he described the ladies' darts league in the Dale as a 'sea of unfaithfulness'. His grandson, a self-styled 'God-fearing Methodist', was still carrying on the family traditions years later, albeit via the ultra-modern channel of the internet, adding a post to a local site saying that it was 'most unlikely' that the family would ever consider selling the building and even less likely that it would ever again become a pub. His father was even more emphatic, declaring that the village was 'dead' anyway. 'The shop and filling station have gone, the people have gone, the youth hostel closes shortly. There's nothing left. If I wasn't farming, I wouldn't be here myself. There'll never be another pub.'

As he predicted, the pub never reopened and, even though thirty years had passed since then, Faith never passed it or heard mention of it without cursing the owner. Tempers had cooled a little over the years, but the split between the 'chapel folk' of the village and the bibulous remainder seemed as broad and unbridgeable as ever. The village pub was only a memory and the village hall and reading room remained chronically underused.

Faith's other pet hate was, on the face of it, a rather more surprising one: Hannah Hauxwell. The story of Hannah's lonely battle against the elements on a Dales farm that was even more remote and bereft of modern facilities than the Inn at the Top had captivated the nation when she became the subject of a Yorkshire Television documentary, *Too Long A Winter*. However, Hannah's tale had left Faith cold, largely, I suspected, because if a documentary was to be made about a woman living under incredibly primitive conditions in a lonely and remote dale, Faith might have had other ideas about the most appropriate subject for it... The television fees and book royalties would certainly have bought an awful lot of Guinness, whisky and cigarettes.

On the rare occasions when we could snatch an hour or so away from the pub together, Sue and I would sometimes drop in on Faith at her tiny cottage. Clinging to a shelf of rock above the gorge through which the river roared and tumbled, the village was a perpetually dank place, the water dripping from the trees as grey and rheumy as Faith's eyes. Her little cottage was always cold and damp, the only heat coming from a fire smouldering fitfully in the hearth, while the acrid smell of urine from her collection of nine cats was enough to make your eyes water as soon as you entered the hallway.

Her son Paul shared the house with her. He was 'a bit touched', as they used to say in those politically incorrect times, though the only visible manifestation of this was his unusual personal grooming. He cut his own hair, shaving his head in a perfect circle about two and a half inches above his ears, so that the resultant disc of white hair – all that remained – sat on top of his head like the icing on a cupcake. He also took his daily shave to extremes, removing the hair on his chest and eyebrows and even going to work on his nose. He came into the pub with his mother one day, wearing a large plaster across the middle of his nose.

'What happened, Paul?' I said. 'Been in a scrap?'

'Oh, no,' he said. 'I just cut myself shaving.'

'What? On your nose?'

'Yes, I always shave my nose,' he said, in a tone of voice that implied surprise that anybody didn't.

He had worked as a postman in his earlier years, covering a twenty-mile round on foot in all weathers to deliver the mail to the inn and all the remote farms around the head of the Dale, but when the Post Office introduced post vans, Paul, a non-driver, was made redundant. He had never worked since and, excluding Faith's daily intake of whisky, Guinness and cigarettes, they lived a life of almost medieval poverty.

On the first day we called in, Faith was just cooking their lunch – a boiled and, from the smell, rather elderly ox heart, that was to be shared between them, without vegetables or any other accompaniment. Too impatient or indifferent to wait for it to cook through, Faith took it off the stove when it was barely discoloured on the outside and so pink on the inside that it could conceivably still have been beating. She hacked it in two and the pair of them then tucked into the tough, rubbery and parboiled heart while, feeling queasy, Sue and I made our excuses and left.

Unlike his mother, Paul was a rare visitor to the pub, but two or three times a year he'd call in, order half a shandy, and then begin the ritual opening of his purse. From his pocket he extracted a large, indescribably filthy, but carefully folded and knotted handkerchief. Placing this on a table, he undid the knots one by one and folded back the handkerchief to reveal another smaller and cleaner handkerchief that was also carefully folded and knotted. Inside that was a small and very battered leather purse. This was opened, the inner pocket unzipped and Paul would then extract the requisite amount – usually in ones, twos and five pences – and then complete the purse ritual in reverse. Had there been any pickpockets operating around the Inn at the Top, they would have found Paul a very tough nut to crack indeed.

Unlike Faith, our other locals and the tourists and hikers who patronized the pub arrived not by Post Office van but by foot, bike and car, occasionally by tractor and sometimes even on horseback; a few of the farmers kept 'Dales Galloway' ponies for use in winter. Although tractors did much of the farm work once carried out by horses, in winter snows that could stop a tractor in its wheel tracks, horses could still 'lead' hay through the drifts to fodder hungry sheep.

One of our locals, Tommy, who had a round, pink-cheeked face that always looked as if it had been polished before he came out for the evening, was so inordinately proud of his shiny, top-of-the-range new tractor that he used to do the seven-mile commute up to the pub in it every night. Unfortunately, though he was an affable and friendly sort, he was – how can I put this? – not necessarily the sharpest set of shears in the shepherd's toolkit, and it soon turned out that his enthusiasm for purchasing shiny and expensive new tractors, while most of his peers in the Dale were still driving the tractors their fathers had bought, was not remotely justified by the returns he achieved on his farm. Within a couple of years he had gone bankrupt and been forced to sell his farm, a devastating blow to anyone in a community that had such deep and long-standing roots in its land.

One group of occasional customers used an even more surprising mode of transport to reach the inn. One early spring morning, I heard a growling, deep bass rumble and felt the ground beneath my feet began to shake. I rushed outside to see a column of armoured cars, tracked vehicles and army lorries grinding up the hill towards us. The commanding officer jumped out and introduced himself. They were based at Catterick Camp and this was one of their annual exercises to put the latest batch of raw recruits through their paces. They then deployed themselves (as I believe they say in the Army) around the inn and, with our permission, the CO and his juniors ran their communication cables in through the pub windows and set up HQ in the taproom.

They then settled themselves with their radio sets and a few drinks and snacks, while their hapless men were still plodding their way towards us on a fifteen-mile route march, wearing full battledress and carrying rucksacks that their kindly NCOs had filled with rocks. When they finally arrived some hours later, the exhausted squaddies were forbidden to enter the inn and had to slump down on the ground outside to consume their army rations, washed down with water from their canteens. Meanwhile, maintaining the noble traditions of the British Army, their officers were still ensconced inside, passing snide comments about their men while lunching on fillet steaks washed down with a couple of bottles of our best claret.

While their officers finished a leisurely dessert, their soldiers were loaded aboard the lorries and shipped off back to Catterick.

'We've got a nice surprise for them when they get back,' one of the officers told me, tapping the side of his nose. 'They're going straight on the assault course.'

He was still laughing uproariously as he went out of the door.

Like the unfortunate squaddies, Sue and I carried on working all day, every day, with rarely more than a few minutes to rest or talk to each other – just like breakfast, lunch and the evening meal were also taken on the hoof – until we fell into bed at night, by which time we were usually too tired even to speak. The next thing we knew, the clamour of the alarm was rousing us to another day, and every day that passed, the pub got busier and busier and busier.

The best times of day for us were the late evenings with our locals and the very first thing in the morning and the last thing at night. In the morning, the moors around the inn were deserted, save for sheep, grouse and the moorland birds that came up there to breed in summer. For a few precious minutes we could sit on the bench outside or stroll over the fell with the dog, watching the sun rise and listening to the birdsong: the liquid, bubbling call of curlews; the breathtaking song of the larks on sunny days, invisible high in the sky overhead; the gabbling of the grouse; the whoops of the lapwings; and the eerie, monotone piping calls of the golden plovers in the morning mist, till the fells seemed full of the sound.

The mist would burn away from the fell-top first and for a few minutes the sun would be gilding the inn, while all around us was a sea of mist, clinging to the slopes and the valley floors, its tendrils tracing the course of each beck and stream. We'd watch the lapwings cartwheeling in the sunlight, the curlews soaring and the larks climbing ever higher into the sky until they disappeared from sight altogether, leaving only their song filling the air. The sheep would begin toiling up the fell-sides towards the tops, away from the stinging hordes of insects below. For those few minutes we could almost convince ourselves that the perfect peace would never be broken, until the first car or hiker appeared over the horizon to shatter the illusion.

Last thing at night, after shutting down the generator, we would also often take the dog for a last stroll in the darkness. On clear nights we gazed up in wonder at an array of jewel-bright stars un-sullied by any light pollution, with the Milky Way a glorious band of light across the heavens. On moonless, cloudy nights, it was so black-dark that the only way we could tell where we were was to listen to the sound of our footsteps on the hard surface of the road. If that ceased, we knew that we had wandered off-course onto the grass verge, beyond which the peat bogs lay in wait. There was a cattle grid a hundred yards along the road from the inn and the rattle of that underfoot told us it was time to turn round and head back to get some sleep. Those brief, beautiful interludes were almost the only moments of relaxation in our endless working days.

However, fearing for my health if I took no exercise and stuck to a diet of beer and whatever food could be crammed down in the gaps between customers, I began trying to fit in a daily jog out on the moor during the quietest part of the working day in mid-afternoon. Many other people used the moors around the inn for recreation, and jogging and hiking were only two of the forms of healthy exercise that could be practised. I was running past an old mine shaft near the top of the moor one afternoon when I came across an amorously entwined couple, so absorbed in what they were doing that they hadn't heard my approach. I ground to a halt and then beat a discreet retreat, but it gave me an instant flashback to one of the more formative of my youthful experiences when, a spotty schoolboy in a class full of spotty schoolboys, I joined my peers on a nature ramble led by our teacher, a shy and sensitive soul known to us only as Mr Wilks.

A confirmed bachelor (as it used to be possible to say, without a hint of innuendo), Mr Wilks was a gentleman well past his first flush of youth who taught Latin, collected stamps, played the clarinet and was so sensitive that the Latin word *pectus* always had to be translated as 'chest' rather than 'breast' in his presence. To utter the translation 'she thrust the dagger deep into her breast' was enough to produce a crimson blush in Mr Wilks and a hasty 'No, No, No! The correct word is chest.'

One June afternoon, Mr Wilks led us out on a ramble through the tangled woodland a mile or so from our school.

'If you walk very quietly, you may hear a cuckoo,' he promised, an observation greeted with scowls, sniggers and snorts from the motley deeply unimpressed crew at his heels.

Undeterred, he pressed on deeper into the

woods, pointing out birds, butterflies, animals, flowers, ferns and other wonders of nature to his near-mutinous charges, who would all have been far happier eating chips and watching television instead.

At length, walking along a narrow track in a little-used corner of the woods, Mr Wilks came to a juddering halt, his stream of bright and helpful observations dying on his lips. Just ahead and to one side of the track lay a couple, naked as cuckoos' eggs and blissfully intertwined in the grass. An arc of incredulous and delighted school-boys extended rapidly to either side of Mr Wilks, all straining their eyes to absorb every magic moment of the tableau vivant in front of them.

The couple, secure in the knowledge that no one ever visited this wild and remote part of the wood and deeply occupied with one other, had clearly failed to detect us before, but were now all too aware of us. Two pairs of eyes stared unblinkingly at us from the grass; thirty-one pairs of eyes stared just as unblinkingly back. All was silence as the seconds dragged by, agonizingly for Mr Wilks, ecstatically for his charges. Thirty eager school-boys silently willed Mr Wilks forward, nearer to the pink-fleshed apparitions so tantalizingly close at hand.

The two lovers remained freeze-framed, awaiting developments, and poor Mr Wilks simply stood like a rabbit trapped by car headlights, unable to go forwards, backwards or in any direction at all. At last he could bear the awful silence no longer. With a strangulated cry of 'This way, boys, I think I hear a cuckoo!' he plunged blindly off the track into a bramble-clogged copse of trees. With much reluctance and many a lingering backward glance, we followed behind him. There was not the faintest trace of a path and the undergrowth was thick, the ground muddy and the air buzzing with flies, but not even the hounds of Hades would have dragged Mr Wilks back the way we had come. Sweating profusely and sobbing with the effort, he forced a way through the undergrowth, eventually re-emerging onto the track a quarter of a mile back towards our starting point.

We walked back to school in near-total silence, each of us lost in our thoughts. For Mr Wilks it was a day of mortification he would long remember – he blushed when reminded of it years later, when I was a sixth-former about to leave the school. For my schoolmates and I it was the first glimpse of forbidden, earthly delights, and it left an indelible impression. With that happy, nostalgic thought, I chose another route back across the moor and then got back to work.

CHAPTER 5

Needs a Bit of Work

In addition to the workload with which any pub landlords, anywhere, would have been familiar, there were other quirks and idiosyncrasies that were unique to the Inn at the Top. The generator, bought in one of Neville's numerous dodgy deals, was ancient and even in its prime only had an output of seven kilowatts. Its peak output was now much lower than that, and nowhere near enough to cope with all the demands a busy pub would put on it. There were lights, power, coolers for the keg beer and lager, a freezer, a fridge, a chill cabinet, a microwave oven, a couple of fruit machines, a jukebox and an immersion heater, though that used such massive amounts of power that it was only ever switched on by accident or in a dire emergency.

During opening hours we were running near full capacity most of the time, which led to some mildly amusing quirks and foibles. If the microwave was switched on, the jukebox would slow down and even Madonna would acquire a bass voice for a few seconds, and if by some mischance someone switched on the immersion heater, the lights would dim, everything would grind to a halt and the generator would go into something close to cardiac arrest until I'd sprinted upstairs and turned the immersion off again, when normal service would be resumed. And on top of all that, of course, we ran out of water surprisingly often thanks to customers leaving the taps running in the Gents or Ladies, and we'd either have to do without until the pub quietened down a little or I'd have to sprint back down the hill to the pumps and get some emergency supplies running into the tanks.

In our early days at the inn, although it was already exhibiting the early symptoms of what would prove to be its terminal illness, the Start-a-matic – the battery-operated system that, as the name suggests, should have started the generator whenever a switch was turned on – had just about kept working. Since our bedroom was directly over the generator shed, we were woken from our slumbers by the generator rumbling into life whenever a customer switched on his bedside light or went to the loo in the middle of the night. Usually it would run for no more than five minutes and then wind down and stop as the customer turned his light off again, but on one occasion the generator started up at four in the morning and just kept running and running. I lay in bed, fists clenched, trying to suppress a mounting irritation at the way our already-too-short sleep was being disrupted, but finally, after half an hour, I got up, put on my dressing gown and went to ask the customer, as politely as I could manage, if he'd like either to a) turn the bloody light off and go to sleep, or b) borrow a torch or candle so that he could read in bed while we got our beauty sleep.

I knocked on his door – no reply. I waited and knocked again – still no reaction. Finally, after a third unanswered knock, I opened the door and strode in. Two near-simultaneous thoughts occurred to me as I rounded the door and took in the scene in front of me. One was that, until that very moment, I had completely forgotten that this particular customer was deaf. The second thought, arriving rapidly on the heels of the first, was that if there was one situation more embarrassing than a pub landlord catching one of his customers in flagrante delicto – 'having it off', for those without the benefit of a Classical education – the other was probably catching a customer in the act of applying his pile ointment.

For obvious reasons he hadn't heard me come in, but the movement of the door had certainly caught his attention. For what seemed like an eternity but in reality was probably only a couple of seconds, I stared at him and he, still with his tube of pile ointment poised for action, stared back at me. Then, mouthing, 'Sorry! Terribly sorry!' I retreated, closed the door and tiptoed back to bed. A few minutes later the light went out, the generator stopped and I went back to sleep, praying that, in my dreams, I would not be revisiting the scene I had just witnessed.

Hard though I tried to keep out of his way the next morning in the hope of avoiding further mutual embarrassment, Sod's Law dictated that we bumped into each other on the stairs. Both of us blushed an impressive shade of crimson, though I did manage to mumble, 'Good morning. Sorry about last night', and then, once more remembering that he was deaf and wouldn't have heard me, I gave up and hurried past. To my relief, and I'm sure to his as well, Sue served him his breakfast and sped him on his way without our paths crossing again. Only when he was safely off on the next leg of his long-distance hike did I tell her the story of the embarrassing incident the previous night.

We were early risers by nature and, since very few delivery wagons were willing or able to negotiate the twisting, precipitous roads that led to the inn, two or three times a week, one of us – or sometimes both if we had no overnight guests – tiptoed away from the still-sleeping inn and drove the winding road over the moors and down into the Dale to fetch bread, milk and the thousand and one things we needed. Quartz-rich spoil from the heaps at the old lead mills in the Dale, the cheapest and most easily accessible material, was used to surface these ancient roads. Always the wind was blowing and often the cloud was down or rain or snow were driving across the fells, shrouding the land from view, but when the cloud lifted and the sun broke through, the quartz crystals in the road surface sparkled like a million diamonds.

A mile or two across the fells, separated from the road by some of the most glutinous peat bogs of even that sodden moor-top, we could see the Nine Standards outlined against the western sky. From that distance they appeared monolithic blocks of stone but when I walked and splashed my way over to them one day, I discovered that they were actually man-made, drystone stacks, with their name perhaps deriving from 'standers': the pillars of rock left in coalmines to prevent the roof from collapsing.

The purpose of the Nine Standards was unknown. Some claimed they were built to appear like an advancing army to marauding Scots border raiders, though that suggested a contempt for Scottish intelligence that even the most prejudiced Englishman would have found hard to maintain for long. The theory that they were boundary markers seems implausible, too – why build nine where one would have done? – and the most plausible, if prosaic explanation might simply be that they were built by shepherds with time on their hands.

Nine Standards had been for centuries a place where shepherds from either side of the fells were accustomed to meet to exchange sheep that had strayed from their 'heaf' – their home turf – or been driven off the tops into the wrong valley by wild weather. Since building cairns on hills is an apparently elemental human need, as the heaps of stone every few hundred yards of the 270-mile course of the Pennine Way seem to testify, perhaps the Nine Standards are simply cairns built for once by men who were skilled at drystone walling to while away the hours waiting for their peers from the neighbouring valleys to appear.

Leaving the Nine Standards behind, we drove on down into the Dale, a gentler, softer place, where the cutting edge of the wind was dulled and the day warmer. Winter arrived a month later down there and ended a month earlier than on the bleak 'tops' around the inn. On our return, we would often pause again at the moor edge, looking back over our shoulders before driving on over the cold and lonely fells.

Alongside some sections of the road there were tall poles every few yards. There were no telephone lines or wires connecting them and we puzzled over their purpose for days until a farmer enlightened us.

'They're snow poles,' he said. 'In winter the drifts bury the road ten, twenty, sometimes even thirty feet deep in places. The poles show the drivers of the snow ploughs and snow blowers and the JCBs we sometimes have to use when the snow's really compacted, where the edge of the

110

road is. If it weren't for the poles, they might be ploughing out the moor, or dropping over the fell edge.'

Just below the edge of the moor, the road passed under a viaduct, part of a disused railway line near the head of the Dale. Half a mile along the track next to it was the grand old station that the local firewood-seller and general dealer, Mick, had converted into his house and place of business. We needed some logs, so one morning I turned off and drove up to take a look at what Mick had to offer. He turned out to be a gnarled, wizened, permanently unshaven old man, a sort of Steptoe without the son, who drove a battered pick-up truck and made a precarious living buying and selling things that even a scrap dealer like our dodgy employer Neville would have looked at twice.

Mick produced cream and scarcely edible butter he had churned from the milk of his Jersey cow and sold logs cut from decrepit railway sleepers, so thick with creosote that the stench of them burning could be smelt miles away. In his enthusiasm for a cheap purchase he also often bought things that even he couldn't sell. When I called round one day, I spent half an hour helping him to unload a wooden henhouse, bought at auction. It was so rotten that it collapsed as we were lifting it down from the wagon. 'Needs a bit of work' was Mick's only comment as we carried the sodden pieces of wood over to a corner of the yard and added them to an already mouldering heap of nameless, unidentifiable items.

Mick's only garb was boiler suits. He possessed

111

three of them, and selected them according to the business of the day. Two seemed to our untrained eyes to be almost equally filthy, but Mick clearly held one in higher esteem, for he would never wear it while tackling really dirty jobs. His third boiler suit was immaculate, a Sunday-best outfit. When he appeared in that, we knew that the day was a rest day and that he was off somewhere important, perhaps to see his bank manager or attend a wedding.

The railway running past Mick's station house was once the highest railway line in England, with a summit height of 1,370 feet where it crossed the Pennine divide. The line was constructed in the 1860s, and originally intended purely for the transport of freight, though passengers were soon being carried as well. The trains took iron ore from the mines of West Cumberland to the iron and steel mills of Teesside, and carried coal and coke on the return journey for the foundries and blast furnaces at Barrow and Workington. By the 1870s a million tons of coke a year were being carried.

The builders of the line had to span some formidable obstacles, including several deep valleys and fast-flowing rivers, and then the long climb up to the summit of the line, on the moor three miles north of the Inn at the Top. Heading in either direction, there was a punishing climb to the summit – a thirteen-mile ascent travelling from east to west and ten miles from west to east, with an even steeper gradient. The stream near the summit was named Welcome Stream by the train drivers, grateful for this sign that the long, hard haul under full steam was over, though the descent on the other side could be just as stressful for them. Heavy-laden goods trains heading west often arrived at the foot of the downhill section with their brakes glowing red with heat.

The station building where Mick lived was a remarkably grand structure for the tiny village it served and was probably originally intended to operate as a station hotel as well. Just along the track had once been an even grander structure – a 1,040-foot-long, 196-foot-high steel viaduct, designed by Thomas Bouch. He was also responsible for the infamous Tay Bridge, but, unlike that structure, his railway viaduct remained intact until it was demolished and sold for scrap in an act of epic official vandalism just after the final closure of the line in 1962. A side line also once ran for a couple of miles across the moor towards a long-disused quarry not far from the Inn at the Top, where the huge stone blocks for the embankment piers and the dressed stone for the station house were cut.

A sparsely used station a little further down the line adopted an unusual, and possibly unique, method for collecting fares from its infrequent passengers. No money changed hands at the station, but the railway worker on duty there would contact the stations further up the line by telegraph and give the number and description of any passengers, and their fares were then collected from them when they got off.

When we moved to the inn, the line's tracks had long been torn up and its beautiful viaducts demolished, but another railway, one of the most dramatic and scenic in the country, also passed close to the end of the Dale, and that one was still open, albeit only just, having been saved from threatened closure by a formidably determined public campaign. There may never have been a genuine economic case for the line, which only came into being in the 1870s as the result of a misguided piece of brinkmanship by a Victorian railway company that applied for permission to build the line, mainly to put pressure on one of its rivals to share its facilities. But the railway company had reckoned without the intransigence of the MPs who had voted for the construction of the line. When the company tried to abandon its plans, having secured the grudging co-operation of its rival that it had been seeking, MPs refused to allow it to do so and instead compelled it to go ahead with construction at prodigious expense.

The line was built over – and under – some of the most difficult terrain and in the face of appalling difficulties and the most intractable conditions that could be found anywhere in Britain: peat bogs that swallowed thousands of tons of rock for embankments without trace, landslips, mudslides, atrocious winter weather and winds so strong that some workers were literally blown over viaduct parapets. One newspaper correspondent sent to investigate the cause of delays in construction had this answer to critics:

Let them go over it in the drenching rain of October, or let those who complain of its slowness in the making, wade through the mire, clay and water and see the slurry slipping away from the metals and add

114

to these difficulties the cuttings through boulder clay and rocks of excessive hardness, the roving habits of the workmen and the wild inhospitable district through which it passes and then the wonder will not be that the works are incomplete, but at the possibility of completing them at all.

Despite all the difficulties, the line was completed in only six years, but at a stupendous financial and human cost. The eventual bill to the railway company was more than twice the original estimate, and the cost to many of the 6,000 men who built the line was their lives, either from accidents or the typhus, cholera and smallpox that swept through their shantytown construction camps, built on the open fells. The total number of deaths went unrecorded, but eighty people died in a smallpox outbreak at one camp alone. The cemetery at the tiny church near the most spectacular viaduct on the line bulges with the railway dead.

The first passenger train ran in 1876 and several villages along the line declared a public holiday and rang the church bells to celebrate a day that many farmers in the Dale and elsewhere felt would be the beginning of a new era of prosperity, with the markets of industrial Yorkshire, Lancashire and Scotland at last open to them. That belief was not shared by the railway company, however, who saw the line simply as an improved express route to the North.

The wishes and needs of the local inhabitants had remained bottom of the scale of priorities of those running the railway ever since. The nadir was reached with the closure of all but three of the stations on the line. Since then, it had seen a revival of passenger traffic, with several small stations reopening, and it was well used by local people as well as tourists, but even though it was now officially reprieved, a lingering doubt about its future remained. Some railwaymen claimed that the line had always been marked for closure since the end of the Second World War. Although in theory it was now safe from closure, in practice its long-term future remained as unpredictable as the Dale's weather, but to close the line, or allow it to decay beyond recall, would be an act of public vandalism that our descendants would find hard to understand or forgive.

Even today, the arguments about the line's economic value remain as heated as the boilers on the steam trains that used to travel the line and as impenetrable as the smoke they left hanging in the long tunnels through the Pennines, but in a civilized country the arguments would not be all about economics. As one critic of the closure plans remarked, 'Hadrian's Wall and Durham Cathedral are not required to justify their existence on economic grounds.' The railway, built through some of the most wild and dramatic scenery in the country, is perhaps the supreme monument to Victorian vision, determination and engineering skill, and deserves to remain forever as both a working railway and a national monument.

CHAPTER 6

What Do You Find to Do in Winter?

In June, as Argentina were winning the 1978 World Cup and England weren't, Sue and I took the chance of a day off before the real mass influx of tourists and hikers began with the start of the school holidays. We set off to explore some of the highways, byways and pathways that snaked through our new moor-top kingdom. We had only to settle the matter of our equipment and supplies and we could begin our voyage of discovery.

I consulted the oracle, William Boot, the hero of Evelyn Waugh's *Scoop*, probably the most comprehensively equipped journalist ever to set forth on an assignment. In addition to a set of cleft sticks, 'Boot of the Beast' took with him:

a well- perhaps rather over-furnished tent, three months' rations, a collapsible canoe, a jointed flagstaff and Union Jack, a hand-pump and sterilising plant, an astrolabe, six suits of tropical linen and a sou'-wester, a camp operating table and set of surgical instruments, a portable humidor, guaranteed to pre-serve cigars in condition in the Red Sea, a Christmas hamper complete with Santa Claus costume and a tripod mistletoe stand, and a cane for whacking snakes... At the last moment he added a coil of rope and a sheet of tin.

Although Boot's baggage seemed to encompass most possibilities, we felt that it was slightly better suited to travel in North Africa than northern England, and we compiled instead a list of the things a true hikesman – a Hiking Boot – would require to face the Pennine hills with confidence: a stout pair of boots; a tin of dubbin; a dozen pairs of thick wool socks; waterproof gaiters like over-grown spats, bristling with hooks and eyes; thick wool knee breeches; thermal underwear; wool shirts and coarse, hairy pullovers; bilious yellow waterproof jacket and leggings; embarrassing woolly hat with bobble; gloves; compass; clear plastic container to be hung round the neck on a string, keeping the Ordnance Survey map dry, visible and dangling always within reach; rucksack; tent; sleeping bag; inflatable mattress; foil blankets; windproof matches; iron rations; Primus stove; billy cans; water bottle; chocolate bars; tea bags; water-sterilizing tablets; needle and thread; Travel Scrabble; army-style survival guide explaining how to extract protein from crushed cockroaches; whistle; torch; first aid kit; shortwave radio; distress flares; Very pistol; length of rope; Swiss Army penknife; binoculars; field guides to the mammals, birds, fish, reptiles, invertebrates, trees, plants, ferns, grasses, flowers, fungi, rocks, minerals and soils of northern England; dictionaries of Dales and Cumbrian dialects; Bible and complete works of Shakespeare.

In our time at the inn, we were to see many similarly equipped hikers and derive much simple pleasure from the sight of them toiling up the fell-sides, like snails with leaden shells. On a cloudless summer day, we even went to the assistance of one Pennine wayfarer, who was literally unable to walk another step. Scarcely able to pick up his rucksack for him, we discovered that, among the customary tent poles, socks and pullovers, were a dozen large tins of baked beans, stew and vegetables. He was in no danger of starvation, just death from exhaustion.

A patch of glutinous ground within sight of the inn proved a particularly valuable source of entertainment. One man who slipped and fell while traversing it was so weighed down by his pack that he was unable to raise himself unassisted and lay there on his back, waving his arms and legs in the air like a demented tortoise, until a rescue party, weak with laughter, came to his aid. Another unfortunate leaned too far forward and found the weight of his pack propelling him relentlessly forward, till he was face-down in the bog. He emerged looking and sounding like the Creature from the Black Lagoon, a peat-smothered hulk, emitting banshee wails of disgust.

If we were to avoid a similarly hideous fate, it was clear that either we would have to use bearers to carry our equipment or else restrict ourselves to the bare necessities. The thought of a Sir Gandalf Twickenham-District-Lines-style expedition had enormous appeal: twelve major sponsors, a thousand tons of supplies borne by a massive motorized convoy and a send-off watched by a battery of the international press, as a moist-eyed society beauty and the heir to some Ruritanian monarchy wrung their exquisitely manicured hands in distress at our departure. It was an appealing image, but it seemed a trifle implausible for a ramble through well-charted English territory and we set it aside, not without some regret.

We toyed with the idea of a *Five Discover the Dale* expedition instead: plenty of scrumptious picnics with hard-boiled eggs, fruit cake and lots of ginger pop, and an Adventure in which we and our companions, including George (short for Georgina), who always had wanted to be a boy, and Christopher (long for Christine), who always had not, would discover secret caves and smugglers, while Timmy the dog chased sheep all over the fells, before being shot by an irate farmer. This, too, failed the plausibility test and we decided reluctantly that this was a journey that we had to make unescorted. We dug out our wellingtons, a map and a couple of Mars bars and set off over the moors.

There are few parts of Britain, and probably no parts of England, that are more bleak and apparently inhospitable than the moors around the Inn at the Top. One of our better-travelled customers called them 'the empty quarter', in an echo of the endless barren rock and sand dunes of the Saudi Arabian *Rub' al Khali*, albeit, as he acknowledged with a smile, with rather lower temperatures and substantially more in the way of annual rainfall. The moor-tops formed a strange, almost lunar, landscape, punctuated by hags and hummocks of peat capped with heather. Surrounding them was the grey, gritstone bedrock, stripped bare by the force of erosion, leaving only sterile, rain-washed ground. If split, the rock was a surprising coral pink, but a few weeks of wind and weather leached the colour from it, leaving it as grey as the clouds streaming over the fells.

Lower on the slopes, spiders' webs, jewelled with moisture from the clouds, glowed among the mat grass in the watery sunlight. A grouse clattered out from beneath our feet, whirring away downwind as we blundered from wiry tussocks of heather into mosses and bogs, the ground quaking gently, as if there was nothing solid in these water-filled hills. At each step, the peat gave up its hold on our boots with a soft reproachful sound.

The track we were following was an old 'greenway' or 'driftway' over the moor. Some of these old tracks had been in continuous use for thousands of years. They may well have been created as early as the Bronze Age by the movement of animals from one grazing area to another, and were certainly in use by the Iron Age, around 600 BC, and through Roman and medieval times, when animals were being moved between grazing lands and to markets on at least an annual basis. Before the nineteenth century the greenways were the prime arteries of trade throughout rural Britain and the narrowness of this one showed that its use had been restricted to stock, men and packhorses. No wheeled traffic would even attempt the muddy, peaty track over the moor, which only had to be wide enough for a packhorse carrying two panniers, or a farm horse pulling a wooden sled, to pass.

Very few people of that era possessed any kind of wheeled transport. As a contemporary writer recalled: 'Only yeomen and the larger occupiers could boast of carts; the produce of the farms, hay, corn and peat, being brought in on railed sledges and the more portable articles on packhorses. Coal and lime were conveyed by the last method across the miry moors and commons, where tracks instead of roads existed till near the end of the eighteenth century', and packhorses were used both as 'general carrier from town to town and the vehicle in transit for grain to the mill or market and for manure, etc., on the farm'.

With transport only possible by packhorse over the greenways, the price of a heavy commodity such as coal or lime could double or treble in the space of a few miles. Wool, hides, iron, lead, charcoal and salt were also transported in this way, with salt a vital necessity at a time when the only way to preserve meat was to salt it. Over centuries the passage of animals and travellers accelerated the effects of erosion on soft surfaces like moorland peat or the rich soils of the valley floors, and some sections of the old tracks became sunken 'hollow ways' several feet lower than the surrounding land. Struggling on foot along one of these ancient greenways, once the prime arteries of trade, the true scale of the revolution in transport created by the development of turnpikes, canals and railways was brought vividly to life. Before the coming of the turnpikes, even a road as well used as the Great North Road could become almost impassable because of autumn and winter mud, and coach travel along lesser roads was so bad that, if a journey absolutely had to be undertaken, it was more usual to yoke up oxen than horses. Travel by horse could only be safely undertaken in summer – safely except for highwaymen, that is.

Just to the side of the track was a pile of stones, the rubble of some ancient mine buildings. Nearby there was a fenced-off mineshaft, its opening sealed by steel girders and railway sleepers, and next to it a curious sunken circle perhaps thirty feet in diameter, the green turf in sharp contrast to the moorland surrounding it. We puzzled over it for some time before we realized its purpose. The circle had been worn over decades, and perhaps even centuries, by a 'horse-gin' driven by a pit pony harnessed to a winding engine, and plodding in an unending circle as it raised and lowered coal tubs from the mine workings deep below the moor. Over time, the hooves of the generations of pit ponies had slowly eroded the circle, sinking it a few inches below the level of the moor, and their droppings had enriched the previously poor soil underfoot, allowing a finer turf to grow in place of the coarse moorland grasses. In that hard age, most ponies doing such work were deliberately blinded so that they would not see the futility of their endless walk to nowhere. The ruined buildings must have been the stable where the pit pony was housed at night and the sheds where coal was stored until it was loaded onto the packhorse trains that carried it down to the farms and the lead-smelting mills in the Dale below.

At the edge of the moor, we picked up a rough track, running down the fell alongside a tumbling tributary of the river that ran through the bottom of the Dale. Halfway down the track we came to the extensive ruins of one of the old lead mines, ore works and smelting mills that had once dominated the upper Dale. In the late eighteenth century, this smelting mill and the nineteen miles of underground mine tunnels that honeycombed the fell-sides around it gave employment to 1,200 men, women and children; probably more people worked in that one mine complex than the entire permanent population of the upper Dale today. The mines were co-owned by many small investors, and whole families worked together to extract the galena – lead ore – from the mine and process it. The men did the heaviest work of mining the ore-bearing rock, while the women and children used iron hammers to break up the extracted ore into manageable lumps, which were then passed through a water-powered crushing mill and a series of hand-operated riddles and sieves, eventually reducing the ore to grains like coarse sand. These were then smelted on 'roasting hearths', fuelled by peat dug from the moors above the mines and coal from the pits around the Inn at the Top.

Water-powered bellows were used to fan the fires and a mile-long system of flues was constructed, running up the fell-side to the moor edge, to carry the deadly poisonous lead fumes away from the hearths. When the wind was in the south-west, the fumes blew straight over the Inn at the Top – just one more health hazard for the landlords there to endure. The flues were built less in the interest of protecting the health of the inhabitants – whose lives were curtailed by inhaling lead fumes and ingesting lead particles to such an extent that in the nineteenth century, life expectancy in the Dale was just forty-six years – than for financial reasons. The long flues gave time for the valuable particles of lead carried in the fumes to settle or condense out as the smoke cooled. Once a year workers, usually children, were sent up the inside of the flues to chip off and collect the accumulated deposits.

As we walked down the track through the old mine complex, the first ruined building we passed was what had once been the peat store, a cavernous building well over a hundred yards long, and originally roofed with heather thatch supported by twin rows of stone pillars. The thatch was long gone but the pillars still stood, though all else had disappeared. In early summer each year, the entire workforce of the mine used to turn out to cut peat from the moor. The cut peats were stacked and partially dried on the moor and then brought down in late summer to finish curing in the winds blowing through the open-sided peat house, which, when full, held enough fuel to last three years.

Every resident of the Dale, including the landlords of the Inn at the Top, had also once had the same ancient right of 'turbary' – peat cutting – and other commons rights including pasture; pannage (the right to turn out pigs to feed on acorns, beech-mast, chestnuts, etc., and by extension, the right to gather food such as nuts, berries, mushrooms and herbs, for human consumption); estovers (firewood, hedging material and other vegetation like heather or reeds for thatching, bracken for animal bedding, or rushes for lights);

125

piscary (fishing); and common of marl (the right to take sand or gravel). These rights pre-dated Magna Carta and even the monarchy, but an Act of Parliament in 1965 restricted those ancient rights to those willing to go through a process of formally registering them and – as must have been the intention of those who framed the legislation – many people did not bother. As a result, like the rights of passage and stance (overnight grazing), lost to the drovers as a result of the Enclosure Acts of the eighteenth and nineteenth centuries, the remaining commons rights were lost, not only to the current occupiers of the land, but to all their successors.

The old lead miners of the Dale had also left other, even larger, though less immediately obvious, traces of their activities. The early miners used a method called 'hushing' to expose the veins of ore, constructing dams and conduits to gather and channel huge quantities of water that were then released to tear away the loose rock from a hillside and reveal the ore-bearing rock beneath. Almost all of the natural-looking cliffs and gullies that we had passed as we made our way down from the moor into the Dale had been formed in this way. There were also massive old spoil heaps, formed from the waste from mining and ore processing and the spoil from the shafts and levels dug to reach the ore-bearing rock and to provide drainage and ventilation to the mine workings.

Even a century after the mine and smelt mill fell silent for the last time, the spoil-heaps were still so contaminated with lead that almost nothing would grow there. Among the exceptions were the beautiful 'heartsease', the small wild ancestors of the pansies that grow in so many suburban gardens, with tri-petalled, purple, white and yellow flowers. Despite their apparent delicacy and fragility, they were as lead-tolerant as any plant and grew in abundance around the spoil heaps of the lead mines. The sight of them in bloom always gave a lift to our spirits as we wandered the paths and tracks of the Dale.

We walked down the track through the deserted ruins, an evocative, eerie experience, accentuated by the harsh cawing of a solitary crow perched on a crumbling wall; apart from ourselves, it was the only living thing visible in the whole of that once-bustling landscape. We passed the crumbling magazine where the gunpowder for blasting was stored, the wreck that had been the 'silver house', where the precious metal that always accompanied the lead was assayed, and the remains of the roasting hearths and the flues, slowly merging with the land on which they lay, though their course up the fell-side towards the moor could still be made out.

As we reached the edge of a village and began to walk along the main – indeed the only – street, we weren't entirely sure what sort of a welcome we'd receive from any unfamiliar natives of this remote and very traditional area whom we might encounter, but in the event our fears proved groundless. While offcomers were not always welcome in rural areas, their presence in the Dale had been less traumatic than in many tourist honeypots. The explosion of property values came later here than the rest of the country, and the strangers bought mainly houses and barns that had long stood derelict.

'There is a big percentage of outsiders here now,' said one of the local farmers we met while making our first tentative exploration of our new domain. 'But they've done good in one respect: they've done up houses that would otherwise have gone to the wall. There's one just over there that nobody had been living in for thirty years.'

He settled his forearms along the top of a gate, preparing for a lengthy chat, a man to whom a rush was only a thing that grew in his pasture. He had a cigarette dangling from the corner of his mouth, carrying a precarious column of ash. He neither inhaled nor removed it from his mouth, content to allow the smoke to drift up into his eye without apparent discomfort. He was dressed in his working clothes, a cap settled on his head like a cowpat on a patch of grass, and oversized trousers held in place by an enormous pair of braces, reinforced by a stout leather belt. His shirt was the old-fashioned, striped, flannel variety, the separate collar long detached and probably lost altogether.

In contrast to the trousers, his short-sleeved V-neck pullover was too small for him and holed below the waterline, riding up over his midriff to expose an ample waistline and the bottom end of his braces. The ancient tweed jacket was functional rather than decorative, with enough encrustations to keep a forensic scientist busy for weeks. A piece of baler twine around his middle compensated for the missing buttons, and stuffing spilled out of the shoulder seams; it would have been no great surprise to find sparrows nesting there.

He talked a good deal of old days and hard times, but when we steered him back to the subject of newcomers, to our surprise, he showed very little of the resentment that farmers were popularly supposed to feel about offcomers.

'Most of the outsiders seem to fit in with the community well enough,' he said. 'There are some people who maybe never fit in anywhere, but most of them seem to be very clannable people.'

'What about the visitors, though, the walkers and the tourists; how do you feel about them?'

'There's a tremendous lot of walkers,' he said, with the amused tolerance displayed by farmers towards those who walk for pleasure rather than need. 'It's trebled these last few years. They can be a damned nuisance. They leave gates open, knock part of a wall down, with going over and this sort of thing, but there's a percentage of them very good, just a few who couldn't care less. It's not so bad if they stick to footpaths, but some tend to wander aimlessly anywhere.'

We pointed out that we had just walked down from near the head of the Dale, finding virtually none of the footpaths marked and almost all the stiles walled up, blocked or fenced off. It seemed less than just to blame the visitors for not knowing where the footpaths were supposed to be, when often it was the farmers themselves that were forcing them to climb over walls.

'I would say it's better if the footpaths are clearly marked; it puts things out of dispute,' he said, steering a careful course around the topic without making any admission of guilt. 'You never mind where anyone's going, if they close gates and don't do any damage, but dogs and that I don't like. These people coming with half a dozen dogs and they won't just keep them on leads. Well, they will if they see you, but turn your back and they're gone again. They're the worst type.'

'Would you ever shoot a visitor's dog?' Sue asked, with a nervous look at our own mongrel, sitting patiently at her feet.

'I'd shoot a dog if it was chasing sheep, because you can't do with that. We keep our dogs under strict control. They are things that can do a lot of lumber, are dogs. These people that walk about with them tend to think you're shouting over nowt, but they don't realize what frightening sheep can do. They can rush off and end up in the river, because it just alarms them. That's what we're up against, though, because they're coming out more, these people, than ever before.'

The vast influxes of hikers and tourists was only one of the changes that had swept over the Dale in the last few years, and we asked him if he could see a time when farmers might be driven out of the area altogether, caught between the hammer of grouse moor owners clearing the moors of sheep and the anvil of offcomers fuelling the house price spiral.

'People that breed sheep will be wanted yet awhile,' he said. 'But things change. I would hope it doesn't come to that – I mean, what else would you graze these hills with? You haven't a lot of alternatives on this sort of ground, unless you're going to turn to flower power like some here.'

His scathing reference was to the farmers who

were now paid a grant by the National Park Authority to restrict their use of fertilizers and delay their hay crop to allow the wildflowers and herbs in the hay meadows to thrive and set seed. There were wildflowers in the Dale that had all but disappeared from the rest of Britain and the hay meadows were some of the most ancient in Britain, a mass of grasses, flowers and herbs that had grown undisturbed for at least a thousand years.

'So do you get sick of the tourists who come to see all those hay meadows?'

'No, I get sick of the ones that think the whole place grinds to a halt as soon as they go home. "What do you find to do in winter?" some of them ask, as if we hibernate when the visitors aren't here. So I tell them: "We sit around the fire and talk about all the daft buggers that come here in summer" – and as a rule that shuts them up.'

We left him shaking with laughter, still draped comfortably over the gate, as we walked away from his born-again hamlet towards the river. One irony of this resurrection of the small communities is that, while the offcomers were enthusiastically buying and restoring the traditional farmhouses, cottages and barns, the aspirations of the traditional inhabitants were firmly directed towards modern bungalows. Bungalow bliss was now part of almost every village, except where banned outright by the National Park Authorities.

While outsiders eulogized traditional stone farmhouses, oak beams and open fires, natives saw only damp walls, whistling draughts, awkward corners to be dusted and buckets of coal to be carried in and ashes carried out. We grew up in squeaky-clean modern houses, all straight lines and sharp angles and yearned for curving walls, lumpy ceiling, uneven floors and plumbing that went bump in the night. We called it character, but the natives would probably have called it 'a right pain in the arse'.

We had walked a few miles by now, well down into the Dale beyond the bottom of the long winding hill that led to the pub. As we paused on the banks of the river, half a dozen wild ducks flighted upwards, including one absolutely pure white one, a Moby Duck that would be fortunate to survive some shotgun-toting Ahab in the wildfowling season. In a field just along the lane were a group of tups feeding on good lowland grass as they prepared for their next bout of prodigious exertions at tupping time in the autumn. The resting tups had no choice about their place of residence, but they and the hoggs – last year's lambs – which had spent their first winter in the lowlands before joining the breeding flock high on the fells for the rest of their lives, had a much more comfortable time than their kin on the hills above. Apart from these privileged tups and hoggs, the only sheep grazing the low-lying land in the valley bottoms were the fat cousins of the hill sheep. The Suffolks, Leicesters and crossbred 'Mules' that thrived down here could not survive on the coarse vegetation from which the Dale sheep and the other hill breeds got their nourishment; life for man and beast was softer and easier here.

The resting tups of the Dale flocks were turned

out to serve the ewes on the same day every year, though that date got later, the further up the fell-sides the farm was situated. The sheep were tupped at the time that ensured the earliest start to lambing after the worst of the winter weather had gone. Most of the farmers of the Dale kept diaries, recording the date when the first lamb was born, when the last snow fell, when the swallows returned, when hay-time began and when it ended, sometimes months later. Through the recording of these dates, they might have hoped to reach a better understanding of the seasons and weather that governed their lives. Like the naming of every feature of their land, perhaps the numbering of all the events of their year gave them some sense of power in the face of the brutal weather and cruel hardships they often faced, or a feeling of imposing some order on the apparently random variations within the endless succession of the seasons.

Some dates in those diaries were as fixed and immutable as the bedrock of the hills, however. The date on each farm when the tups were turned out had not changed, perhaps for several centuries, certainly for as long as any of the farmers alive could remember, but it was not a precise science and the unpredictability of the weather could often make a nonsense of those careful and long-established plans. In some years there would be warm spring sunshine in March; in others, thick snow might be still lying on the ground at the end of April. Just the same, that constancy of the farming cycle from year to year was one of the enduring and endearing features of rural life. Come war, plague or famine, the tups would continue to be turned out to serve the flock, the lambs to be born, the sheep clipped and the hay crop cut and gathered, in a sequence as unyielding as the natural cycle that dictated its course.

Great historical figures might have diverted the course of events by their actions and been celebrated long after their deaths as a result, yet there was as much quiet satisfaction in putting a tap root down to that constant natural sequence, flowing like the river through the Dale. Those of us who lived in towns and cities tended to sublimate that loss of contact with the natural cycle into obsessive gardening and fantasies about rural retirement, but even those who made the move to the country could find that there was far more symbolism than substance in the appeal of that kind of rural living.

It was easy to romanticize the way of life of the farming community in the Dale, and the reality of hard work, battling the elements for an often precarious living, was in harsh contrast to *Good Life* suburban dreams of 'one goat, one acre' self-sufficiency. One acre would scarcely support one sheep for one month up on the fells around the Inn at the Top. There had always been new blood in the area alongside the families who had been there for centuries, but we hoped that at least some of the new breed of offcomers would bring long-term benefits to the area. As farm sizes continued to grow and large landowners preferred grouse and trees to sheep-farming, the indigenous population was continuing to decline. Those moving into the area were needed to replace those leaving, but only if they used the shops, schools and buses, and lived and raised children there, rather than, as so many did, arriving on summer Friday nights with a car full of shopping brought from elsewhere rather than purchased in the shops of the Dale, and disappearing again on Sunday for their real homes in the cities. The presence in summer of large numbers of such people might have given a brief illusion of life and renewal to the villages of the upper Dale but in reality was just another nail in their coffins.

It was already too late for the tiny village that was the nearest one to the Inn at the Top. Three-quarters of its houses were now holiday lets, weekend retreats or second homes. Its school, pub, post office and shop had all gone and its bus service was reduced to a once-weekly mockery, leaving it little more than a ghost village, coming to life for a few brief summer weeks, eerily quiet the rest of the year. The next village, too, would perhaps suffer the same fate one day. We both hoped that the decline could be halted before the upper Dale ceased to be a community and became nothing more than a fossilized landscape, preserved by the National Park as a playground for tourists rather than as a place where people could live and work.

However, we were also aware that the quiet satisfactions of being a part of the Dale's community might not always compensate for a lack of challenge or mental stimulation in the work we did, nor for the sheer backbreaking drudgery of running a pub, particularly one open from what

135

often seemed to be dawn to dawn. 'I'd love to retire to a country pub,' our unwitting tourist customers would say as, behind the bar, we exchanged looks varying from amusement to incredulity. Yet even without the drudgery, there was also a potential downside to the peace and tranquillity that made rural life so attractive – boredom. It was never a problem at the Inn at the Top, where there was a constant flow of new faces among the ranks of local characters, but we could pause on the doorsteps of two or three of the Dale's other pubs and, before opening the door, predict precisely who would be in, what they would be doing, where they would be sitting, what they would be drinking, even what they would be talking about.

To people who felt trapped in a high-pressure, frenetic city life, the reassuring constancy of that aspect of the rural life might have seemed like heaven, but living in the midst of it in the depths of winter, with no strangers to enliven the scene, it might begin to seem more like hell. For every offcomer who settled for good, there was another who stayed a while, then packed up and moved on. Only time would tell which of those we would be, but for the moment the Dale felt like home to us.

CHAPTER 7

The Yorkshireman's Creed

We strolled on along the bank of the river, watching its rapid, tumbling descent slow as it left the steep slopes of the upper Dale and flowed past the patchwork of pastures and hay meadows that filled the valley floor, maintaining a precarious hold on the lower slopes, a ribbon of fertility in a barren land. At the foot of a small rock outcrop we could see one of the things that had contributed to that fertility, a lime kiln. They were an ubiquitous sight in the high country, sited near an outcrop of lime and used to burn the stone, often with 'crow' coal mined from shallow drift mines near the roof of the fells, like the one near the Inn at the Top.

The care with which even the most prosaic construction, like this lime kiln, had been built in a former age was astonishing to us onlookers from the age of the breeze block. The cornerstones were carefully dressed and the kiln mouth gracefully arched, all the more remarkable for the fact that the builders would almost certainly have been not craftsman stonemasons, but local farmers.

The kilns were relics of the days when farmers all burned their own lime for their fields and when many miners and smallholders would claim a small piece of 'intake' land along the edge of the moor. It would be laboriously cleared of stones, which were used to wall it, and then limed heavily to bring it into good grazing condition, supporting a couple of beasts, or adding to the vital hay crop. Now, most of the intakes at the moor edge were long abandoned and reverting steadily to moorland, with the drystone walls crumbling and rushes and coarse grasses invading from the adjoining fells, and if a farmer needed lime for his land, he tended to get it from a plastic sack.

Across the fields I could see a farmhouse standing in the shadow of a clump of Scots pines, memorials to the droving era, when two or three were planted as a sign to drovers and packhorse trains far across the fells that food and shelter for the night could be obtained there. A former owner of the Inn at the Top might once have contemplated the idea of planting some Scots pines there, but even trees as hardy as Scots pines could not survive the icy blasts of the winds that howled around those bleak fell-tops and the nearest tree to the inn was no closer to it than the nearest inhabited building – four miles.

As we walked on, following the river down the Dale, one of the oldest and darkest mysteries of the British countryside began to trouble us. It was not the origins of stone circles nor the significance of ley lines, nor even why the armed forces insisted on choosing the most beautiful stretches of land on which to drop bombs, having first surrounded them with miles of barbed wire, but rather why some farmers so painstakingly filled even the most wild and inaccessible nooks and crannies of the landscape with rubbish.

Climb every mountain, cross every dale, you can guarantee that you won't find Julie Andrews, but among the crags, fells, forests, meadows and riverbanks, you will find everything up to and including the proverbial kitchen sink, nestling shyly among the primroses. In their determination not to expend money or effort disposing of rubbish, as long as there was a hole or some obscure corner of the farmyard to fill, a steep bank to tip it down or a copse in which to hide it, some farmers at least were a happy breed.

Granted, they were far from the only culprits. From valley bottom to fell-top, thoughtless walkers tended to discard empty drinks tins, cartons, orange peel and chocolate wrappers at random, or wedge them into cracks in the drystone walls, but lower down the slopes, farmers often seemed to be the worst culprits of the lot. Plastic was an ever-popular favourite, particularly the fertilizer bags and black polythene 'big bale' silage wrappers, so lavishly used and so cheerfully dumped. But it was the more surprising items of rubbish that made a country stroll such a voyage of discovery.

Rusting cars were a familiar feature of many a riverbank. They reached their journey's end by some strange migration; like lumbering grey beasts searching out the legendary elephants' graveyard, old cars seemed inexorably drawn to the riverside in the twilight of their years. In the River Eden just outside Carlisle there was one that nestled peacefully in the shallows, filled to the bottom of its missing windows with silt, and a carpet of grass covering the whole interior and spreading out over the bonnet; one spring a family of ducks even chose it as a nesting site

Though that car was clearly more decorative than functional, farmers often seemed to use old cars to shore up riverbanks, even though the same function was performed far more naturally and elegantly by trees, whose roots bound the banks together far better than the legions of Escorts, Toyotas and antediluvian Morris Minors. I suppose that was progress for you, but it did seem strange that such astute reusers of surplus equipment couldn't find a way to recycle their rubbish as well. Given farmers' inventiveness in finding new uses for redundant objects, could they not have shown the same sort of ingenuity in disposing of their garbage? What a shame that the fate of their rolls of rusty barbed wire, old TVs, plastic fertilizer bags, corrugated-iron sheets and old tractors was to blight the countryside which they so often claimed to be preserving and tending for us ungrateful townies.

Of course I may have slightly overstated the perfidy and ecological criminality, etc., etc., of the average farmer, so before the stream of hate mail reaching me from rural areas grows to EC food mountain proportions, let me attempt to redress the balance a little: the vast majority of farmers – those horny-handed sons of the soil – are lovable, ecologically sound creatures, looking after the land out of the goodness of their hearts, without thought of profit or reward. They look on each and every tourist or walker crossing their land as a potential boon companion on life's highway, to be helped, cared for and seen off along the carefully marked footpath or bridleway with a smile and a friendly wave. Truly the typical farmer is the very salt of the earth and those who block stiles and footpaths, dump rubbish in beauty spots and pollute streams and rivers with their nitrate fertilizers or silage run-off are a totally atypical minority. There, that should hold them for a while...

In fact many farmers in the Dale really did take a genuine pride in the beauty of the land they farmed and were friendly and helpful to visitors, though this tended to be more true in areas that were not swamped by a tidal wave of cagoules, rucksacks, hiking boots and unrestrained, yapping dogs every weekend and throughout the summer. Farmers in tourist honeypots like the upper Dale could be forgiven for displaying a little irritation with walkers when they had just had to round up their sheep for the fourteenth time that week because some visitor had left a gate open again.

In that disposable, throwaway age, when recycling, if mentioned at all, was probably thought to be connected with repairing pushbikes, the farmers of the Dale also deserved to be commended for the endless resourcefulness they showed in improvising new uses for old things. Wellington boot soles torn off and nailed to gates as primitive hinges, redundant railway wagons pressed into use as moor-top hay barns and the million and one uses they could find for scraps of baler twine were impressive enough, while their discovery of a use for old tyres was worthy of a Nobel Prize for *Litter*ature ... (sorry!)

To see a mound of worthless worn-out tyres, impossible to give away, sell or destroy, and immediately think of a use, suggests an ingenuity that even a Third World rag-picker might envy. Farmers used them as weights to hold down the covers on their silage clamps. Faced with the same problem, my solution would have been to douse them with petrol, toss on a match and run like hell ... which suggests that I should probably have been the last person to be pontificating about farmers and the countryside, but I digress.

All the farmers of the Dale also seemed to be able to turn their hands to just about any trade. If their work was not always marked by the elegance of the true craftsman, they could pretty much fix anything, acting as mechanics, joiners, electricians, plumbers, fitters, builders, fencers, wallers and a dozen other skills, as well as farming. They could tinker with a tractor, breathe life into a moribund hay-baler, build a shed, calve a cow or find a sheep buried under a snowdrift, but there was one set of skills that none of them had ever managed to master. The division between man's and woman's work was so deeply ingrained that, asked to cook his own dinner or wash his own clothes, even the fabled ingenuity of the farmer was not equal to the task. When Ben Alderson's wife made her annual trip to a town on the other side of the Pennines to do the Christmas shopping, his neighbour's wife sent his meals round for him, because without them, he would have starved.

The farmers' thriftiness could also manifest itself in less than wholly attractive ways. Farmers, and in particular the farmers of the Dale, had an often deserved reputation of being supremely careful with their money. When they paid for a drink they always asked 'How little?' and never 'How much?', for example, and there was a famous story of a farmer from the Dale offering an odd-job man a turkey for Christmas in payment for his work. When December came round, the man returned to collect his fee, only to be told that there was nothing for him.

'I thought you said you were going to give me a turkey,' he complained.

'Aye, lad, I was,' the farmer said, 'but it got better.'

Some of the farmers who came to the inn exhibited a similar stinginess that sometimes bordered on the pathological. Local tradition dictated that, when he arrived at the pub, a farmer would always offer to buy any of his peers whose glasses were empty or near-empty a drink. As a result, many a time I saw a group of them nursing a quarter-inch of tepid beer in the bottom of their glasses for five to ten minutes, watching and waiting for the door to open and some unsuspecting fellow farmer to enter. When the hapless newcomer duly appeared and approached the bar, the others would immediately drain their beers and present the row of empty glasses for refilling. This collective tight-fistedness might have been one of the reasons the farmers always stayed in the pub so late; there was no chance of any of them being willing to leave before everyone else had bought their round.

Most of them were cut from similar dour, hard-wearing cloth, but there was no finer exponent of this unlovely trait than Richard, one of our nearest neighbours – albeit over five miles away – a prime contender for the title of the world's tightest man. Such an accolade was a considerable achievement in a farming community where thrift was both a birthright and a source of personal pride. 'Summat for nowt' was the ultimate achievement in the eyes of many farmers in the Dale and I suspected that many of them knew the Yorkshireman's Creed by heart:

'Hear all, see all, say nowt.
Eat all, sup all, pay nowt.
And if tha ever does owt for nowt,
Do it for thissen.'

But Richard took his thrift to extremes that no other could match. It would have taken an anaesthetist and a surgeon to extract his wallet from his pocket and he regularly befriended tourists in the pub, I suspect not through any great interest in them, but because he knew that they were quite likely to buy one of the 'local characters' a drink, and wouldn't be too upset if he didn't buy them one back.

One lunchtime he was leaning on the far end of the bar, nursing a drink, when a hiker bought himself a couple of soft drinks and a packet of crisps and then set off out of the door on the next leg of his route march. A couple of minutes later, I noticed that he'd left his change on the bar. It wasn't a huge sum – only about fifty pence – so I left the money where it was. If the hiker didn't come back for it, I'd drop it in the collection box for the local Fell Rescue team.

While I was serving another customer, out of the corner of my eye I saw Richard pick up his

144

pint, take a sip and then put it back on the bar about six inches to his left. He then sidled along the bar until he was facing his glass again, and then took another sip and repeated the process. In between customers, I kept an eye on his progress as he inched along the bar like a caterpillar approaching a particularly tasty leaf. At last he reached the middle of the bar and his forearm came to rest on top of the money. There was a faint chink and when he began to make his slow way back along the bar, there was only an empty space where once there had been fifty pence in small change. I waited until he was almost back in his corner and then said in a loud voice, 'Oh, look. Someone has stolen that money from the bar. I was going to put it in the charity collection box, but now it's gone.'

The farmer at the other end of the bar winked at me and one or two customers gave me baffled looks, but Richard sat motionless, staring straight ahead and saying not a word, though I was gratified to see his neck turn an impressive red, shading into purple. Five minutes later he drank up and disappeared out of the door ... and he didn't even leave me a tip.

The other farmer caught my eye.

'He wouldn't give a dog the skin off his kipper, that one,' he said. 'Good thing I kept my hand on my drink or he'd have supped that as well.'

Richard was back the next day, as if nothing at all had happened, but he was soon revealing an even more alarming way of displaying his stinginess. He was leaning on the bar one evening, warming up a tourist for his next drink, when the conversation turned to sheepdogs and what to do with the ones that didn't have what it took to join the family business.

'There's maybe only one or two in a litter that are up to the job,' he said.

'So what happens to the others?' the tourist said. 'Do people keep them as pets or sell them?'

'No, most farmers shoot them,' Richard said, 'but I couldn't do that.'

I stopped what I was doing, genuinely surprised. Was this not only the world's tightest man but the world's only sentimental farmer as well, a man so soft that he had surrounded himself with sheepdog puppies that he couldn't bear to kill?

'No,' he said. 'They're not worth the price of a shotgun cartridge, so I take them in the barn and hang them instead.'

In a silence too deep and rich for mere words to convey, the tourist finished his drink and disappeared into the night, never to return.

Richard was unlike his fellow farmers in other ways too. Most of them regarded the news as of only marginal importance to their lives, paying little attention to the problems of Vietnam, Cambodia or any other faraway places with strange-sounding names, coming alert only at the mention of farming, livestock or subsidies. Much more important was the common currency of rural life: gossip – zealously acquired, jealously hoarded, shrewdly traded.

Some found the gossip, the insistent curiosity, the half-heard remarks or the sudden silences when the subject entered a room, hard to take. Yet it was surely more natural for members of a com-

146

munity to talk about topics of which they had an intimate knowledge than to spend hours pontificating about the latest war or financial crisis, about which, like the rest of us, they probably knew next to nothing at all. However, one farmer, the tight-fisted Richard, showed a far from typical interest in current affairs. He seemed to pride himself on his sophistication – he even had neat creases in the trousers of his spotless boiler suit – and often took a contrary stance to the prevailing farmers' views, meeting my eye and giving a faint, world-weary shake of his head at the Neanderthal attitudes of some of his peers.

When he was propping up the bar one quiet early evening, he chatted to me for a while about the state of the world and then suddenly asked me, 'So, what line of work were you in before you came here, then?'

'I was – well, I suppose I still am – a journalist.'

'Oh, so you tell lies for a living, then?'

I shrugged. So much for the journalist's sword of truth and the trusty shield of righteousness.

'Not really, but you can put it like that, if it makes you happy,' I said.

'Well, I'll tell you something you can put in your paper: they want to throw Callaghan out and get that Maggie in. She'll send all those immigrants [though that wasn't the word he used] back where they came from, give the hard word to all those buggers in the unions and she'll get all those scrounging sods off the dole and make them work for a living like farmers have to. If they can't stand on their own two feet they should go under. No one featherbeds farmers; if

147

we don't work, we starve.'

Every pub seems to have one, a pet bigot who occupies a corner and bores the pants off every passing customer with his tediously predictable opinions on an equally predictable range of issues; but Richard was quite well disguised: an urbane and reasonable manner to draw in the unwary victim, and then a blast of noxious opinions, delivered at close range, like a spray of slurry from his muck-spreader.

I was going to switch to autopilot, smiling and nodding occasionally, but his last remark was too much to take.

'Do me a favour,' I said. 'You farmers get more state handouts than anyone else. You get subsidies for your livestock, grants to plant things, grants not to plant things, grants to grub out hedges and trees, grants to put them back again, payments to grow crops, payments for not growing crops, grants for equipment, grants for buildings, grants for fencing, grants for walling. When you're not filling in claim forms for grants, you're poisoning the streams and rivers with your silage runoff and your nitrate fertilizers, and disfiguring the landscape with the rubbish you dump in every available corner and the ugly sheds and buildings you put up, for which, unlike the rest of us mere mortals, you don't need planning permission. When you go to auction, you get guaranteed prices for your stock and your crops as well, and even then you whinge about it all the way home in your brand-new Volvos. You make being on the dole look like an honourable occupation. Your wives do twice the work that

148

you do and don't bellyache about it at all. If you lot tried standing on your own two feet, you'd fall over.'

I paused for breath, and he seized the chance to try to reclaim the moral high ground.

'British farming leads the world,' he said. 'We're the most efficient industry in the country.'

'The most efficient at screwing money out of the government and the EC, you mean.' I shot back. 'Bank robbers and tax evaders are just as efficient and they don't moan half as much as you lot do.'

He changed his tack: 'You'd all be running to us in wartime though, wouldn't you? You'd need us then to keep the nation fed. And another thing, instead of complaining about our subsidies – and they're little enough, I can tell you – what about complaining about all the money we send out to Africa and places like that? They want to let all those buggers in Ethiopia starve if they can't grow enough to feed themselves. They'll only breed again otherwise.'

I was genuinely shocked. Such views seemed even more obscene expressed in terms suggesting a logical and efficient solution to a difficult problem than they would have done spat out by some crazed fanatic in a black shirt.

I was, of course, familiar with the expression 'The customer is always right', but by now I was past caring.

'You miserable sod,' I said. 'I hope your sheep are barren, your hay crop rots and you fall off your tractor and break your rotten neck. And even then you'll probably get a subsidy for your

149

bloody funeral.'

I stomped off into the beer cellar at the back to cool down and by the time I returned he'd gone. Yet the following night, to my considerable surprise, he was back on his perch at the corner of the bar as if nothing had happened, though from then on, whenever we spoke, which was as little as possible, we both stuck to platitudes about the weather.

As well as fleecing the maximum in grants from the government and the EC while simultaneously bleating louder than any sheep about the iniquitous taxes they were compelled to pay, some of the farmers in the Dale were also past masters at extracting compensation for sheep killed or injured by cars, dogs, trains or even planes.

The sheep that roamed the fells around the inn were not exactly blessed with good road sense and there were regular accidents, but very few of the motorists who had knocked over a sheep or lamb would have dreamed of driving off without trying to establish who owned it and then contacting him to tell him what had happened. A lot of people were genuinely upset if they killed a lamb – and even the most careful drivers might encounter a 'kamikaze' lamb determined to throw itself under their wheels – and Sue often found herself comforting and consoling some distressed motorist who'd gone into a state of near shock after having run one over.

By now we knew most of the markings of the different flocks that grazed the fell around the inn almost as well as their shepherds and, when the motorists had calmed their jangled nerves, we could send them to the right farmhouse to report the accident and offer reparations. Curiously enough, whenever they did so, they were almost invariably informed that, according to the aggrieved and grieving farmer, the sheep they had killed just happened to have been 'the finest one in my flock'.

After a shrewd glance, taking in the visitors' clothes, car and potential income, a suitably inflated compensation figure would be proffered and usually accepted without demur – visitors to the Dale were not usually very knowledgeable about livestock prices. Many, anxious to preserve their no-claims bonus, would then pay up in cash and, having trousered the proceeds and waved off the chastened visitors, the farmer would make a couple more quid by selling the dead animal to the 'knacker men', who collected casualty stock from farms to be sold for processing into dog food.

When I challenged one of the farmers about the morality of profiting from the soft-heartedness and gullibility of passing tourists by overcharging them for sheep they ran over, he merely shrugged his shoulders.

'Not everyone who knocks down a yow bothers to tell us about it,' he said. 'Some folk say nowt and just drive off straight away. So if we make a couple of pounds extra out of the ones who do tell us when they've killed one, it still isn't enough to compensate for the amount we lose on the others.'

As well as compensation for sheep killed on the roads, those who farmed at the western edge of the moor could also try their luck with the company that operated the railway that passed the Dale-head. One of our locals regularly lost sheep, killed by trains after straying on to the track.

'The fences are bad on both sides of the railway,' he told me. 'If you've sheep on it, you can get a lot killed. We had three rams killed on it last summer.'

'I've heard stories about farmers dropping dead lambs over the fence on to the railway at night, so they can claim compensation; what about that?'

He grinned at me. 'You listen to too many stories. No, I don't think so, there wouldn't be a lot of that goes on. The railway might maybe think so, but we tend to do more fencing on that stretch than ever they do, just to keep stock off, because if you relied on them, you'd wait forever, like.'

On the face of it, seeking compensation for sheep losses caused by aircraft would seem a claim too far even for the most optimistic farmer, yet a couple of our customers also claimed to have secured compensation from the RAF when some of their ewes were startled into aborting their lambs by the terrifying din of low-flying military jets, skimming the moor-tops while on a NATO exercise.

Having been startled out of my wits myself while jogging on the moor one day, by the bowel-loosening roar of a fast jet suddenly appearing out of a calm blue sky what seemed like no more than fifty feet above me, I could certainly vouch for the shock they could induce. However I couldn't entirely avoid the cynical thought that some of the farmers we knew – Richard was only one of those who came to mind – wouldn't have been above collecting every dead lamb they could find, whatever the cause, before heading off to the RAF base to lodge a claim. And had a sheep been killed by a lightning strike or similar Act of God, I could think of at least one of our regulars – no prizes for guessing which one – who would have been straight round to the parish church to file a compensation claim with God's representative on earth.

CHAPTER 8

How're You Going to Keep Them Down on the Farm?

However successful the schemes or scams of some farmers might have been in extracting additional income from visitors, businesses or publicly funded organizations, none of the farmers of the Dale ever complained or – uniquely for farmers – sought compensation on the far from infrequent occasions on which their highly trained sheep-dogs, worth up to a thousand pounds each, died after eating illegal poison baits laid by game-keepers. The keepers' aim was to kill birds of prey and other predators on the grouse that the Lord of the Manor – 'Lordy', as he was derisively known by everyone behind his back – and his paying guests shot in industrial quantities during each shooting season. Lordy and his keepers always denied any involvement in or knowledge of such poisonings, of course, just as he proclaimed himself an avid conservationist for preserving grouse and pheasants ... which was true, if you ignored the toll on other wildlife – foxes, stoats, weasels, buzzards, hen harriers and other birds of prey – that were exterminated to stop them preying on the cosseted game birds.

This wholesale extermination also led to biblical plagues of rabbits, which, freed of the depredations of their natural predators, bred like ... well, rabbits. One of the more surreal sights to be seen in the Dale was of soft-hearted tourists swerving from side to side as they drove along the narrow lanes, trying to avoid the rabbits hopping about on the tarmac, while farmers in their Land Rovers following behind were also swerving from side to side, but with the opposite intention: aiming to run over the rabbits that were devouring the precious grazing for their sheep and cattle.

Lordy's plans for what was effectively his own private Dale also included profound changes in the way in which the land was managed, and that in turn had severe implications for many of the people whose families had lived and worked there for generations. I used to walk or run for miles across the moors and the only obstacles in my way were peat hags and mountain streams, but now it seemed as if every ridge or summit I reached had a new wire fence running along it. Boundaries had once been defined by natural landmarks and by watersheds – 'as Heaven water deals', as the old documents say – but those ancient boundaries across the moors were now being reinforced by miles of wire fencing, stretching into the distance. The wires carried the signals of a profound change in the pattern of upland life.

The boom in income from grouse shooting had persuaded some of the larger landowners, including Lordy, to buy up the 'stints' – the grazing rights on the moors – and remove the sheep. The land was fenced to prevent stock straying from the adjoining moors, although it had the added benefit, from the landowners' point of view, of also restricting access for hikers and other would-be intruders on their selfish pleasures. Any farms not already owned were bought and the tenants were either persuaded or 'sweetened' with a bribe to move out. The farms were then split up – or 'asset-stripped', in City terminology – with the farmhouse sold to an offcomer as a private house, the pasture and meadow land rented to one of the handful of remaining farmers, though 'ranchers' might now have been a more appropriate term, and the grazing rights on the moor retained by the landowner, but not used.

The practice had already blighted the Dale, applying the *coup de grâce* to farming communities that had survived little altered for a thousand years. The belief was that fewer sheep would mean more grouse, but the case was far from proven, or universally accepted by the inhabitants, by no means all of them farmers with axes to grind, though they were the most vociferous critics.

155

'I wouldn't think there'd be more grouse if you take the sheep off,' a local farmer told me as we talked one day. 'There'll be a balance, won't there? Always will have been. The heather will get too rough without the sheep, because the grouse won't keep it down, there has to be something that's going to eat it.'

In hard winters the sheep also fed the grouse, in a sense: by scraping away the snow cover with their hooves, they exposed the heather to the grouse as well as themselves.

'But haven't you farmers been overstocking?' I asked. 'If you can get a subsidy on every sheep you have, surely that encourages you to keep a few extra?'

'No, I wouldn't say so. Most farmers here tend to keep what they can handle. They are all to winter; you needn't have them if there are more than you can winter. I wouldn't think there would be many more sheep than ever there was.'

Below the fell-tops, at the moor edge, stood the evidence of an earlier land grab by the large landowners: the ubiquitous Pennine drystone walls. Most dated from the eighteenth and early nineteenth centuries, when an avalanche of Enclosure Acts passed through Parliament. The House of Commons proved no friend to the holders of common rights, for those who could not afford to pay their share of the cost of enclosure forfeited them. By a cruel irony, men forced off their land into dependency on others often found the only available work was in building the walls enclosing the land that had once been their own.

The House of Lords predictably proved to be

156

no better friend to the drovers, overturning their historic rights of stance and passage across the moors and commons in a test case in the 1840s. The comments in the *London Daily News* at the time would have needed little alteration to fit the activities of the present large landowners:

Rights of road, especially footpaths and driftways over enclosed land, have been almost annihilated in England, and the Highland proprietors of Scotland seem to be rapidly effecting the same thing. There is too much reason to fear that the encroaching proprietor with an ultimate right of appeal to a tribunal of his own class will be more than a match for the public. This right of stance, which has existed for centuries, is not displaced to make way for cultivation or improvement of any kind, but to foster the barbarous and puerile passion for artificial wild sports, and the feudal spirit of the House of Lords assists the purblind owners of Highland Estates to push their proprietary right to this mischievous extreme.

The wholesale exclusion of the public indulged in by the proprietors of great estates down the centuries was still continuing. Quite apart from the panoply of legal measures that the estates had used to close off their millions of acres of moorland to the walking boots of Joe Public, there were a host of tricks that they and their minions employed to keep the public off the commons and the open heaths that were being enjoyed by our ancestors when the antecedents of many of today's lords and lairds were grubbing in the dirt.

New gates were often put on tracks, green

roads and drove roads that had been used since time immemorial; during the shooting season they would be padlocked shut. Signs warned wayfarers that they were on a private road and could go no further. Few outsiders were brave enough to challenge such official-looking notices and where the right of way was not marked on the Ordnance Survey map – and many, though ancient, were not – it was subject to these de facto restrictions and eventually lost altogether.

Access to the moors and woodlands was denied so that the landowners and their paying guests could enjoy their field sports without interruptions, particularly the driven shooting, which remained the last truly feudal spectacle still on show in Britain. Driven grouse shooting was bad enough, but at least the 'low flyers' – grouse – accelerating with a couple of beats of their wings and skimming the surface of the moor to drop out of sight among the peat hags, had some chance of evading the guns – not much, but some. Not so the pheasants. Hand-reared in protected pens and corn-fed, they lacked the full wild instincts to escape and might even move towards humans they saw as food providers. In any event they were so well fed and lumbering that many seemed hardly able to get airborne at all. To describe shooting these hapless creatures as 'sport' was like describing the first day of the Battle of the Somme as 'a fair fight'.

The 'guns' were often City traders or foreign businessmen, equipped from head to toe in brand new shooting gear and often so inexperienced and/or incompetent that they were almost as much danger to each other as they were to the game they were there to shoot. Some shoots even had to erect steel poles at either side of the gun butts, to stop the overexcited 'guns' from swinging round as they tried to down a bird and shooting the man in the next butt instead. When a party of such types was loose on the moors, the sound of shots was punctuated at regular intervals by the metallic clangs as the barrels of their twelve-bores came into violent contact with the steel poles. The guns paid through the nose for the privilege of their day's 'sport' and all they got in return was one brace of birds. The others were retained by the estates and sold to game dealers, who were as ubiquitous on the 'Glorious Twelfth' as flies round fresh cowpats.

As well as their attempts to restrict public access to the fells, Lordy and other estate owners also scarred the views with miles of ugly new shooting roads driven across the moor. Of course, greenways, driftways, pedlars' tracks and drove roads had all once criss-crossed the moors, but they were constructed by usage over centuries for purposes beneficial to every community. The shooting roads bulldozed over the fells were there primarily to allow plutocratic 'guns' to reach the shooting butts without the indignity of actually having to walk to them. They were delivered to their butts by forelock-tugging estate employees, hoping for a tip to augment their modest wage, just as the grouse or pheasant were delivered to the guns by the beaters, all part of a day's energetic country sport.

These feudal aspects of the Dale infuriated me

but I soon learned not to voice my opinions too loudly – not through any fear of retribution from Lordy, but rather because my customers and now friends did not need lecturing by some 'Johnny-come-lately, here-today-and-probably-gone-to-morrow' pub landlord about the inequities of the society in which they and their forefathers had lived out their entire lives. As I heard one of them say, 'For good or ill, it's the way things are round here, and there's no point in wasting time worrying about it.'

If the world's tightest man, Richard, had showed some of the less attractive aspects of the Dale farmer's personality, his near-namesake Dick epitomized the virtues. His father had first brought him to the inn in a horse and cart in the 1930s, and Dick told us that he had never passed the inn since then without calling in for a drink. His eyes were hazel and hawk-sharp, his face weather-beaten and his hair iron grey, with a cap so permanently perched on it that it seemed to be stitched there. He had a chest like a barrel and a neck you could have bent iron bars around, and, even at sixty years old, his relentless stride up the fells had me gasping for breath as I tried to keep up. His smile was as warming as the glow of a fire on a winter's day and his sense of humour as subtle as peat smoke in the wind. I never heard him speak a harsh word to or about anyone, and I heard nothing but admiration, liking and respect for him. The cliché 'one of nature's gentlemen' was, for once, wholly apt.

He was also a very kindly man, and, having

taken a bit of a liking to us, he gave us some wise advice.

'A few people round here aren't over fond of the two who own this place,' he said, jerking his head in the vague direction of Newcastle on Tyne. 'If you run this like the proper pub it used to be, people from the Dale will support you all the way. But take my advice, no matter how well you're doing, never buy a new car. If folk hereabouts see you putting on the style and driving round in a big flash car, they'll be thinking "It's my money bought that car", and they may turn against you. But if you drive round in a second-hand Datsun or a beaten-up old Land Rover, even if you've got a hundred thousand pounds in the bank, you won't be rubbing people's noses in it and they'll still come here and support you.'

He winked and went back to his mates in the corner.

Dick was as shrewd and observant as any hill farmer and weighed his utterances as carefully as a parsimonious shopkeeper, often pausing in mid-sentence for a few seconds to re-examine his thought before committing it to words, but he was also refreshingly free of the narrow, bunkered world view that can afflict people in small agricultural communities. Perhaps the rolling fells and broad acres of the land he farmed encouraged broader perspectives; perhaps the river, ever-enduring but ever-changing, reminded him that even the thousand years that his ancestors had farmed by its banks were less than the cry of a curlew in the life of the Dale.

Many Dalesmen shunned strangers, disinterested in the world outside their heaf, but Dick had a healthy curiosity about people and would often join strangers in conversation, chuckling with delight at the ways of the world beyond the Dale. Despite this, he had made only one journey out of the area in his life, travelling to London for the Smithfield show. He got off the train at King's Cross, stood aghast in the middle of the hordes of scurrying travellers and commuters, saw the traffic clogging Euston Road outside, heard the noise, saw the dirt, smelt the exhaust fumes hanging in the air and caught the next train back to the North, without ever leaving the station.

Like their owners, the sheep of the Dale also did not stray far. The young hoggs – the previous spring's lambs – were wintered downcountry on the softer lands of the valley floor, but for the mature sheep of the breeding flock, the moors straddling the Pennines were the only home they would ever know. They remained up on the tops in all but the wildest weather, surviving on a diet that would have starved their fat lowland cousins and, if buried by snowdrifts, had even been known to eat their own fleeces to survive.

However, such skilled foragers also found other ways to supplement their meagre rations and one enterprising ewe took to scrounging handouts from the tourists who flocked to the Inn at the Top. The ewe had discovered that if she stuck her head in through the open windows of cars parked outside the inn and allowed herself to be petted by the tourists, they would give her crisps, sand-wiches and all sorts of other snacks that were probably very bad for her digestive system but which she consumed with evident relish. Each year she also trained her lambs to practise the same trick, so a large and ever-growing flock was soon lying in wait for unsuspecting visitors to the pub, and then pursuing them like the persistent 'Spare change?' beggars on city streets.

It was hard to begrudge the sheep a little increase and variety in their spartan diet on those lonely, windswept tops.

'We keep them up there all winter,' one farmer told us. 'We'll never have had them off the moors in the thirty years I've farmed here.'

They were 'heafed' to the moors, in the local phrase, only straying from them when driven against their will. So strong was the pull of the heaf that when a farm changed hands, the sheep were always sold with it as part of the deal.

Despite the pull of the heaf, sheep often strayed from their own range, particularly when driven before the ferocious winds of winter storms, and shepherds from either side of the moor met regularly to exchange such waifs and strays and return them to their rightful owners. Given that scores of farms might have sheep stints – grazing rights – on the same unenclosed moorland, and that gales and winter storms could scatter and mix together sheep from different flocks like confetti caught in a gust of wind, a system of identification marks to establish each animal's ownership was absolutely essential. Every farm's sheep had their own distinctive markings to the ear, fleece and/or horn, and each year's young lambs were always given their flock marks before being released on to the open fell with their mothers for the first time. The origins of most of those marks had been lost in the mists of time, but they were handed down with the farm and many of them had been unchanged for centuries. *The Shepherd's Guide*, published every few years, acted as the farmer's bible, enabling him to use the marks to identify sheep that had strayed on to his patch and return them to the correct owner, albeit having first charged him for any grazing or winter feed that the animal had consumed while in his care.

A variety of 'lug marks' could be made: either a series of small rectangular or triangular shapes clipped or cut out of the edge of their ears with a knife, a pair of scissors or the tips of sheep shears, or holes made with a tool like a leather worker's hole punch. The system of lug marks had been in use since medieval times, when the punishment of 'greater outlawry' was imposed by the courts on those who cut off sheep's ears, removing the lug marks that established the true owner of the animals. While some system of proof of ownership was still obviously essential in modern times, some animal-lovers felt that lug marks were a cruel and unnecessary practice, but despite the criticisms lug marking persisted, I suspect largely because, unlike coloured dyes, which could be washed out with detergents, the earmarks could not be eradicated by an unscrupulous sheep rustler.

Brand marks could also be burned into the horns with a hot iron, but sheep quite often lost one or both horns as part of the normal wear and tear of life on the fells, so another mark would always be used in conjunction with the horn marks, the most common markings being 'smits' –

daubs of colour on the fleece, most often applied in crude strokes or 'pops' (blots of colour), though letters or symbols such as swords, crosses, triangles and bugles were also used. Smits were traditionally made with a thick, sticky grease, coloured with haematite or graphite, but in modern times that had been replaced by proprietary fluids in a variety of bright primary colours that were easier to scour from the wool with detergents after the fleece had been clipped. At tupping time, ewes also received a different coloured mark on their rumps, for tups were fitted with a coloured 'pencil' on a harness around their chests, to ensure they left a mark on each ewe they 'covered' (mated with), allowing the farmer to determine the parentage of every lamb born the following spring. Such pairings were scrupulously recorded in each farmer's flock book, and they could often trace the lineage of their sheep further back than their own ancestors.

Dick would often sit in his chair by the fire in his farmhouse kitchen, with a glass of whisky at his elbow, and turn the pages of his flock book, just for the sheer pleasure of recalling the individual sheep he had bred.

'Now this yan,' he'd say, as he turned another page. 'She was not a bad yow. Not so bad at all.' And factoring in the traditional understatement of the Dale, I could guess that the ewe had been a champion.

At one end of the mantelpiece in his living room was a fading sepia portrait of Dick and his wife on their wedding day. At the opposite end there was a photograph of Dick with the first of his tups ever to be crowned supreme champion at the sheep show at the Inn at the Top. I was tempted to ask which picture he was most fond of, but eventually, and probably wisely, decided not to push my luck.

To my inexpert eye, just as all cats were grey in the dark, all the sheep of the Dale were indistinguishable from each other – horns, black face, black legs, and peat-stained, off-white fleece – but Dick, who had a flock of 300 sheep, knew each one of them by sight and could recite the parentage and grandparentage of most of them without even having to refer to his flock book for confirmation.

Dick did try to initiate me into some of the mysteries of what made one Dale tup or yow a champion and another just an also-ran, but he lost me almost as soon as he began the litany of necessary characteristics.

'They need to be good at back o't'head and good at t'leg, a good loin as well, and if the back of t'head matches t'top of back legs, you're not so far away. They want good hard hair an' all – do you know what I mean by that?'

I shook my head, but he was already on to the next point: 'And I like to see a good bit of black in t'legs. That's not the modern fashion–' Fashion?, I thought – who knew there were fashions in sheep? 'But to me it's not right,' he continued. 'I like to see a good bit of black in t'legs. Put all that together and you're not far off. That's what we breed towards but of course it's not as easy as that sounds. You'll not have many champions in a lifetime. I've had nobbut four or

166

five in mine, and I've lived a while, haven't I? But no matter how many you've had, you always want another one.' His eyes took on a faraway look. 'I've a tup hogg just now that's not so bad at all. We'll not be so far away with him if the judges concentrate on the sheep and not what their owners have to say about them. Well,' he said, coming back to the present from his dreams of Show Day glory. 'One thing's certain: talking never bred a prize tup or yow. Howay, there's work to do.'

The Dale farmers had once been as strongly heafed to the land as their stock, but, while the older men like Dick had rarely been out of sight of their land from one year to the next, their sons now took themselves off for package holidays in Spain every summer. Poor communications and the slow spread of electrification had held back the pace of change in the Dale for many years, but television culture was now eroding local dialect and tradition as relentlessly as the river that ran through the Dale cut away at the soil. The hoary old wartime song got it wrong; forget about 'Paree', the real question was: 'How're you going to keep them down on the farm, now that they've seen TV?'

CHAPTER 9

I Were Tupped There and I'll Lamb There

As winter had finally given way to spring and then summer – in each case, a good month later than their arrival in the Dale at the foot of the fells – we soon discovered that, despite or probably because of its isolation, the pub was a magnet for every tourist and hiker for twenty miles around, and was jam-packed from early morning until well after dark throughout the tourist season.

It was a good thing the pub had its altitude and location to trade on, however, for visitors certainly didn't come to admire the building's beauty. Even before Stan and Neville got their hands on it, the inn's most loyal locals would have struggled to describe it as being of outstanding – or even any – architectural merit. Early in the twentieth century, one writer called it:

One of the most abject, uncompromisingly ugly buildings that ever builder built. The ruins of a toll house stand nearby, silently inviting that it was once worth the while of somebody to levy and collect tolls in what is now as unfrequented a place as it is possible to conceive, but railways long since knocked the bottom out of that, and for some years until the autumn of 1903, the licence of the inn was allowed to lapse.

Few would have argued with that description, but architectural merit was not high on the list of priorities of those who built the inn. It stood there in blunt defiance of everything that wind and weather could throw at it, and had survived both natural forces and a series of man-made disasters, culminating in the fire of 1973, which gutted the building. However, what beauty there was to be found there was not merely in the eye of the beholder but in the grandeur of the wild and wonderful moorland that surrounded it.

The origins of the Inn at the Top had been lost in the mists of time. The current building dated from the late seventeenth century, but alongside it once stood another, older building, also an inn at one time, and some cottages, the ruins of which were finally demolished in the 1970s, and behind them were the remains of yet another, even older, building that was probably the original inn. All that could be said for sure was that, as long as people had lived on this remote hilltop, they had provided food, drink and a bed for the night for travellers, and the inn's fortunes were closely tied to those of the traders, travellers and labourers who used it. Traces of that history were everywhere: in the drovers' tacks that still crossed the moors, the ruins of toll houses from the Age of the Turnpikes, and the abandoned mines that were worked for coal from at least as far back as Roman times until the mid-twentieth century; and to work at the inn was to be daily immersed in that history.

It was one of hundreds of inns that once stood in remote and lonely places, usually at a cross-roads of two moorland tracks, greenways or drift-

169

ways. The Inn at the Top's name derived from the Old English word for a branch in a track or from the Celtic word for fire, either because of the coal that outcropped there or because the hill on which the inn stands was one of the sites of the symbolic fires that the Celts lit at their great festivals to commemorate the changing of the seasons: Samhain at the start of winter and Beltane to herald the summer.

From monastic times to the nineteenth century, traders travelling from settlement to settlement and between the markets and fairs in the surrounding towns, would break their journeys at the inn and the scores of miners who dug 'crow' coal from the numerous pits around it also slaked their thirsts there. Many miners actually lodged at the inn and all of them visited it for the share-out of their monthly pays, most leaving at least part of their earnings behind as they made their unsteady exits some time later. In addition, farmers and a stream of practitioners of now-vanished trades – chapmen (itinerant dealer or hawker), pedlars, badgers (corn dealer), broggers (wool dealer) and the drivers of packhorse trains – called at the inn, while many of the drovers bringing cattle and sheep in their thousands south from Scotland to the English fairs and markets also stopped to eat, drink or exchange news and gossip on market conditions and prices.

While some of the tracks across the moors were primarily created and used by trains of packhorses, the majority were drovers' roads, followed by men employed in what Sir Walter Scott described in *The Two Drovers* as 'the tedious, laborious, and responsible office' of driving cattle, sheep and occasionally horses prodigious distances from the remote fringes of Britain – the Scottish Highlands, the Welsh mountains and even from Ireland – where they had been reared. Many drovers were Scottish Highlanders who made the same journey year after year. They either bought their cattle from farmers and sold them for their own profit, or worked for a share of the proceeds and were trusted by the owners to drive the animals to market and return with their money.

The drovers had to be men of outstanding skill and character since on them rested the enormous responsibility of steering so many beasts over hundreds of miles in the most difficult and often dangerous circumstances. The drovers were also known as 'topsmen', since their route lay over the tops of the hills and moors, always taking the most direct route across the high moorland, where the going underfoot was better for the animals and they avoided not only the tracks in the valley bottoms that heavy rain could rapidly convert into near-impassable morasses, but also the turnpikes where the stiff tolls charged would erode or eliminate the drovers' profit. The long-range views from the tops also made it easier for the drovers to navigate and to avoid ambush, for the toll bars on the turnpikes were by no means the only hazard they faced.

Most of the great drove roads were originally established by the movement of stolen cattle, from which the Highland drovers also acquired their expertise. Before the introduction of railways in the nineteenth century signalled the end of the Droving Age, rustling was practically the national sport in Scotland and cattle were one of the most negotiable forms of currency; in the Highlands even the rent was fixed in terms of cattle. Rustling and thieving continued throughout the droving era, and drovers who emerged unscathed from the long journey south with their livestock had to run a further gauntlet as they returned home after delivering their animals to market. They were often carrying huge sums and were a tempting target for robbers. Local court documents from August 1692 recorded two 'people unknown' robbing a drover of the then-stupendous sum of £144 – about £10,000 in today's money – on the bleak high moors not far from the Inn at the Top. Suspecting, probably rightly, that the thieves were opportunistic locals, the court ordered the inhabitants of the district to repay the man 'without any further trouble'.

The early drovers were often robbers or raiders themselves and might arrive at their destination with more cattle than the numbers with which they had set off, having rustled a few from farms they'd passed along the way. The worst of these characters were barred from the droving trade during the reign of Elizabeth I, when laws were introduced requiring all drovers to be annually licensed by three Justices of the Peace, but a century later the legitimate drovers still remained vulnerable to the depredations of thieves and rustlers. The legendary Scots 'hero' Rob Roy, for example, born in 1671, was a brigand who exacted a toll of stolen animals from all those who tried to cross the territory that his clan controlled.

When Sir Walter Scott wrote about the drovers' art in *The Two Drovers*, early in the nineteenth century, he noted that Highlanders were still:

masters of this difficult trade of driving, which seems to suit them as well as the trade of war. It affords exercise for all their habits of patient endurance and active exertion. They are required to know perfectly the drove roads that lie over the wildest tracts of the country and to avoid as much as possible the highways which distress the feet of the bullocks and the turnpikes which annoy the spirit of the drover; whereas on the broad green or grey track, which leads across the pathless moor, the herd not only move at ease and without taxation, but, if they mind their business, may pick up a mouthful of food by the way.

Scott's view of a mouthful of food clearly does not quite match that of Robert Louis Stevenson, who complained in his novel *St Ives*, set during the Napoleonic Wars, that 'a continual sound of munching and the crying of a great quantity of moor birds accompanied our progress, which the deliberate pace and perennial appetite of the cattle rendered wearisomely slow'.

Those Highland regions were ideal for rearing, but not for fattening stock – the short growing season and the harsher climate than the lowlands meant that they could not grow wheat nor other crops to fatten their stock for slaughter, nor sufficient feed to over-winter most of the cattle they reared. The drovers were the link that bridged hundreds of miles of wild country, bristling with robbers and rustlers, bringing the cattle to markets such as the great English livestock fairs, like those held at the foot of the fells close to the Inn at the Top, from where a purchaser would be reasonably confident of getting the animals he had bought back to his home area without being molested by thieves.

The animals would then be fattened on the softer grazing of the lowlands or the stubble of the harvest, before plodding onward in their final journey to the markets, including London's Smithfield, where they would be sold for slaughter. The relative affluence of England and the insatiable demand for 'the roast beef of olde England', both to feed the burgeoning population of England's industrial towns and cities and to be salted down and stored and shipped as rations for the armed forces patrolling and garrisoning Britain's fast-expanding empire, ensured a continuing market for cattle that English farms alone could not supply.

The demand for Scottish, Welsh and Irish cattle made it economic for drovers to bring cattle from the furthest corners of the British Isles, but careful handling of their livestock was crucial if they were to be in saleable condition at the end of their marathon journey. As well as the financial incentive to look after them, negligent or cruel drovers were subject to the law. Anyone 'exercising any cruelty to cattle by use of any pointed stick' was liable to a fine and imprisonment.

The herds of driven cattle announced their approach from a good way off, both by the noise – men shouting, dogs barking and cattle lowing – and in dry weather by the dust clouds the hooves of the animals raised around the herd. The average distance Highland cattle would cover in a day was only about ten to fifteen miles and the drovers had to do their best to arrive each evening at a good 'stance' – a place where grazing and water were available for their animals and, with luck, shelter for themselves. A clump of three Scots pines was a signal to drovers way out on the fells that rest and food for the drover and his stock could be found. Inns also planted holly trees – an ancient sign of hospitality, still remembered in the pub name The Holly Bush. In places where there was no suitable shelter, they slept in the open, in all weathers, taking it in turns to stay awake to guard the herd against two- or four-legged predators, and many drovers did not once sleep under cover during a journey that might last three months or more.

Drovers also carried much of the food they needed with them, although, as Sir Walter Scott noted, it was a very plain diet: 'A Highland drover was victualled for his long and toilsome journey with a few handfuls of oatmeal and two or three onions, renewed from time to time, and a ram's horn filled with whisky, which he used regularly, but sparingly, every night and morning.' The oatmeal the drovers carried was often eaten cold, mixed with water from a spring or upland stream, and the resulting porridge was known as 'crowdie' – a name that older inhabitants of the Dale could still remember being used for the feed of crushed grain mixed with water that they used to give to their hens. The drovers would also make a form of black pudding by nicking a vein in one of their cattle with their knives, collecting a little blood and then mixing it with their oatmeal and onions.

The drovers tended to work with small herds, one experienced drover and a boy and a couple of dogs driving up to fifty cattle, though individual drovers sometimes banded together like cowboys in the American West, easing the individual's workload and providing greater collective security against raiders, with herds of up to 2,000 head of cattle being driven along together. Some drovers might be on the road for as much as six months, much of the time sleeping rough alongside their animals. Nor was there any guarantee of turning a profit for all their time and work, and to boost their income many of them gathered the loose wool they found on the moors they crossed, then carded it, twisted it into yarn and knitted it as they walked along, selling the woollen socks and hose they produced at the hamlets and villages they passed. The drovers also brought news from parish to parish and some priests even read out the 'Drovers' News' at Sunday service. Some drovers herded animals on the return journey as well; Irish drovers often took donkeys with them, since they were much used on Irish farms, and strings of thirty or forty donkeys were not an uncommon sight on the drove roads passing the Inn at the Top.

Improvements in transport and agriculture – and, perhaps, in law enforcement – coupled with the loss of the traditional rights of 'passage and stance' across the uplands as the Enclosure Acts closed off more and more of the old droving routes, eventually killed the droving trade and

176

most of the livestock fairs that went with it. By the 1830s, steamships were already reducing the journey time to market by days and even weeks, and the spread of the railway system through the remainder of the century eventually left no cattle breeder, no matter how remote, more than a few miles from a railhead from which his beasts could be shipped to market in speed and safety. The Droving Age was virtually at an end, though there were still a handful of men, like our regular customer Jed, who made a living well into the twentieth century by carrying out a relatively local droving trade, collecting sheep from around the upper Dale and driving them to market twenty or thirty miles away.

Drovers, traders and travellers were far from the only customers pausing at the Inn at the Top in the old days, and it was the focus for all manner of other activities. Bare-knuckle fights were staged at the inn in the eighteenth and nineteenth centuries, with the champions from either side of the Pennines meeting in contests to decide the supreme champion. Farmers and miners came from miles around to watch the fight and bet on the outcome. There were few rules and rounds could last anything from a few seconds to ten minutes or more, each one continuing until one of the fighters was knocked down. His second – a man whose only medical equipment was a wet cloth or rag and a bucket of cold water – then had sixty seconds to get his man back up to the mark – a line scratched in the earth at the centre of the ring. If he was not 'up to scratch' when the bell rang for the next round, his opponent was declared the winner. Some fights lasted for hours, no doubt much to the delight of the landlord of the inn at the time, who would be selling drinks to the spectators as fast as he could pour them. After the fight, the champion and sometimes his defeated opponent would often spend a couple of days carousing at the inn, during which time most of the contents of the prize purse would also find their way over the bar.

However, by the late nineteenth century, the traditional customers of the Inn at the Top were fast disappearing. The coming first of turnpikes in the eighteenth century and then of the railways in the nineteenth signalled the beginning of the end for both the drovers and the itinerant pedlars and packhorse traders, as livestock and goods were increasingly moved by road and rail. Turnpikes were hated by virtually everyone – drovers, pedlars, carriers, miners and farmers – who saw in them benefit only for the rich, or who felt, often with good reason, that their own livelihoods were being threatened. Toll bars and toll houses like the one across the moor from the inn were sometimes destroyed by angry locals and the 'pikemen' who collected the tolls were often threatened or attacked. A vengeful Parliament responded with punishments ranging from public whipping to transportation to the colonies or 'death without clergy'. The turnpikes remained until the 1870s and 1880s – the last disappeared in 1888 when Parliament gave the responsibility for maintaining main roads to the county councils – and the old droving and packhorse trades went into permanent decline.

The local coalmines were in decline too, losing their prime market, the lead-smelting mills in the Dale, as the lead companies failed one after another. The veins of ore in their own mines were almost worked out and they also faced growing competition from mines in Spain and other countries with much lower production costs. The coal pits around the Inn at the Top were also seeing more and more of their domestic market being taken by the higher quality coal from the Durham collieries as the railways came closer and closer to the Dale.

Only the farmers and a few pitmen remained as potential customers for the Inn at the Top and competition for their beer money was intense. In addition to the handful of inns that still exist in the Dale today, there were two or three dozen other pubs and beerhouses back then, and like many of its rivals, the Inn at the Top's trade declined steadily during the nineteenth century. It was so poor by the turn of the century that the inn was abandoned by its landlord in 1899 and lay empty and near derelict for four years.

At the same time as this decline in its trade, however, the nineteenth century was witnessing the beginnings of a new phenomenon. In previous centuries, the landscape of the wild and remote areas of the country, like the moors surrounding the inn, did not conform to the then-widespread ideas of beauty in the landscape, which required the influence of the human hand to be clearly visible. Beautiful scenery was equated with rolling parkland or formal gardens, while the fells and moors of the North Country were seen as too wild and threatening by travellers, as illustrated by the opinions that have come down to us from the journals of the 'Tours' taken and recorded by the wealthy gentlemen of the time.

However, as ideas of beauty changed and the Romantic view of wild nature began to gain wider acceptance, people started to take walking tours in the Dales and Lakes, and other remote areas. This new form of recreation was soon accelerated by the spread of the railway network, which brought increasing numbers of people, particularly from the industrial areas of Yorkshire, Lancashire and the North East, within reach. Although the prime purpose of the railways was to move freight, they also carried growing numbers of cyclists and walkers, and by the turn of the twentieth century the first motorists were also beginning to discover the lonely roads that led to the Inn at the Top.

Apart from its striking setting, the inn also benefited from the shrewd eye for publicity of some of its landlords and owners, none more so that a legendary character in the lore of the Dale, the landlady of the inn for over three decades, Susan Peacock. There had not been enough tourists to save the inn from being closed and abandoned to dereliction for several years around the turn of the century, but in 1903 Susan and her first husband, Richard Parrington, a former landlord of another pub in the area, bought it and set about restoring it. They had brought two children with them, Olive and Maggie, and a third, Edna, was born at the inn in 1906. Her mother refused to leave the inn to give birth, rejecting the suggestion with what became a famous reply: 'I were tupped there and I'll lamb there.'

Richard died when his new baby was only a year old, but the redoubtable Susan stayed on at the inn with her three children and later married a local miner, Michael Peacock, who worked the coal outcrops around the inn, providing fuel for the fire and some for sale to neighbouring farms. The entrance to the pit, worked on the 'drift' or 'day hole' system – accessed by means of a level or sloping tunnel, rather than a shaft – was no more than a hundred yards from the inn, and was usually a one-man operation with Michael Peacock acting as 'miner, overman, underground and surface manager, winder, salesman and clerk – working the whole pit in himself, in fact, and is also a flockmaster', as one admiring visitor noted in the 1920s. 'The mine is worked on most primitive lines, there is no danger of gas or flood, and the miner lights his working place by a candle stuck in his cap.'

At one time there had been half a dozen working mines on the moors around the Inn at the Top, and the inn itself had doubled as the manager's house for a colliery that lay a hundred yards or so to the east of the inn; the now-vanished building behind and to the west of the inn was once the manager's house for a rival colliery. The inscriptions LW 1676 and WPE 1759 carved in the rocks behind the inn marked the boundary line between the land to the west and south of it owned by Lord Wharton, the Lord of the Manor in the seventeenth century, whose rights and possessions included not just

181

the colliery but the entire Dale, and Wingate Pulleine, who owned the mineral rights, including the colliery, in the neighbouring manor to the north and east of the inn.

Coal had been dug from the pits since at least the thirteenth century and mining may go back even further than that, for the Romans mined lead in the Dale and may have used the coal from such a convenient, nearby source to smelt it. Records show that coal from the pits around the inn was being supplied to Richmond Castle in the late fourteenth century and many other castles and cathedrals, in France as well as England, were roofed with lead from the Dale, smelted with a mixture of the peat dug from the moors and coal from the pits at the inn.

The coal was moved by packhorse at first, adding prodigiously to the cost, but the road over the moors was turnpiked in 1770, largely to make it cheaper and easier to transport the fuel to a wider market. At its nineteenth century peak, coalmining near the inn took place using relatively deep shafts, with winding gear and pumps powered by horses, or by 'horse-levels'- tunnels driven into the hillside with a gradient of no more than 1 in 100, giving access to the coal seams and providing a means of drainage. Even when we came to the inn, there still remained what was left of a horse-level and the associated pit buildings just off to the side of the road a couple of hundred yards south of the inn. Although the entrance to the level had long been blocked up to prevent curious tourists or cavers putting themselves at risk inside the old mine workings where roof-falls were a constant danger, water stained orange by rust from the rails laid for the coal tubs inside the mine still gushed from a narrow opening at the foot of the hillside.

The miners working the pits around the Inn at the Top showed precious little workers' solidarity during the General Strike of 1926. While coal-mines around the country ground to a halt as miners joined millions of fellow manual workers in striking for better pay, the pits near the inn not only continued working but doubled their output and put up their prices to cash in on the sudden increase in demand for the local coal. Business was so brisk for Michael Peacock that he took on an extra man to help him meet the demand for coal selling at six shillings and eight pence a ton (33p), twenty per cent cheaper than the coal from the nearby official pit.

That short-lived boom proved to be the last hurrah for all the pits, including Michael's. Demand for the local 'crow coal' evaporated once the national strike had ended and the better quality deep-mined coal from the North East was once again available, and the last commercial pit around the Inn at the Top closed in 1934. When coal was nationalized following the Labour landslide in the 'Khaki Election' at the end of the Second World War, along with the huge deep mines of the major coalfields, the newly formed National Coal Board also inherited responsibility for hundreds of disused small mines like the ones on the moors around the inn. They were often in a perilous condition with unfenced or barely fenced shafts and drifts and pit entrances that any passer-by could enter. Coal Board employees did their best to make the old pits around the inn safe, sealing the shafts on the open moor with steel girders or railway sleepers and dynamiting the entrances to the pits and levels.

In later years the coal that had been such an asset to the inn in previous eras became more of a threat to its future, when the Coal Board applied for planning permission in 1958 to construct an opencast mine. Had they done so it would have devastated the area and finished the inn as a tourist attraction – it might even have been demolished – but furious opposition led by the National Park Authority persuaded the Coal Board to withdraw the application.

The coal is still occasionally worked today, though more usually by landlords in search of publicity than in a genuine attempt to achieve self-sufficiency in fuel. In any event, it is poor shaley stuff, prone to spitting and cracking as it heats up, sending fragments of shale flying in all directions and making a fireguard a near-essential piece of equipment

While Michael Peacock had been digging coal from that same mine back in the 1920s, his wife Susan was beginning to develop the inn. She was astute enough to recognize its tourist potential and produced black-and-white souvenir postcards proudly proclaiming it to be the highest inn in the country, and her strong personality and forthright opinions also soon earned her a reputation far beyond the Dale. She became something of a national celebrity after appearing on a BBC radio programme *Harry Hopeful's Day in the Yorkshire*

Dales. Although her accent and use of dialect must have made her near-incomprehensible to some Southern listeners, unused to hearing vowels as broad as the acres of her native county, she took the opportunity to tell the listening millions that some of the people in the Dale needed 'a reet shekkin' oop'. She proved so popular with BBC listeners that Harry Hopeful returned for a follow-up interview not long afterwards and she also appeared on a couple of radio panel discussions.

Publicity from these and other interviews established the inn as an obligatory stopping-off point in a trip to the Northern Dales, where visitors were often treated to a few more of Susan's brusquely expressed opinions, alongside the ham and eggs or tea and scones that were the only fare on offer. The ham and eggs were locally produced – a pig and a few scrawny hens could be seen scrabbling for food in the yard behind the inn. Susan also kept a goat, which, like all its breed, was a confirmed omnivore and ate everything the tourists could proffer, from sandwiches to liquorice allsorts. Many visitors also stayed for bed and breakfast at three shillings and three pence (16p) a night and many others made special journeys just to say they had been to the highest inn in the country, though one visitor then described it as 'not an inn at all in the sense of having a grubby place called "Bar" and a shiny place called "Saloon". You can sit and have a drink in the kitchen and talk to the lady of the house as she does her cooking, which I take to be the proper kind of inn for mountain solitudes.'

Susan Peacock was an absolutely indomitable

character, not above banning people on sight if she didn't like their looks, but she was beloved by the Dale's inhabitants. Those who knew her were still talking fondly and frequently of her fifty years after her death. The tales about Susan would fill a book on their own, but one in particular was told whenever the conversation turned to her. During the hungry times of the twenties and thirties, there were many 'gentlemen of the road', also known as tramps, travelling the country, living rough and surviving on their wits. Many of them were veterans of the Great War, who had either never found work since returning home from the war or, scarred by their experiences, had found it impossible to settle again into their former way of life.

One such character, Tom Brockbank, spent several years living rough in the area, and he was a frequent visitor to the inn. He just as frequently made trouble, once pinching one of Susan's chickens and cooking it over the fire kept burning at the coal pit at the top of the hill leading down into the Dale. One night he was in the inn, very drunk and belligerent. Susan decided he had drunk enough and refused to serve him. In retaliation Brockbank threatened to smash every picture in the place, whereupon Susan pulled out her husband's revolver – a souvenir of his war service – chased Brockbank out of the inn and fired two shots after his hastily departing figure. Fortunately both of them missed; either Susan was a poor shot or, probably more likely, she'd aimed high. These and other exploits earned Susan a place of honour in the folklore of the Dale. She reigned as queen of the inn for thirty-four years, until her death aged sixty-one in 1937. Her funeral was the biggest ever seen in the Dale, with forty cars following the cortège on its journey, and hundreds of people gathering to pay their last respects, far more than the little village church could accommodate.

Sue shared her Christian name with this celebrated former landlady of the inn, who was still fondly remembered by several of the older farmers, and when one of them, our mentor Dick, began calling Sue 'Susan', he was paying her the most handsome compliment he could have chosen, implying that she was the modern-day reincarnation of the inn's most celebrated landlady. The original Susan's husband, Michael, and her daughter, Edna, stayed on at the inn and ran it until 1945. Edna's memorial to her mother is still visible, carved on the rocks behind the inn. Susan loved the Inn at the Top above all other places, and she, more than any other, ensured it would survive as a local pub for the community of the upper Dales, as well as an attraction for the summer visitors.

Susan Peacock's next-door neighbour, 'Awd Joe', also known as 'Turnip Joe', lived in the now-demolished cottages alongside the inn between the wars and was another notable local character, remembered in particular for two things. As a schoolboy, his family was so poor that his school lunch consisted of two slices of bread with a piece of raw turnip for a filling – hence his alternative nickname. In later, and more affluent, years for him, he was the only person in the district with a wind-up gramophone. As a result he was in great

187

demand for social evenings at farmhouses around the area and would often set off to walk over the tops to the villages down in the Dale, carrying his gramophone and a stack of 78s strapped to his chest. At the end of the evening, often as late as two o'clock in the morning, he would gather up his gear and walk all the way back across the moors, snatching a couple of hours' sleep before going on shift at the colliery,

Joe once decided to give up on the high life and move down to a cottage in the tiny hamlet of half a dozen houses at the bottom of the hill, but he lasted only a couple of weeks before abandoning the place and returning to the hilltop, complaining that the little hamlet was 'much too noisy' for him. In his old age he eventually grew so frail that he had to go to live in sheltered accommodation in a small town further down the Dale, and there, for the first time in his life, he encountered mains water and had to be shown how to operate a tap.

Not all the legendary characters associated with the Inn at the Top were homegrown. Patrick 'Pat' Lisle, who owned the inn for a few years in the 1960s, was a larger-than-life character in every sense, and an even more flamboyant land-lord than Susan Peacock. A wartime evacuee to the area from Tyneside, Pat was also a man for whom the description 'likeable rogue' might have been invented: a serial entrepreneur, according to his friends and admirers, or a chancer and a sort of Northern Arthur Daley, if you believed his enemies. At his peak he weighed twenty-seven stone, leading me to wonder how on earth he had ever managed to fit into the narrow space behind the bar of the Inn at the Top, and he also managed to squeeze his considerable frame behind the wheel of his vintage Bentley.

He had begun his working life as a goods porter on the railways and somehow managed to combine that £10-a-week job with operating as an illegal bookmaker. This was in the years before 1961, when off-course betting and bookmaking in Britain was finally legalized, though it had been unofficially practised by men like Pat in almost every town and city for over a century before that. In my own small hometown I could vividly remember the building in a back street that had frosted windows, a succession of working men entering and leaving, and a seemingly permanent fug of tobacco smoke hanging over it. Intrigued, I asked my father about it one day.

'Oh, that's the bookie's he said. 'And when you grow up, I don't ever want to see you wasting your money in there.'

Everyone in town knew it was a bookie's, including the local police, but, whether they preferred a quiet life or simply because they enjoyed a bet themselves, they were happy to turn a blind eye and it was never raided.

As well as bookmaking, at other stages of his career – if something so punctuated by abrupt and apparently inexplicable changes of direction, wrong turns and U-turns really qualifies for the term – Pat had also worked as a travelling artificial inseminator – of cattle – a signalman on the railways and the secretary of the local branch of the National Union of Railwaymen. At various other times he had also owned a bakery, a draper's, a

189

baby clothes shop on an army camp, three betting shops, a racehorse called Belfry, and three pubs including the Inn at the Top. In Pat's eccentric life, no windmill ever went untilted for long.

He also had something of a minor political career, though as a Labour Party activist in one of the most conservative – with both small and capital 'C' – areas in the country, opportunities were limited. Nonetheless he stood as a candidate in the local elections and became the only Labour member of the Rural District Council, where he served for eleven years and was eventually given the token post of Chairman of Road Safety. With the slogan 'Never fear, Patrick's here', he also stood for Labour in the General Election of 1966, contesting one of the safest Tory seats in the country. During the campaign he was filmed by the BBC's Trevor Philpott for a *Man Alive* programme. While the television cameras rolled, Pat canvassed one venerable farmer from the upper Dale.

'Will I be getting your support, sir?' Pat asked.

The old farmer looked him up and down. 'Will thou hellers like,' he said. 'And I'll bet you half-a-crown that you'll lose your deposit.'

Pat took the bet and demonstrated his supreme confidence by giving the farmer odds of five hundred to one. Any suggestion that it was pure hubris, brought on by the presence of the television cameras, was made to look a little foolish when Pat kept both his deposit and the farmer's half-crown by picking up almost a quarter of the vote. It was a respectable showing but not enough to win the seat, though he later claimed to have been relieved by the result.

'The way they drink in Parliament, I'd be dead by now,' he explained.

In 1970 Pat was declared bankrupt, blaming 'drink, fast women and slow horses' for his plight, and over the next few years he claimed to have successfully given up all three. He went south for a while, but didn't last long there – the pub he bought burned down in mysterious circumstances – and he returned once more to the North, where he made an unsuccessful attempt to obtain planning permission to turn a farmhouse he'd bought into a hotel. Once more he sought election to the parish council – perhaps to try to reverse the verdict of the Planning Committee – and during the campaign he reported six rival candidates who, in breach of electoral law, had failed to include the name of the printer and publisher on their election leaflets. Despite that valiant attempt to improve his odds, he still failed to win the seat. With his health deteriorating, he finally went 'uncharacteristically quiet', and if he launched further madcap schemes in the years before his eventual death news of them did not reach the ears of the regulars at the Inn at the Top.

Characterful landlords and landladies like Pat Lisle and Susan Peacock knew full well the publicity value of owning the highest pub in the country and Susan in particular put the Inn at the Top firmly on the tourist map, a place it had occupied ever since. It was by some distance the busiest pub in the entire Dale and we were therefore the busiest landlord and landlady. We spent our working days within three or four yards of each other but rarely managed more than a few minutes together in the course of an entire day. My kingdom was the bar and Sue's was the kitchen. In the evenings, when visitor numbers were lower and the pressure less intense, she produced some fabulous meals, but different qualities were required at lunchtimes when the place was packed with tourists and hikers who all wanted to be fed with a minimum of delay. In the early stages of running the pub, we'd talked about the need to find a menu that lent itself to rapid-fire turnover, offering food like hot beef or hot pork sandwiches, stews and chillies that could all be cooked in advance and dished up at high speed, or even limiting the lunch menu to a broad selection of cheeses, pâtés and good bread. In that way, one or two people could have fed an army, but those ideas somehow fell by the wayside and every lunchtime saw Sue and her beleaguered helpers working flat out but still falling further and further behind the ever-growing piles of food orders.

Most of our customers and certainly most of the local farmers had an uncomplicated view of food. They wanted it hot, they wanted it now and they wanted plenty of it – 'farmers' portions', as we called them, in tribute to the good trenchermen of the Dale, whose prime yardstick of a good meal seemed to be the quantity of food on the plate, rather than its quality. Eating Out in the Dale could sometimes seem more like Eating Owt – anything – as long as the plate was overflowing. We heard more than one farmer praise his meal by saying, 'That were a grand meal. I couldn't finish it all.'

Sue really did have a commitment to good food, well cooked and well presented. She was a Jamie Oliver twenty years ahead of her time, and had such a hatred of 'chips with everything' that she disconnected the deep-fat fryer and threw it away. But she would still be trying to artfully arrange the garnish on a dish when, to my admittedly jaundiced eye – and I was the one who was copping the complaints about waiting times from hungry customers – what was needed was a bit less art and a lot more speed. Had I been older, wiser and more inclined to keep this opinion to myself, even if it was correct, marital relations would probably have been less strained…

Although the coal board had sealed off the old pits and shafts around the inn soon after nationalization of the coal industry in 1946, erosion and subsidence had over the years combined to reopen some of them. When we took over as landlords of the inn, one of the old pits – the one that Michael Peacock had worked – could be accessed from a hollow no more than a hundred yards from the back door of the inn. Inspired by one of our bar staff who had been down the mine a few years before, I carried out my own exploration of the mine early one morning. Sue wasn't even slightly keen on the plan.

'It's an absolutely ridiculous idea,' she said. 'I can't think of anything more dangerous. It's been abandoned for decades, for God's sake. What if there's a rock fall and you get trapped down there?'

She was right, of course, but I wasn't going to admit it.

'Nothing's going to happen,' I said. 'I've read about these mines. There has never been any "fire damp" [explosive gas] in them, so it's not going to blow up and it's not going to cave in either. But if I'm not back in two hours, call out the Fell Rescue team; it'll make a nice change for them from scrambling around on top of the moors.'

She was about to say more but gave a weary shake of her head instead; muttering something about hell and handcarts, she left me to my folly.

I had borrowed a potholer's helmet from one of our customers, telling him vaguely that I was going to explore an old cave. I also took a torch and, feeling a bit like a character in a Greek myth or a Victorian 'cautionary tale', I was carrying a huge ball of string as I walked down the side of the inn, climbed over the wire fence and walked across the fell. It was only a short distance to the dip in the ground that hid the entrance to the mine. The opening was no more than eighteen inches high by a couple of feet wide and partly concealed by a curtain of overhanging grasses growing above it. I tied one end of my ball of string to a rock just to the side of the entrance, switched on my torch, lowered myself to the ground, took a deep breath and wriggled forward into the mine. I had to belly-crawl for the first few feet but then the space opened out and I was able to get to my knees and then to my feet, though I had to stoop to avoid banging my head on the roof and walk with an awkward, back-breaking crouching gait. It was painfully clear to me at once that Michael Peacock and the other old-time miners had been considerably shorter than my six feet four inches.

Before I moved on, I glanced around, taking stock of my surroundings. The main 'drift' ran straight ahead, sloping downwards at a gentle angle and following a winding course as it went steadily deeper and deeper underground, following the path of the coal seam, a broad, jet-black band three to four feet deep. A maze of lateral workings opened on either side, roughly at right angles to the main drift, and interrupted every few yards by another tunnel running parallel to the one in which I was standing.

Although miners had been extracting the coal from this pit for hundreds of years, I was astonished to see how much still remained there. The mine had been worked on the 'pillar and board' system, with huge pillars of coal left in place as 'standers', bearing the crushing weight of the rock strata above, while the winnable coal was extracted from relatively narrow sections between them. Had I been able to look down on the mine workings from above, I imagined that it would have looked rather like a chessboard – albeit one extending for several miles underground – with the black squares the remaining coal and the white ones the areas that had been worked out.

I began to move along the drift, stepping over and around the big lumps of rock that had fallen from the roof over the years that the mine had been abandoned and were now littering the floor. It was not a reassuring sight and I was tempted to turn tail and abandon the exploration there and then, but sheer cussedness and, if I'm honest, the fear of losing face with my barman if I bottled out of even going as far down the mine as he had, persuaded me to keep going.

As I moved on, I kept my torch in one hand and the piece of string in the other. It was sometimes difficult to pick out which was the main way through the mine from a number of similar openings – at times the drifts and lateral passages seemed to veer off at all angles to each other – and I was very glad that I'd had the foresight to bring the string with me. When I stopped and looked behind me, it was already difficult to tell from which of the multitude of passageways I had just emerged and I said a silent prayer of thanks for the reassuring sight of the string disappearing into one of them.

At times I could walk in that awkward, stooping, Quasimodo-like gait, but at others, so low was the roof – or, more accurately, so high were the mounds of loose fallen rock on the floor of the tunnel – that I knocked my helmet against projecting rocks a dozen or more times, and often had to crawl on my hands and knees to get through. In places the headroom had been reduced to as little as a couple of feet, and I inched my way into the gap, not sure if it would narrow still more and render any further progress impossible, but each time it opened out again and I was able to move on. The sharp edges of the shaley rock were painful to my knees and I wished that, as well as my torch, helmet and ball of string, I'd added a pair of carpet-fitter's knee-pads to my exploration equipment before setting off for the mine.

There were no other living things to be seen – quite a relief, because in my imagination I'd populated the old mine with colonies of rats – and no sound whatsoever in the darkness, save for the faraway drip-drip of water. I kept moving on, a little further and a little further, following the drift as it twisted and turned, but always going deeper under the ground. I had been following it for about forty minutes when it came to an abrupt halt at a 'sump' – a point where the tunnel dipped and water seeping down through the rock strata had accumulated, flooding the workings and blocking the way ahead. I knew that the mine continued for a considerable distance beyond the sump because I had seen copies of the plans of the old mines collected by the National Coal Board after nationalization, but I could follow it no further.

I didn't know whether to be disappointed or relieved by that. I was enjoying exploring where almost no one had set foot for at least fifty years and I still had hopes that around the next corner I might yet find an old miner's lamp or pickaxe or some other souvenir, but I was also tired from scrambling over the loose rock, my knees and elbows were bruised and sore from squeezing through gaps and crawling over piles of loose shale and my back was aching from the strain of walking bent nearly double, so on balance I felt glad to have reached the end of the line.

Before I began making my way back, I sat down for a moment on a flat rock at the edge of the water and stared into its inky depths. I felt a little drowsy but put it down to lack of sleep and the exertion of getting this far down the mine. I'll just rest here a while, I thought. I turned off my torch for a bit, just to see what it felt like to be in darkness as complete and absolute as anywhere on earth. As I did so, I began to smile and then giggle at the thought of sitting there in the pitch blackness, all alone at the bottom of an abandoned coalmine. I imagined someone walking down the tunnel towards me, carefully winding my string back into a ball as he approached and saying, 'You dropped your string'. It wasn't that funny, but I found myself laughing out loud at the thought. Just then a warning voice in my head told me something wasn't right. I needed to get up, get moving and get out of that mine fast.

I relit my torch and began to make my way back, stumbling along, still holding the precious string in my hand. I found it very hard going and the slope I was climbing was not enough reason for that. I now noticed for the first time that my breathing was fast and shallow, and my head had begun to ache so sharply that it felt like a stabbing pain behind my eyes. I was afraid now, and stumbled on, trying not to panic. To my relief, though I hadn't been aware of any deterioration in the air as I moved down the mine, I sensed a little improvement as I moved back up the slope. Although still laboured, my breathing was not so ragged, and I found I could move slightly quicker, tracking back along the string. A little further on, I felt the faintest current of air across my face, and heaved a sigh of relief.

It took me a lot longer, perhaps an hour, to

make my way back to the entrance than it had done to reach the bottom of the mine, but at last I saw the faint glow of natural light ahead. I crawled the last few yards and extinguished my torch. Just before I came out of the mine, I picked up a fist-sized lump of coal and carried it with me as I wormed my way through the narrow gap and emerged into the open. As usual, there was a cold wind keening over the moor and, hot and damp from struggling through the mine, I shivered as I felt the bite of wind. I took a giant lungful of air. It was the sweetest I had ever tasted, proof alone, if any were needed, of just how foul the air at the bottom of the mine had been. I shuddered at the thought of what might have happened if I'd ignored that faint warning in the back of my mind and kept sitting there on that rock a little while longer.

I resolved to say nothing of that to Sue. I told myself it was because I didn't want to alarm her, but that didn't even fool me; the unpalatable truth was that I didn't want her saying 'I told you so' and pointing out what an idiot I'd been. As I came back into the inn, I plonked the piece of coal on the bar and met her questioning gaze.

'I'm glad I've seen it,' I said, 'but I won't be going down again. It's a bit too hard on the knees and elbows.'

She gave me a suspicious look and then went back in the kitchen without further comment.

I spent the next twenty-four hours fantasizing about reopening the pit as a tourist attraction and making a fortune selling lumps of coal as souvenirs, but then, in a rare and uncharacteristic burst of common sense, fearing that some tourist's child might be tempted to explore the mysterious-looking hole in the ground and get lost down there, I phoned the Coal Board and told them that subsidence had caused the old entrance to the mine to open up again. The following day a mine safety team came out, cordoned off the area and then blew in the entrance to the mine with explosives. Unless further subsidence reopens it once more at some time in the future, I would be the last man ever to set foot in the mine and take coal from it.

I kept my piece of Inn at the Top coal in pride of place on a shelf next to the fire for a couple of weeks, but one lunchtime a hiker, busily poking the fire and adding fuel and logs, picked it up and had thrown it into the flames before I could stop him. I dashed out from behind the bar to try to retrieve it, but it was already ablaze and I left it there.

'What's the matter?' the hiker asked.

'Oh, it's silly I know, but it was a souvenir and really precious to me.'

'No,' he said. 'It was only a lump of coal. Look, there's plenty more in the coal bucket.'

CHAPTER 10

The Customer is Always Right

The weeks and months of long hours and hard graft at the Inn at the Top were beginning to take their toll. Exhausted and sleep-starved, I stared at the face in the shaving mirror every morning and began to wonder about the identity of the stranger staring back at me. Although Sue somehow managed to retain most of her normal charm and human warmth – except when unduly provoked by her husband – my previously sunny disposition gave way to periodic bouts of irritability that were occasionally punctuated by random bursts of complete, unreasoning fury.

At busy periods, which effectively meant all day every day throughout the summer, the only way to keep pace with the demands of the ceaseless hordes of people coming through the doors was to perform every task at top speed. When manning the bar, I would be simultaneously serving one customer, handing change to the previous one and taking the order from the next, and nothing would infuriate me quicker than a customer with an order for ten drinks who, despite having waited his turn for five minutes, would reach the front of the queue and only then start enquiring what his companions would like to drink.

'You're next, what can I get you?' I'd say, while

201

finishing serving the previous customer.

'Er ... now then, what does everybody want?' he'd reply, as he turned his back on me to consult with his friends and family. I'd spend the next thirty seconds to a minute drumming my fingers on the bar while a member of his party vacillated between a sweet sherry and a bitter lemon, before finally deciding on 'a Snowball – but I don't want one out of a bottle, can you make me one?' The faint sound of a landlord's teeth grinding could be heard as I mixed the ingredients, hurled a maraschino cherry in the top and pushed it across the bar, and of course, even though that had taken at least half minute, the next drink in the order had not even been thought about until I'd finished that one, leading to yet another delay. Punctuated by regular pauses for thought and enquiries for cocktails or obscure and exotic beverages that no pub in the country possessed, the whole order would be given one drink at a time, preventing any time-saving tricks like leaving the lager tap running into a pint pot while pouring a glass of wine or getting a measure of spirits out of the optics.

Despite the customer's best efforts, the round would eventually be complete, and, months of high-speed bar work having honed an ability in mental arithmetic that would have left Carol Vorderman gasping in my wake, I'd say 'That's fourteen pounds twenty-seven please', or whatever the cost was. There would be a pause. 'That can't be right, can it?' the customer would say and, as the crowd waiting their turn to be served grew ever more mutinous, I'd have to go right through it again, arriving once more at the same figure. There would often still be much sucking of teeth and puffing out of cheeks before the customer accepted that the price was right and finally departed the bar.

I was bemoaning this to another pub landlord in the area – we do love to whinge about our customers on our days off – when he put me on the right track to minimizing such time-consuming recounts in future.

'If anyone makes me add it all up again,' he said, 'I always make sure it comes to at least a pound more the next time. And if they still want to argue, it'll be another two quid more expensive the time after that.' He winked. 'They soon get the picture and pay up.'

My irascibility with slow-thinking or bolshy customers – whoever coined the phrase 'The customer is always right' had clearly never worked in a pub – and my occasional air of barely-suppressed simmering fury, soon led my locals to supply me with a new nickname: in honour of another character whose wafer-thin veneer of charm and civility barely concealed the raging demon within. My new name, used both behind my back and to my face, was 'Basil' – as in Fawlty. My soubriquet was well deserved and it was little consolation that I was only one of many impatient and intolerant landlords in the area; if the road to hell is paved with good intentions, the road to a good country pub was often lined with ghastly imitations.

Country pubs were often free houses and their opening hours could vary from the sublime to the ridiculous. For every country pub that remained open all day, I could show you another that didn't open at lunchtimes or opened late in the evening or closed on every alternate Thursday when there was an 'r' in the month. I could even have taken you to one moorland pub that was only open after eight in the evening and on Sunday lunchtimes.

Having found a pub that actually was open, the aspiring customer then had to negotiate an entrance porch that was often helpfully adorned with notices: 'NO BIKERS', 'NO HIKERS', 'NO CHILDREN', 'NO MUDDY BOOTS', 'NO LAUGHING'... all right, I admit I made the last one up, but it was only a slight exaggeration of the often grim reality. Those who remained undeterred could press on into the pub, where, if they were very lucky, it might even have been possible to eat. Those not expecting to dine before 12.30 or after 1.30 were not often disappointed, though there remained a few charming remnants of the 1950s where lunch began at one o'clock and was usually over by a quarter past, and a few more where, whatever time you turned up, the only food on offer would be potato crisps.

The Third Immutable Law of Public House Ownership stated that the more beautiful the pub, the more ugly the temper of the landlord. That idyllic little country inn, nestling in an unspoilt landscape, would often turn out to be operated by a cross between Martin Bormann and Attila the Hun. There was a perfectly logical reason for this unpleasant state of affairs: people bought country inns because they thought running a pub would be easy, a bucolic idyll where they could while away their time, chatting to

204

locals, polishing horse brasses and proffering the occasional half-pint. Any landlord – if he could spare the time – could bend your ear for hours about similarly deluded fools who thought a pub would be a suitable retirement home. The reality was that both husband and wife would work an absolute minimum of one hundred hours a week.

Under the pressure of this endless drudgery, most pub landlords – present company included – turned within a few short months from charming, friendly hosts into careworn, bone-tired and hyper-irritable grouches. The ogre behind the bar would be shouting at you for no apparent reason, simply because he was trying to take revenge on the world for luring him to a heaven on earth that had turned out to be a living hell.

Some landlords responded to the deplorable situation in which they found themselves by abandoning all attempts to attract new customers to their pubs, and some even gave up trying to retain the ones they'd already got. In a village further down the Dale from the inn, there was a pub which the irascible landlord operated solely for the convenience of himself and a dwindling handful of regulars. On our own night off, Sue and I watched him one evening, staring balefully at a party of four young people unwinding after a day's hiking. Their noise, laughter, jokes and general good cheer were visibly becoming too much for the landlord and finally one of them gave him the opening he was seeking with an apparently innocent remark about having had a 'bloody marvellous day'.

'That's it!' the landlord screamed. 'I'll have no

swearing in my pub. Get out!'

The stunned hikers stared at him in disbelief, then drank up in silence and left. As the door closed behind the last of them, the landlord turned to one of his regulars, winked and said, 'That got rid of the buggers.'

Another similar character, a Scot who ran the other pub in the same village, stared with mounting fury at a party of about a dozen students who were plying him with orders at a frenetic pace, filling his till but infuriating him with their sheer exuberance. His chance came when they decided to move on to 'shorts' and, amongst other things, ordered 'nine whiskies, one with lemonade'. The landlord, a true Caledonian outraged at this affront to his country's national drink (no, not Irn Bru; the other one), leapt from behind the bar, stormed across the room and shouted, 'I want to know which bastard ordered the whisky with lemonade. He's barred.' When they wouldn't tell him, he threw all of them out.

My own irrational rages were mainly sparked by the unreasonable demands of the sort of pernickety customers who would have sent the wine back after the Miracle at Cana because it wasn't chilled enough or, faced with the miracle of the loaves and fishes, would have complained that it was only a two-course lunch. In general I was far more tolerant of the quirks and foibles of our regulars, even though some of them could also be pretty annoying, but I made an exception for those I felt were abusing the generosity of our extended opening hours.

The only threat to the cosy conspiracy that

existed between ourselves and our customers came from the local licensing magistrates, by repute a distressingly stern and unbending crew. Rumour among our locals had it that most of the magistrates were Methodists and therefore, as one of our regulars put it, 'miserable buggers – they don't drink themselves and they do their damnedest to make sure no one else does either'.

By the time we took over the running of the inn, the local magistrates had issued strict instructions to the police to inspect every pub in their licensing area a minimum of twice, and preferably three or four times, a year. If they found anything amiss on any of their after-hours inspections, they were to apprehend the culprits and then return at frequent unannounced intervals until the errant landlord and his sinful customers had all learned the error of their ways.

Fortunately for us, the nearest police station was almost twenty miles away, at the far end of some of the most narrow, steep and twisting roads in the country. They were doubly difficult after dark, for there were no street lights, no white lines and no cats' eyes, and the road – single-tracked in parts, with a few passing places – dipped, swooped, twisted and turned so much that it was a real heart-in-mouth, stop-start journey even for those who knew it well. Those who didn't could only progress at snail's pace, slowing almost to a halt at every bend or hillcrest, and there were plenty of both on the way up to the inn.

There was never any trouble serious enough to require police intervention at the inn and the local force were understandably reluctant to make the long and harrowing journey up there any more often than they absolutely had to. As a result we became the only pub in the entire United Kingdom to be raided by the police by prior appointment. Every two or three months, the phone would ring at about ten o'clock of a weekday morning and an anonymous but unmistakably policeman-like voice would say 'Mr Hanson? Mr Neil Hanson? Just a word to the wise, sir. The police will be paying you a visit at eleven o'clock tonight.' He didn't add 'Evening all' or 'Mind how you go' before breaking the connection, but even the dimmest bulb in the box could have been in no doubt as to the caller's chosen occupation.

The first time this happened, sure enough, at eleven o'clock that night, headlight beams could be seen piercing the darkness of the road to the east of the inn and a few moments later a police car drove up and parked on the forecourt. Peering through a chink in the upstairs curtains, I watched two policemen get out and try the door. They found it locked and the entire pub in darkness ... albeit with the generator still running and a surprisingly large number of cars still sitting in the car park at the side. After testing the door again and spending a couple of minutes trying to peer through the windows of the darkened bar, honour was satisfied and the policemen got in their car and disappeared back down the hill. As soon as the glow of their headlights had faded, we turned the pub lights back on, the doors were reopened and a couple of dozen farmers and hikers who'd been waiting out the raid in total darkness and silence, standing in the kitchen clutching their pint pots, were ushered back through to the bar and normal service was resumed.

One member of the local constabulary, however – my locals had nicknamed him 'Sergeant Gravelknees' in honour of his habit of crawling around car parks on his hands and knees, searching for cars with bald tyres – was far from happy with this flagrant abuse of the letter of the law and he resolved to take matters into his own hands. So it was that around midnight one night the door burst open and Sergeant Gravelknees strode into the pub, accompanied by an apologetic-looking constable. They netted a rich haul, catching me in the act of pulling a pint and about twenty customers in the act of drinking one. Among them, by a pleasing irony, was one of Sergeant Gravelknees' own colleagues, out of uniform and enjoying a big night out with his mates. Curiously, he was the only one of all of us who did not receive a summons to appear in the magistrates' court a few weeks later.

Deciding that, if we were going to go down, we might as well do so in style, we hired a coach for our day in court, and after a hearty breakfast at the pub and a glass of buck's fizz to put us in the mood, we all piled aboard the coach and set off for the magistrates' court in the market town twenty miles away. We put in a brief appearance in the courtroom, where my customers were fined £25 for drinking after hours and I was fined £250 for letting them. Sue got off scot-free since my name, not hers, was inscribed as licensee over the pub door. Having got that unpleasantness out of the way, we all adjourned to the nearest pub where we made the heartwarming discovery that, since it was market day, the town's pubs were all, quite legally, open all day. After a very long and liquid day out, we returned at midnight to the inn, where our customers managed to squeeze in one last nightcap before summoning their transport for the unsteady journey home.

Whether by coincidence or not, Sergeant Gravelknees was transferred out of the district soon afterwards and our previous mutually beneficial arrangement with the local police was resumed. However, anxious to avoid another swingeing fine, we took the precaution of applying to the magistrates for a two-hour extension on the night of the annual sheep show – the biggest night of the pub's year. To our horror, when we attended the court for the hearing, the chairman of the magistrates told us that he was turning down our application. But after a few beats of silence, belying the 'miserable buggers' reputation our locals had given him and his fellow magistrates, he gave the ghost of a wink and added a rider: 'Since I understand that the pub is already open twenty-four hours a day, I can't for the life of me see how it would be physically possible to extend the drinking hours any further.'

Generous, not to say excessive, though our opening hours were, there were always one or two customers who wanted to push the envelope even further. There was one particular local – let's call him Bert – who lived some way away on the far side of the moor. Although he was a sheep farmer and had a reputation as 'a good tup man', he was not well liked by most of his peers and, though nothing had ever been proved, was suspected of a string of crimes and misdemeanours. It was believed that he had been involved in the ultimate crime in the Dale – sheep rustling – in the past, and, almost as bad in his peers' eyes, there were suggestions that on more than one occasion during 'tupping time' he had sneaked onto another farmer's land in the dead of night and used some of their prize tups to 'cover' his own ewes. The crime was magnified when the shearling tups and tup hoggs said to have resulted from those unholy unions went on to win prizes at the local shows and were subsequently sold at auction for high prices.

Despite the rumours, he was a lively and gregarious character, and his major crime in our eyes was not so much his cavalier ways with other people's livestock as his habit of rolling up at the pub well after the legal closing time, having spent the evening filling some other landlord's till, and then staying for hours nursing a half-pint or a single whisky. His wife worked late shifts at a hotel thirty miles away and, unbeknownst to us, Bert sometimes arranged with her to pick him up from the inn on her way home at three in the morning. We didn't mind late opening – it went with the turf at the Inn at the Top – but staying open till three in the morning, especially for a customer who ignored all pleas and entreaties to drink up and go, and was not even spending enough money to pay for the lighting, struck me as taking liberties. The near-saintly Sue disagreed and on several occasions, to avoid an ugly scene, she intercepted me as I was storming round from behind the bar ready to toss him into the carpark, and told me to go to bed while she sat up with him until he'd gone.

The final straw came one night when, well after two o'clock, Bert accepted a lift home from the only other customer still standing and disappeared into the night. With sighs of relief, we cleared up, turned off the lights and fell into bed. In the depths of the night I was woken by shouts and the noise of someone pounding on the door of the inn. Bleary-eyed and cursing, I stumbled downstairs to find Bert's wife standing on the doorstep.

'Where is he?' she demanded.

In other circumstances, I might have been more sympathetic, but half-asleep and freezing cold because I was standing in the doorway in my pyjamas, I had no sympathy to spare for anyone but myself.

'I've no idea where he is. At home, I should think. If you'd paused before knocking the door down,' I said, reaching for sarcasm, the traditional standby of those short on wit and temper, not to mention sleep, 'you'd have noticed that all the lights were off and the doors locked, which is usually a bit of a clue that we've closed up and gone to bed.'

'But he phoned me earlier on and told me to pick him up from here. I've come twenty miles out of my way to get him.'

I shrugged – and regretted it at once, since it only served to send a further icy draft down my neck – and said, 'Well, he got a lift with someone else and left at least an hour ago.'

'The selfish bastard,' she said. 'I'll kill him

when I get home.'

'Good idea,' I said. 'And when you've finished, tell him he's barred. I'm sick of him pitching up here after closing time and staying half the night. I don't want to see him here again, even in daylight.'

When not having to be strait-jacketed by Sue to prevent me pitching more late-drinking farmers out on their ear, my bursts of spontaneous irrational fury were mainly targeted against the long-range hikers who called at the pub – one of the way-stations on a celebrated long-distance walk over hill, dale and glutinous peat bog. I have never had the least inclination to submit myself to the self-imposed tyranny of such a marathon walk. I cannot deny that there must be a tremendous sense of achievement in completing those peat-encrusted miles and I am sure there must be people who have actually enjoyed the experience; the trouble is that I never met any.

For most long-range walkers, whatever their feelings and intentions as they set off, full of optimism, from one end or other of the trek, a few days of rain-sodden bog-trotting were usually enough to reduce the Arthurian quest to the status of a prison term. Each day was a grim battle of attrition between the hiker and a number of implacable adversaries: the weather, the peat bogs and hags (steep-sided hummocks of peat that rise out of the surrounding morasses, driving hikers into an exhausting, endless series of slippery climbs and slimy descents), and, most sinister of all, the blisters pushing up through the soles of the hiker's feet, like the first shy daffodils of spring.

Pub landlords are traditionally the receptacle for their customers' woes and I have probably shared more conversations with long-distance walkers than most people, so I can report with authority that their most favoured topics of conversation were neither the beauty of the landscape nor the joy of walking free as the wind among the hills. Number One in the long-range walkers' Top 40 was invariably the state of their feet. Number Two was the wetness of their socks and its possible contribution to the condition of Number One (see above). Remedies for the former problem were eagerly discussed and compared, but the remedy for the second was usually to try to suspend them from the mantelpiece over the blazing open fire.

'Do you mind taking your wet, stinking socks down from my fireplace?' I enquired of a hiker one day. 'I'm sure they smell like roses to you, but they don't to me. If you open your eyes just a tiny bit wider, you might notice that you are far from the only customer in the pub and many of the others are trying to eat their lunch.'

A tad too sarcastic for some tastes, no doubt, but it did seem the best way to get the point across, though in that, as in much else in life, I was clearly wrong.

'Oh, so you don't like hikers then?' came the reply. 'Why did you get a pub in the middle of the moors, if you don't like hikers?'

'It's not the hikers I object to,' I said. 'It's just the obnoxious personal habits of some of them.'

He took down his socks and stomped off in high dudgeon, but it wasn't long before another one was trying the same trick. This may have partly explained the jocular motto we adopted with reference to the food we served: 'If the tourists won't eat it, feed it to the pigs; if the pigs won't eat it, feed it to the hikers.'

The real problem with the long-distance hiking marathons, as far as I was concerned, was that they swiftly became reduced to an endurance test. The point of doing it was to have done it; to sit back at journey's end and say 'I did the Wombles of Wimbledon Way', or whichever marathon they had chosen. Yet was there any real point in travelling through some of the most spectacular landscapes in Britain if your eyes had been firmly fixed on the patch of peat bog in front of your boots all the way? Call me lazy, call me soft, call me anything you like, but my sympathies were definitely with the all-too-rare long-distance cheaters who used to call at the inn.

One fine summer morning, the postman roared up in his van, depositing not only Faith on her eternal quest for Guinness, whisky and cigarettes, 'for the love of God', but also three portly middle-aged men in full hiking gear. They shot straight into the bar and set themselves up for the rigours of the day with three or four pints, all the while keeping an anxious eye out of the window on the track leading over the moors to the south. About an hour later, one of them suddenly called out, 'Look out! Here they come!' They swilled down their pints in one and with a pleading look at me one of them asked, 'Is it all right if we just nip out the back door?'

I ushered them out through the kitchen and

215

they hurried off and hid among the rocks behind the pub, invisible but for the clouds of smoke from the cigarettes they were chain-smoking. A few minutes later, two more portly, middle-aged men entered by the front door, puce-faced from the exertion of marching up the moors from the youth hostel in the village five miles away at the bottom of the hill, where they had spent the night. They ordered a drink and sank down gasping by the fire to examine their blisters (see above).Ten minutes after that, the three stooges, having finished their cigarettes and carefully smeared their boots and leggings with peat and mud, came marching in at the front door, extolling the virtues of healthy exercise. They exchanged greetings with their suspicious-looking companions and called for pints all round.

'Have this one on me; you've earned it,' I said, with only the faintest trace of a smile.

If long-distance hiking left me cold, I wasn't a big fan of camping either, although, like my occasional irrational hatred of the former and its practitioners, it was not something I ever felt able to admit at the inn, where around one in four of our summer customers wore hiking boots and carried a rucksack containing a tent. Even as an eight-year-old I knew that scouting could terminally damage your street credibility and apart from a couple of Mediterranean holidays in my teens and a freezing twenty-four-hour 'outdoor adventure' with my children a few years ago, I've never spent a night under canvas in my life. My idea of the perfect end to a day's walking on the fells would be to be met at a prearranged rendezvous by a chauffeur-driven limousine and whisked away to a sumptuous country house hotel for a hot shower, a relaxing sauna, the best dinner that money could buy and an untroubled night's sleep between freshly laundered sheets in a large, comfortable bed.

To trudge all day across the moors in driving rain and howling wind with half a ton of rucksack on my back and then spend most of the evening wrestling with a tent and trying to remember where I put the tin opener, before eating un-identifiable stewed meat and vegetables cooked over a pitiful Primus stove, didn't seem like much fun to me, though thousands begged to differ. Even worse would be to wake after a cold and un-comfortable night to find that all the clothes you were about to put on were just as wet as they were the night before. The only refuge from the wet, the cold and the ferocious, blood-sucking assaults of the local midges was likely to be the pub, and prudent campers, just like other walkers, should always ensure that the day's journey ends at the front door of a public house. It always pays to remember where you've pitched your tent, however...

Most hikers tended to camp overnight on the level ground beside the inn, where the coarse moorland grasses gave way to a springy, sheep-cropped turf, but one night, two students on their 'Last Great Adventure' before going away to college decided to pitch their tent in splendid isolation a quarter of a mile onto the moor. They then strolled down to the inn, enjoying the last rays of the setting sun. They ate some supper, spent the remainder of the evening at the bar and then wandered off into the night breathing fond if beery farewells to us and the assembled company.

Our locals were just settling back with yet another of their perennial 'just one for the roads' when the two hikers reappeared.

'I wonder if you have a torch we might borrow?' one said. 'It's rather dark out there and we can't seem to find our tent.'

To describe the moors around the pub on a moonless night as 'rather dark' was like describing Genghis Khan as 'a bit of an uncouth type'. The nearest street light was getting on for twenty miles away and there was none of the reflected glow from the clouds you get near a town. On a moonless, overcast night, it would be easier to sort coal by braille at the bottom of an unlit mineshaft than to find your way across the moors around the inn.

'All right,' I said, getting my torch down from the shelf behind the bar and handing it over, 'but one of you will have to bring it back, once you've found your tent. I need it myself to find my way back from the generator shed after shutting down for the night.'

This was only partly true; it was also, I confess, for the sheer malicious pleasure of seeing how he would then navigate back to the tent in pitch blackness once more.

The farmers propping up the bar were hugely enjoying the hikers' predicament and were offering all sorts of helpful advice as they again headed for the door.

'You want to take a big ball of string with you next time,' one said. 'Then you can tie one end to

218

the tent, unravel it when you go for a walk and follow it back afterwards.'

The hikers marched out red-faced. Through the window we could see the torch beam criss-crossing the ground to either side of the track running up the moor until they eventually found their tent. Five minutes later one of them returned, bearing the torch.

'Excellent,' I said, as he handed it to me. 'Now, you've only got one small problem: how are you going to find your way back again?'

His expression suggested that this particular problem had not occurred to him until that very moment. He gave the torch a last longing look. 'I don't suppose...'

I shook my head.

'Sorry. Like I said, I need it myself when I switch the generator off.'

He turned and made his way out into the darkness. We let him have a few seconds' start and then all rushed outside to follow his progress. We saw his footsteps falter as soon as he reached the edge of the pool of warm orange light spilling from the inn and disappeared into the utter blackness beyond. After a splash, two squelches and a couple of muddied oaths, he began calling out to his friend: 'Hello? Helloooooooo!'

There was a pause and then a distant answering 'Helloooo! Is that you?'

'Of course it's me. Who the hell else would it be?'

'All right, all right. What do you want?'

'I want to find the bloody tent, of course.'

'It's right where you left it!' shouted one of the farmers, getting into the spirit of things.

Ignoring the interruption, the two continued to try and echo-locate each other.

'There's no need to get so shirty. It's not my fault; I wanted to pitch it by the pub. Anyway, just follow the sound of my voice.'

'That's what I'm trying to... Shit!'

There was a pleasingly moist squelch as our hero strayed off the track and sank up to his knees in a neighbouring peat bog, followed by some muffled straining and cursing as he extricated himself from that one only to disappear into another.

'Shit, shit, shit! Where the hell are you? Keep calling to me.'

By now we could hardy hear for laughing as the two of them kept hallooing to each other across the moor, like a latter-day Heathcliff and Cathy. Heathcliff's attempts to locate the tent by sonar were not assisted by the constant shouts and bursts of laughter from the spectators and it must have been another ten minutes before the three of them – the two hikers and their tent – were finally reunited.

As we returned inside, wiping the tears of laughter from our eyes, I saw something lying on the bar. I hurried to the door.

'Helloooo!' I called into the darkness.

There was a silence and then a tentative reply from the tent: 'Hello? Are you talking to us?'

'Yes. I've got some bad news for you. You've left your wallet on the bar.'

He was still swearing when he blundered into the bar again and we could hear him cursing all the way back, visiting most of the same peat bogs on his way.

CHAPTER 11

Five Litres of Worm Drench

Although weekends and bank holidays at the inn often resembled King's Cross in the rush hour, the very busiest days of the year were purely or primarily local occasions. One such was the summer night of the annual 'Sports', when the inn, strangely deserted at 9.30p.m., was bursting at the seams half an hour later as a couple of hundred farmers and other assorted locals, who'd been participating in, or spectating at, a range of quirky sports including harness-racing, Cumberland wrestling, knur and spell, and throwing the welly, tried to get served simultaneously.

An even more frenetic night was the last night of the autumn tup sales, the major sale of rams on the eve of 'tupping time' – the breeding season. The sales coincided with the date of an ancient fair held in the town at the bottom of the hill and dating back to 1353, though it was now little more than a tourist curiosity. Where the streets were once lined from end to end with pens of livestock, farmers' carts full of poultry and produce, and the jostling stalls of cheapjacks, quack medicine vendors, fortune-tellers and other traders, there were now no more than a handful of stalls, most selling twentieth-century tourist tat, while in an effort to provide some entertainment for visitors,

strolling players, bearing a more than passing resemblance to various local characters and shopkeepers, staged whimsical, medieval-themed street
theatre in the main street and the market square.

Women in peasant costume, with artfully black-
ened teeth, gathered to gossip on local events like
the spread of the Black Death. A pardoner offered
forgiveness for people's sins in exchange for a
suitable fee, and he also had a number of
'blessings' on sale, including a fragment of 'the
true Cross' and a piece of wood from Noah's Ark.
A cuckolded husband whose wife was said to have
bewitched her young lover, had her carted off to
be tried as a witch, and a stall holder who had
short-changed his customers was put in the
stocks and pelted with leeks, cauliflowers and
cabbages – much the most popular entertainment
of the day among the children of the town, who
joined in with gusto. The players also staged a
'Court of Piepowder' – a corruption of the
Norman phrase *pied poudré* – like those that had
once dispensed summary justice among the
dusty-footed pedlars, broggers (wool buyers),
badgers (pedlars of corn and general goods),
salters, carriers and the other itinerant traders
who thronged the streets in medieval times.

While the visitors were entertained on the main
street of the town, an almost equally ancient and
far more important ritual was being followed on
the parallel road, where the tup sales were taking
place in the auction mart. I dropped in there
during the afternoon to find out what all the fuss
was about, squeezing into a chink between a
couple of the farmers who were arranged cheek

by jowl in tiers right around the auction ring. Try as I might, as he sold the tups to their new owners at a bewildering speed, I found the auctioneer's spiel to be even less comprehensible than the old drover, Jed, speaking dialect with his teeth out and a mouthful of tobacco juice sloshing around in his cheeks.

I did manage to make out the words 'Lot 187' but all I heard after that was what sounded like 'Awerra-bid-awanna-bid-awanna-bid-heeja-bid-werra-bid-awarra-bid-wanna-yanna-awrayadun–' delivered at blinding speed, and then terminated by the thud as the hammer went down and the next tup was prodded and pushed into the sale ring as the previous one was ushered out. It made no sense at all to me, but the farmers seemed to know what was going on, and that was the main thing, after all. It was almost equally impossible for me to see who was actually bidding. No farmer liked another to know his business and, presumably by prior arrangement with the auctioneer, those making bids were doing so with gestures or nods or shakes of the head that were so discreet they were almost imperceptible. Only when the hammer had gone down was the identity of the successful bidder revealed, and only then because the auctioneer announced it before moving on to the next lot.

Before the sale began, all the farmers had been running the rule over the livestock held in the pens alongside the auction mart and there was a genuine buzz of excitement as one of the star attractions – the winner of the supreme champion rosette at that year's sheep show at the Inn at the

Top – was led into the sale ring. It was eventually sold for well over £40,000 – not a record, but not far off – prompting a few muffled cheers and rather more whistles of disbelief. 'Yon's a handsome tup, no denying that,' a farmer near me said to his mate.

'Aye, but it'll be a dear do if he doesn't "get" well [sire good lambs], wunt it?' his dour companion muttered back.

None of the farmers' usual carefulness with money was in evidence that night, the last night of the tup sales, when even the most staid and cautious of them could be seen banging handfuls of notes down on the bar of every pub in the area, as all celebrated their good fortune at the sales or spent the rest of their 'luck money'. In the old days, a 'luck penny' was handed over to seal a deal, a practice similar to the acceptance of the King's shilling when joining the army, though there was also a superstition in livestock dealing that handing back a penny would make the animal lucky.

Like much else in the Dale, it was a tradition that dated back to the Norse, who believed that luck was something that could be transferred through an object or in return for a gift. 'The Luck of Edenhall', in the neighbouring Eden Valley, associated with a glass goblet, was one of several 'lucks' associated with particular places. Luck money traditionally also changed hands in exchange for any sharp-edged gift, like a knife, but it was at the tup sales that the practice was still most widespread.

The first tup to make four figures was in 1954, when one sold for £1,800. Harry, the auctioneer who sold it, was a regular at the inn and still remembered it well. He had a fund of tales about the auction mart, laughing himself into a coughing fit over the exploits of the farmers, their cunning and their legendary meanness, but his jokes did not wholly conceal a deep affection and respect for them. 'The farmers gasped at the price, they thought one would never be worth anything of the sort again, but prices have gone up ever since and the record now stands at £50,000.'

Though prices had genuinely risen to record levels, the price bid was not always what it seemed, for 'luck money' could play a big part. 'There has always been a luck penny,' said Harry 'but now pennies have got to be pounds. I think it's a bit to do with reputation. Some of these high prices are caused by jealousy; if your tup makes a thousand quid, maybe I'd want mine to make a thousand too, so I might offer a fair bit of luck money back.' Certainly there were rumours of as much as one-third luck money being handed over on one or two deals, and it was not too hard to believe them, for, like their sheep, hill farmers were a proud breed. To be seen to be bested by a rival in front of all your peers would have been hard to bear.

Pride could be even more expensive to a farmer than that, however. The top prices were paid for the 'shearling' tups, the previous year's tup lambs, which were sold on their looks and pedigree, rather than on their performance since, as shearlings, they had yet to sire any lambs. Tales were told of farmers paying huge prices for tups that either produced poor offspring or failed to show the proper enthusiasm for the job for which they have been bought. It must have been a trifle galling, to say the least, to have paid £50,000 for a shearling tup that, whether as a result of a vow of celibacy, a different sexual orientation, or some general malaise, then turned out to be less than interested in the opposite sex. Rather than admit such a failure, it was claimed that some farmers had shot such tups and sent them away with the 'knacker men', never to be seen or mentioned again.

One other noble tradition connected with luck money was that it needed to be spent; it was bad luck to take your unspent luck money home with you and the last night of the tup sales was a raucous night in every pub for miles around. Farmers who, for the rest of the year, found it hard to bring themselves to pay for their own drink, never mind that of anybody else, could even be heard shouting 'Drinks for the house!' A great stillness lay upon the land the next morning, with scarcely a farmer to be seen as, over the whole Dale, the celebrants of the previous night nursed their aching heads in darkened rooms.

The same scene was repeated in miniature every week on market day, when a modicum of drink would be taken, even by those farmers with no reason to celebrate. It was a deep-rooted tradition, for while researching in the county archives one day, I came across an entry in a farmer's diary from the mid-nineteenth century; which suggested that only the mode of transport had changed: 'To market with the wool. We got overmuch ale. Brother Edmund fell off his horse and lamed his leg.'

Though farmers kept up the tradition every week, the last night of the tup sales was when they went for broke. 'I remember one time, we'd got finished off at the mart and I'd popped into the pub for a drink,' said Harry. 'Quite a few of the farmers would pop in there for a quick one or two after the sales, leaving their tups penned up in the mart. Well, it got to about nine o'clock and the foreman came in to say there was a tup of one of the farmers still in the mart and he wanted to get home. The farmer just shouted, "Fetch it in here, then", and carried on drinking with his mates. I walked down with the foreman and we dragged the tup back up to the pub between us. He wasn't really keen to go in there, but we got him in somehow and one of the farmer's mates announced, "That tup doesn't look so cheerful, Jack." The last I saw they were trying to get a bottle of Guinness down it to cheer it up.'

However, even the last night of the tup sales was small beer compared to the sheep show day in May, when the inn was packed from ten in the morning until midnight. Sheep fairs were a popular attraction in the Dale until the 1930s when the poverty and misery of the Great Depression left the inhabitants with little appetite for organizing them and no spare money to spend at them, and they ceased to be held at all. In 1951 that local tradition was revived with the launch of the sheep show at the Inn at the Top, and it has been held on the last Thursday of May every year since then. The timing is not accidental; it falls in one of the few lulls in the shepherd's year, after the rigours of lambing-time are over and before the stress of hay-time begins to loom too large on the horizon, and also at a time when their tups have recovered from the stresses of winter and, fed on the new spring grass, are in the peak of condition. For many of the farmers it's also the first real chance to catch up with friends they may not have seen since the tup sales the previous autumn.

The inn was chosen as the site for the sheep show because, when the Breed Association for the black-nosed, white-faced sheep – later adopted as the emblem of the Yorkshire Dales National Park – was formed in 1919, the inn was the centre of the circle of fifteen miles' radius within which the breed was originally developed. The native sheep of the Dale were the aristocrats of hill sheep, hardy enough to survive on the poorest moorland grasses and to over-winter on the tops in all but the very wildest weather. The ewes also had exceptional mothering abilities. As a result, the pure-bred Dale sheep have not only become the most numerous and economically important hill-sheep in England, but the cross-bred offspring of a Dale ewe with a Blue-faced Leicester tup, known as a 'Mule', is also the most numerous lowland sheep.

The Inn at the Top's show, where the Dale's wonder sheep and rams strutted their stuff, was completely unlike other Dales shows. This was not a show for dilettantes; there were no Women's Institute tents with produce or handicrafts, no prize vegetables, cakes and biscuits, home-made chutneys, handwriting contests, stick-dressing, painting or any of the other myriad rural activities that were celebrated at every other village show;

228

in fact, there were virtually no stalls at all. It was a sheep show pure and simple, and the people – and there were hundreds and hundreds of them – had either come to see the sheep or just to catch the atmosphere of a unique event.

Several hundred people turned up on the day of the show and, except for a handful of passing tourists and hikers in brightly coloured cagoules, every one of them was wearing the Dale uniform of flat cap, tweed jacket and trousers, check shirt, and boots, not wellies, often with leather gaiters, all in duns, fawns, olive drabs, dark greens and peaty browns that, from a distance, made them almost impossible to distinguish from the fells on which they stood. The farmers prepared their show animals in a mixture of fanatical secrecy and leaks and deliberate misinformation that even MI5 would have found hard to equal. The rivalries between the 'big tup men' were intense and deep-seated, stretching back years, and some were not above a bit of skulduggery to improve their chances or hamper a rival. Beauty treatments were carried out for several days before the show – not on the farmers but on their prize yows and tups. Farmers borrowed their wives' eyebrow tweezers to pull offending white hairs out of the black muzzles of their sheep, rinsed their fleeces in peaty water to give them that year's fashionable shade of pale brown, did a little judicious shaping of the fleece with the clippers to make the animal look more like it had the perfect body shape underneath, and some allegedly even rubbed boot polish into the black bits to make them blacker still or cover up grey or white patches. Top contenders were kept under lock and key, for if local rumour was true, jealous tup men were not above trying to nobble a rival's championship contender.

The prizes for winning each class were as modest as a few pounds and as prosaic as 'Five Litres of Worm Drench' but success or failure was no trifling matter and the real value of a first prize rosette in each class, let alone the one for the overall winner – the supreme champion – was far above its modest monetary value. To be awarded the prize of supreme champion at the show could add a five-figure sum to a tup's price at the autumn sales.

The judges received a constant barrage of nods, winks and helpful advice and asides from owners and spectators alike as they were trying to do their job; 'You mun judge for thissen of course, but yon's by far the best yow I've ever had – better'n her I won with four year ago', was one of the more subtle attempts to sway the judges I overheard when I escaped the bar for five minutes to see what all the fuss was about.

Our mentor, Dick, was one of the most respected 'tup men' in the Dale, but had a deadly rival, Granville, who farmed on the other side of the moor from the inn. Within the limitations of the standard wardrobe of Dale farmers, Granville was a bit of a fashion plate. Whenever he was out and about, he was always immaculately turned out, wearing brown brogues and a three-piece suit with a watch-chain across the waistcoat. But if he was on the cutting edge of Dale fashion, he also seemed to me something of a blowhard, continually finding ways to let everybody know how superior his farm, his tups and yows, and presumably by extension, he himself, were to every other farm and farmer in the area. Dick never expressed a hint of criticism of Granville's big-timing and show-boating, but after Dick's tup had been crowned supreme champion at the sheep show with his rival relegated to runner-up, the quiet smile of satisfaction he allowed himself as his gaze alighted momentarily on Granville, spoke volumes.

The judges' wisdom, or lack of it, was almost the sole topic of conversation on show night and for many nights afterwards, with the farmers discussing the respective merits of various tups with ever-increasing volume and intensity, broken only by a chorus of the local anthem 'Beautiful Dale' emanating from some farmers' choir in a corner.

The music at the show was provided by the Middlesmoor and Lofthouse Silver Band, who had played at every single one. They were passing by chance when the show was first being held, on their way back from a concert in the North East, and stopped to see what was happening. A few minutes later, they had unpacked their instruments and started playing and they had been coming back to play ever since. The rosy glow from the conductor's nose – almost the same hue as the maroon jackets they all wore – and the alacrity with which they downed instruments and headed for the bar as soon as their concert had finished, suggested that a love of music, or indeed sheep, was only part of the reason why they kept on returning, year after year. On a warm spring evening, if I could snatch a few moments away from the bar, there was nothing finer than to sit up on the fell, listening to the sound of the silver band drifting on the breeze apart perhaps from sitting bleary-eyed round the kitchen table the next morning and starting to count the mountain of cash taken over the bar the previous day.

CHAPTER 12

All Fur Coat and No Knickers

Perhaps it was just because we had drunk, not wisely, but too well on the night of the show but, inspired by this community celebration, we resolved to visit another one that occurred a week later in a small town twenty miles away on the far side of the Pennines ... it seemed like a good idea at the time. Stan and Neville and their wives had arrived to hoover up the takings from the show, so we took up the offer of a day off.

'I know,' I'd said to Sue, as we recovered from the show's long day's journey into night, 'let's go over to the Horse Fair. We'll get up before dawn, drive over there and we can take some great photographs of Fair Hill, just as dawn is breaking. I might even be able to flog an article on it.'

The idea didn't seem quite so outstanding at 4a.m. on the first morning of the Horse Fair, when we left the warm embrace of our bed for

232

the cold shoulder of a damp night and followed the narrow, twisting road that crossed the bleak moorland to the west. For centuries, perhaps from as early as Roman times, miners had scrabbled into this sour and sodden land, digging out lead from the dales and coal from the fell-tops, which was then carried by trains of packhorses, and later horses and carts, down to the smelting mills in the valleys below.

The miners would walk for an hour or more simply to reach the mine workings high on the fells and, after a day's backbreaking labour in foul air and soaking wet conditions underground, they would face the same long walk back in their dripping clothes. In the grey light of a damp, false dawn, it was not hard to imagine the miners trudging over the green roads across the moor. Even on this June morning there was an edge to the wind keening across the moor; in winter it cut like a knife.

From the lonely outpost of the Inn at the Top, the road crossed the moors for five miles, passing no human habitation but the old toll gate house, dating from the late eighteenth century and un-occupied throughout the twentieth. At intervals the road was punctuated by the tall wooden snow poles that marked the line of the road for the snow ploughs and diggers that often had to fight their way through a white anonymous winter landscape, every feature shrouded in feet of snow. On this grey morning, however, there was only the mist, carrying the sounds of the sad piping of the golden plovers and the anxious calls of the sheep to their lambs.

As we reached the moor edge, the mist lifted for a moment, giving a brief, familiar glimpse down into the valley below, a view stretching to the mountains of the Lake District and the shores of the Solway Firth, a lush prospect of rich farmland and vivid green grass. After crossing the dun-coloured moorland with its mosses and sour peat hags, fit only for heather and cotton grass, it must once really have seemed the promised land, flowing with milk, if not honey, some of the finest dairy land in England.

Dropping down from the fells towards the valley floor, the drystone walls gave way to hedges, with the road burrowing between high earth banks. We passed the gaunt knuckle of a ruined castle and reached the sleeping town, just as the grey and drizzly dawn was breaking. A new bypass had been driven straight along the old Roman road just below Fair Hill, where gypsies – or travellers, to give them a more all-embracing name – had gathered for the Horse Fair for centuries. No doubt it was the best line for the road, though some might have suspected darker motives; not everyone in town loved the Fair. The travellers' caravans were a little more remote from the town as a result, but not beyond the long arm of the law. We drove up towards the cluster of caravans, Romany wagons, flatbed trucks and Transit vans that covered the site, huddled together as if for warmth against the cool of the night. As we pulled up, a police van at the corner of the site, parked perhaps, in case this was another load of hippies on their way to another alternative Stonehenge, disgorged six policemen eager for whatever diver-

234

sions a pair of dawn visitors like ourselves might offer.

'What are you doing here, son?' asked a sergeant, who looked a full twelve months older than myself.

'I'm going to take some photographs,' I said, producing my tripod as Exhibit A for the defence.

'What for?' the sergeant asked, warming to his theme.

'For an article I'm writing.' I was tempted to add a few enquiries about whether I was violating a curfew or whether a state of emergency had been declared, but no one likes a smart-arse, least of all a bunch of grumpy policemen who need their sleep, so I left it there.

The sergeant was not to be shaken off the scent so easily, however. 'Why do you want to take pictures of a load of gypsies?' he enquired.

'Because they're interesting,' I said innocently, igniting the fuse that had been smouldering in the sergeant from the moment he was assigned to holding the frontier against these latter-day barbarian hordes.

'Interesting? What's interesting about a load of scruffy, dirty layabouts?' he demanded, before immediately proceeding to answer his own question. 'Nothing. If you want to show something interesting, why don't you take pictures inside that barn over there?' Here his arm waved vaguely in the direction of Lancaster, some fifty miles away. 'Show all the filth they leave in there.'

I thanked him for his advice and said I'd consider it when I'd got a few shots of the caravans, and then we left him to his rantings. I got the photographs I wanted, but I couldn't oblige him with the filth in the barn – I hadn't brought my flashgun.

This free and frank exchange of views sums up the ambivalent relationship we have always had with travellers. We've only to pass an old-fashioned Romany wagon on a country lane for our eyes to mist over, as we began a monologue of the 'My God, that's the way to live, for two pins I'd give up the job at Bonkley's Bank, let Tarquin's school fees and Fiona's riding lessons go hang and set off for a life on the open road' variety. The lure of the open road usually lasts only as far as the next bend in it, however, and our admiration for the Romany way of life tends to disappear with considerable rapidity as soon as a caravan comes to a halt near our own town or village.

In the opinion of every self-appointed lounge bar expert up and down the country, travellers are dirty, devious thieves, rogues and villains who would steal the washing off your line and the gold fillings out of your teeth as soon as look at you. The Horse Fair was as good a place as any to find out the truth of this, for it attracted travellers from all over Britain. Some local residents shared the opinions of the Fair Hill police contingent about this annual invasion of their sleepy little town, finding it about as welcome as Al-Qaeda dropping in for their summer holidays, but for others, particularly publicans and shopkeepers, the Horse Fair could be the time of a welcome, if temporary, Midas touch.

The Fair was claimed to be the largest of its

kind in the world and dated from 1685, set up under the protection of a Charter from James II for the 'purchase and sale of all manner of goods, cattle, horses, mares, geldings'. The Charter referred to a Fair held in April, although the 'New Fair', as it is still known, dates from 1750, when the month was changed to June.

Fair Day itself was always the second Wednesday in June, the week after that other great old travellers' gathering, Derby Day at Epsom. Travellers began arriving on the weekend before the Fair and, for a couple of weeks before that, every byway, country lane and piece of common land for miles around seemed to contain a caravan. An open-air church service was always held up on Fair Hill on the Sunday before Fair Day; on the night before the Fair there was more secular entertainment, harness racing, in a nearby meadow.

The travellers also practised another, less official form of harness racing, done both for pride and for prodigious sums in bets, in which the participants raced at dawn along the dual carriageway of the bypass, or even, on one notorious occasion, the motorway a few miles away, while a convoy of vans and cars blocked off the course to traffic at either end. The police knew it went on, but were usually powerless to intervene, for by the time they arrived on the scene, the race was over and the participants and spectators were heading for home, offering nothing more tangible than an air of injured innocence if stopped and questioned.

Having got our photographs and spent two cold hours waiting for the nearest transport cafe to open, we indulged in a substantial and lengthy breakfast, before heading down into the town centre. We took up position on the bridge in the heart of the town and watched as a succession of travellers brought their horses down to the river to wash them in the broad, smooth-flowing water as it drifted through the town. While most of the horses were being preened to be sold, some horse owners were just doing it for 'flash'– showing off a fine horse, or themselves. We saw the same lad bring his horse down to the river three times, per-haps hoping to stir interest of a non-commercial kind among the girls watching from the bridge. A sizeable crowd had gathered, some casting an eye over potential purchases, but most just there for the show. Boys rode their horses bareback into the river in turn and then washed them down using a plastic bottle of washing-up liquid, a touch of new technology in an age-old ritual.

Despite the other attractions, the Fair was first and foremost a time when travellers indulged in their favourite sport of horse-trading, both with their fellows and with outsiders; the latter ranging from people looking for a pony for their children to the upland sheep farmers who had used the distinctive piebald 'Dales Galloway' ponies for centuries. In the afternoon, the horse-trading began in earnest. A vast crowd thronged the road where the horses were run and spec-tators needed swift reactions. One minute we were surrounded by people, the next there was a cry of 'Oi! Oi! Oi!' and the crowd parted like the Red Sea to reveal a horse and rider bearing down at breakneck speed. Sue had already taken a couple of prudent steps back, but the effect of the

238

horse's sudden appearance was sufficiently shattering for me to attempt the UK all-comers' record for the standing jump, to the great amusement of the battle-hardened veterans all around me, who swayed nonchalantly to one side, like roustabouts and 'tattooed love boys' on a fairground 'Waltzer' – perhaps they were – before resuming their conversation. I retired, red-faced, to calm my shattered nerves and salve my wounded pride, before returning to the fray.

Having torn through the crowd two or three times to advertise his wares, each vendor settled back to await offers from suitably impressed purchasers. It seemed appropriate for us to eavesdrop on the negotiations for the horse that had almost run me over, so we joined a small group gathered around the two principals, who were about to enter serious negotiations. The ensuing bartering was long and heated, with both participants egged on by the enthusiastic crowd, who seemed to derive as much pleasure from the wrangling over price as they had from watching the horses. Buyer and seller were subjected to a barrage of entirely unlooked-for advice, as the spectators, like apprentice marriage guidance counsellors, tried to bring the two warring parties together.

To seal a deal all that was required was to spit and slap hands on a price, but both parties needed to satisfy their honour by walking away in disgust at least three times, and all the while the onlookers kept up their barrage of advice. 'Bid him another ten.' 'Away, it's all he's worth, shake hands.' 'That horse keeps his teeth in a jar by the bed, he's not worth half that price.'

Finally, as the sun sank lower in the sky the two parties allowed themselves to be drawn together. With feigned reluctance and a small amount of aggrieved muttering, hands were slapped and the sale was made. No cheques were accepted; a man's word was his bond and the only negotiable currency was cash. Even then the business was not quite complete, for the small matter of 'luck money' had to be attended to.

We watched the two participants step to one side to complete the deal. There was no paperwork, for no one has ever encountered a horse dealer who is registered for VAT. The buyer produced an enormous roll of £10 notes, held together by a rubber band, from an inside pocket and counted off the agreed price. The seller licked his thumb and riffled through the notes at a velocity that reminded me of a farmer's description of an illiterate, but wealthy rival: 'He can't read or write, but by God, he can count.' The luck money was handed back, the two men shook hands, slapped each other on the back and the small knot of spectators drifted away, smiling to themselves; we all love a happy ending.

Both parties would normally commemorate the closing of the deal by retiring to the pub to celebrate their good fortune or drink away the memory of their folly, providing they could find a pub that was open. For some local publicans, the Horse Fair was a time to board up the windows and go into hiding, perhaps allowing the regulars in through a back door for a pint or two. Of the seven pubs in the town, five stayed open but two were firmly shut. It was an attitude I could never understand, for those that welcomed the travellers' money reckoned that the bulging tills were handsome compensation for any damage left behind when the travellers had moved on.

The publicans also had a fund of good stories for the long winter months to come. One told me of discovering a set of false teeth in the corner of the Gents, which he rinsed and put on the shelf. The next morning a traveller staggered in, hungover and toothless, having lost his false teeth in a mighty sneeze and been unable to find them in his drunken condition of the night before. When he seized on the proffered set, however, they would not fit. A similar accident had presumably befallen someone else, who had scooped up the wrong teeth and failed to notice the mistake. No one had ever returned the other set, so, unless it found use as a set of pastry crimpers, somewhere in Britain was a traveller who had not eaten a meal in comfort since the night he got drunk at the Horse Fair.

Even at the pubs that did open, the landlords took the precaution of hiding their ornaments and taking up their carpets. That may have been prudence or it may have been merely pandering to old prejudices, but attitudes among a proportion of the people on both sides of the divide were so deeply entrenched that only surgery would remove them. However, for every virulent gypsy- or 'giorgio' (non-gypsy)-hater, there was another willing to live and let live, and there had been no serious threats to the future of the Fair since 1965, when complaints about nuisance and the near-blocking of a road by travellers' vehicles led to an attempt to end the Fair forever. A deputation of travellers argued successfully for its continuance then, and support for it, even among local residents, remained far more widespread than the complainants would have liked to believe.

My local informant from the nearby small town had few complaints about the gypsies, however. 'There was always a bit of thieving when the gypsies were about, but it wasn't necessarily always the gypsies that were doing it. There were a few bad lots amongst them, but that's like any group of people, isn't it? I think the gypsies got badly liked when quite a number of a bad type – the Irish would maybe call them tinkers – came over and got them a bad name. Most gypsies, if you're straight with them, they'll be the same with you ... mind you, they want watching if you're doing a deal!

'A few were a bit dirty and smelly like, but I got to be good friends with some. Things have changed now, though. There's one bloke who comes geared up like a gypsy, but the rest of the year he runs a nightclub in Leeds, so he tells me. He still trades in horses when he comes every year, though. I think he just gears up for the occasion. He's naturally bred from that type of people, you can tell by the look of him.'

As well as being a forum for horse-trading, the Horse Fair provided one of the few chances for the travelling community to meet during the year, and much family business was settled there. Marriages might be arranged or celebrated, and disputes and old scores settled, often by the rough and ready justice of a bare-knuckle fight. Fights between travellers and outsiders were also not unknown,

242

but even having added travellers to the already volatile mixture of young farmers, soldiers from the nearby firing ranges and liberal quantities of alcohol, trouble was surprisingly rare.

In the main, the travellers had come to meet old friends and enjoy themselves. What they wanted was to be left alone to get on with it, but the clash between two mutually uncomprehending cultures always made that implausible. The travellers needed grazing for their horses. At one time, virtually every village had an unfenced common or a goose green with a pond that made an ideal halt for gypsies and other travellers, but even where they still exist, almost all are now enclosed. From common land and rough grazing, the gypsy habitat has largely changed to industrial wasteland and scrap metal. In the recent past, even though unfenced commons had almost all disappeared, horses could usually be turned out to graze on the roadside verges, but even they were now in short supply in modern Britain and the travellers often took advantage of farmers' fields instead.

Their dogs were expected to feed themselves and were turned out in the evening to bag whatever game they could find, leading to more conflict with farmers and gamekeepers. Any theft or disappearance in the area was also automatically laid at the travellers' doors, though some at least might well have been carried out by local 'hooks' using the presence of the travellers as a convenient smokescreen.

It was hard to escape the feeling that the police and some of the townsfolk would have been happy to see the Horse Fair disappear into history, and their actions and attitudes seemed designed to give that process a push. Police were drafted into the town in vanloads like the one we encountered at dawn, and we saw them stop and interrogate the same travellers as many as three or four times on their way down into the town. Council workmen cut the roadside verges the week before the Fair, removing the grazing for the travellers' horses, while many residents complained long and hard about dirt, noise, theft and violence.

While some moaned about crime, however, others counted their profits. The china shop in the town probably sold more Crown Derby in one week than the China Department of Harrods manages in a year, for the travellers had no great liking for banks or stocks and shares. Good china was both a convenient means of storing wealth and of displaying it to those privileged to be invited into the caravan.

The old, horse-drawn Romany caravans had all but disappeared, and even the few still seen on Fair Hill had often spent the year in mothballs, emerging only for the annual trek to the Horse Fair. The true status symbol among travellers was the motor-drawn caravan, smothered in chrome, with etched, engraved and brilliant cut windows, and, inside, the inevitable Crown Derby on display. It seemed a bizarre contrast to an outsider: a life spent on mud-covered, scrap-infested wastelands, often with no running water or sanitation, but inside the spotless caravans there was cut-glass and Crown Derby: 'all fur coat and no knickers', as we used to say in the North.

As well as the horse-drawn caravans, the old

244

standbys of clothes-pegs, fortune-telling and knife sharpening had all but disappeared too. The staple trade of the modern traveller was in scrap metal, and there were countless non-Romany travellers involved in it as well. There were still a few women telling fortunes on Fair Hill, however, and we joined a queue of giggling schoolgirls to discover what fate had in store for us. When my turn came, the crystal ball pronounced me a gentleman, though my Oxford-educated tones may have helped the diagnosis, and I was promised fame and fortune. I warmed rapidly to both fortune-telling and my own fortune-teller in particular at this point, though fulfilling her further prediction that I would father two fine children might have proved troublesome, since I'd had a vasectomy ten years earlier. Perhaps she really was on to something, however, because many years later I had the vasectomy reversed and I'm now indeed the father of two fine children, just as she predicted...

As the evening darkened, travellers began to gather around campfires and an occasional burst of a traditional song could be heard, though the predominant musical accompaniment was provided by the rather less traditional ghetto-blasters that most of the travellers' children seemed to be toting. We left the travellers to their pleasures and drove back towards the Dale, the inn and sleep.

For all the often spurious charms of fortune-tellers and horse-traders, the Horse Fair remained a great event – earthy, noisy, dirty, and very much alive. The levels of crime and violence at the Fair were grossly exaggerated; there was probably more aggression in five minutes on a congested London commuter train than all day at the Horse Fair and it was an event that put the town firmly on the national map, generating money for the area not only while the Fair was in progress but throughout the rest of the year as well. Its fame brought tens of thousands to the town every year, whether drawn by the Horse Fair or by the associations of the name. Without it, the town might well have become just another bypassed, obscure rural town.

Some local residents delighted in tales of the criminal outrages that took place around the Horse Fair, but my own straw poll of potential 'disgusteds of Acacia Crescent' suggested that those most opposed to the Fair were those who had retired to the area from elsewhere. The same dead hand of irreproachable geriatric gentility had bid fair to choke the life out of many small towns and villages in the rural retirement zones. This case above all was one for that wrinkled old hand to be given a savage crack across the knuckles.

The Horse Fair is the last of its kind in Britain. Long may it survive, however dirty, smelly and noisy it may be. Let the lace curtains twitch their exasperation for one week a year; for those seven days the town is alive, celebrating a tradition that goes back centuries and which provides a brief, bright splash of colour in the dun-coloured year of the fells.

Another even greater and equally ancient fair was held for centuries at the foot of the moors not far from the inn. It was another magnet for gypsies and the crowds that thronged there were

246

also irresistible to pickpockets and thieves. Those that were caught were held in a stone lock-up, that still stands forlorn in the corner of a field. While the Horse Fair ten miles down the road was a continuing attraction for travellers and tourists, no crowds now flocked to the one in the little town near the inn. Once the biggest horse fair in the North of England, it was now virtually moribund, a far cry from the time when, for days before the fair was held, 'strings of ponies could be seen along every road and green track, as well as great herds of Scots cattle drifting slowly down from the Highlands'. In the middle of the eighteenth century as many as 100,000 beasts changed hands each year at the fair, most brought hundreds of miles in droves from the Highlands of Scotland. That great fair had been dying a lingering death since the end of the droving trade, but a small, sad remnant still lingered on. 'Last year it was wet,' my local informant, William, told me. 'It usually is, mind, and there were only thirty or forty people there. There used to be cattle, sheep and horses, and cheapjacks by the score, lining the road for quite a distance. Gypsy women were there every day, selling bits of lace, clothes pegs and all sorts, telling fortunes. At night they'd dance on the road. There was a bus every half-hour out to the fair at one time, there's hardly a bus to anywhere now.'

Another once-prominent marker of the yearly cycle, agricultural hirings, held at the start of spring and, on a lesser scale, before hay- and harvest-time, had also ended, though it continued in the area long after the tradition had died out in the rest of the country. Men and women would line up in the street, chewing a straw or sticking one in their hat-band to show that they were for hire. A deal would be struck with an employer for a sum of money, plus the worker's keep, and the bargain was sealed with a coin which, in common with the luck money on livestock, would almost inevitably find its way into a publican's till.

Apart from the serious business of finding work, hirings also provided one of the few social events in the drudgery of the agricultural workers' year. Some got drunk, some fought, some got married and some took the King's shilling and enlisted, often after indulging in one or more of the other activities. The drinking and carousing led to the hiring fairs coming under strong pressure from the Temperance Movement and from moral re-formers, who argued, not without some justifi-cation, that unscrupulous employers were also hiring young female servants with more than the normal agricultural duties in mind. Pimps and bawdy-house keepers also found them a fruitful source of new recruits.

Though the long-term agricultural hirings largely died out between the wars, hirings for hay-time continued until about the 1950s. 'A lot of local people would hire the Irish at hay-time,' one farmer told me. 'The same ones would come back year after year. There were still odd Irish-men coming over until the middle and late fifties, but that's all finished now.'

I had always found the moors around the inn beautiful – I loved their bleak, elemental desolation – but I discovered that I also liked these grey villages and small towns that clustered at the foot of the moors, though I could understand those who found their charms more elusive. The nearest small town to the inn was a particularly acquired taste. It had a bit of the grim air of a garrison town, perhaps unsurprisingly, since it had virtually never been out of the sight of armed men in its history. Even now, an army firing range was a constant, audible presence just along the road, but if most of the towns and villages in the area were stolid Cumbrian respectability cast in stone, behind the town's quiet, occasionally forlorn, exterior, there was a lot of character to be found and even a bit of a lawless, Wild West feel, including what locals called 'rogueing', and an occasional fist fight, though that wasn't necessarily too surprising, given the potentially explosive cocktail of alcohol, young farmers, local girls and visiting 'squaddies' from the army ranges.

The owner of the town's one and only nightspot – which doubled as an overnight stop for lorry-drivers – had a simple method of keeping order in those troubled times. As I was having a drink there one night, a fight broke out, a by-no-means unknown occurrence. With practised ease and an air of indifference, the owner simply switched all the lights off, plunging the windowless room into darkness. Only those in direct physical contact with their opponents could continue to fight, and after a short cooling-off period, which I took the precaution of sitting-out under the table, still clutching my drink, the sound of blows, grunts and breaking glass ceased, the lights went back on, the music restarted and everyone carried on with their evening.

Even after the bypass was built around the town, the main road over the moors a few miles to the north of the Inn at the Top continued to be a provider of sorts for the locals. When lorries were blocked in by snowdrifts or overturned on the icy bends, spilling their loads, they provided winter pennies from heaven for the locals. The word would quickly be out around the town and, like Cornish wreckers, the locals were off up the hill, collecting whatever came their way. Salt, fresh herrings, washing soda, flat caps – 'there are still a few around', according to William, my local informant – were among the booty, but their greatest haul rivalled that stripped from the SS *Cabinet Minister* in Compton Mackenzie's *Whisky Galore*.

'The best of the lot was a load of whisky. The wagon tipped over on that bad bend up towards the moor. We got the driver away to a farm for a cup of tea – he wasn't really hurt, just shaken up a bit – and then we got amongst it double quick. A hundred proof whisky for export, it was, beautiful stuff. There were a good few bottles smashed on the road, but we had plenty to go at. It was hidden all over the spot – hay barns, milk churns, hen houses, you name it. The police made a bit of a show of searching for it, but they knew they were on a loser, so they just did enough ratching about to keep their bosses happy and then gave up. Mind you, I wouldn't be surprised if a bottle or two didn't go their way as well.'

Lorries snowbound up on the moor still offered tempting targets, though the police now often

250

mounted guard on them, especially on valuable cargoes. William also revealed that, before its closure by the mad axeman of the railways, Dr Beeching, the old railway line – the highest in England – had been the source of a few windfalls of a rather less providential nature. 'The bloke who operated the signals at the summit of the line had a couple of sons,' William told me. 'They'd go down to the goods yard during the day and see what the train was carrying, then he'd stop it at the signal when it came up that night and the lads would be in amongst it, helping themselves to whatever they fancied.'

However, the favourite local pastime, undoubtedly was, and probably still is, poaching. 'When the railway was open, you'd sometimes see a couple of grouse feathers sticking to the telegraph wire up above the railway line,' William said. 'If you looked around, there would be a dead grouse lying somewhere around there. We used to sit in the cabin up at the summit and pot grouse with an air rifle, and we would shoot them up on the moor with rifles, or sometimes net them. The net was laid flat during the day, but at night we'd raise it on poles and then go round the moor driving the grouse into it.'

William had promised to tell me a few poaching tales and teach me how to tickle trout, and one afternoon when I'd slipped away from the inn for a couple of hours, he led me out along the bank of the river, heading up to one of his favourite spots for fish. He quickly spotted a trout keeping station in the current close to the bank, and issued me with my deceptively simple

251

instructions: 'Just tickle along under it until you get to the gills, then stick your fingers into the gills and flick it out.' I lay down on the bank, inching myself forward with the stealth of a commando approaching an enemy position, slid my hand into the water and, waving my fingers in what I felt was a passable imitation of a few strands of weed, I moved my hand towards the trout.

At the first touch of my fingers on its flanks, it took off as if hit with an electric cattle prod. Clearly my technique required a little polish. I tried twice more in the course of our wanderings that afternoon and failed ingloriously both times, though perhaps I should not have been too surprised. My lack of manual dexterity is such that it usually takes me three attempts to tie my shoelaces.

William had watched my bungling efforts with a mixture of amusement, exasperation, resignation and despair. 'If you'd been here in the hungry times, the nineteen-thirties, you'd have starved to death within a week,' he said, taking over the tickling duties and promptly plucking out a plump brown trout with nonchalant ease. I sighed and resigned myself to the role of Boswell to his Johnson.

'Trout are fine for eating, but salmon were the way to make a few bob. Everybody used to be out after a salmon or two when they were running, you could take them easy with a torch and a gaff. We'd use one of them carbide headlights off a motorcycle – damn good lights. We'd take one of them, shine it on the water, just wiggle a gaff along under the salmon and then – phtttt! This

252

was a good spot, we used to get them down below the waterfall, just along there. By day you could use one strand off a rabbit snare. Clear water and very sunny, you'd just loop it over them until it got to the gills and then click!

'You can do the job with salmon roe too,' said William, 'though it's an awful job to get it done right. They all have to be pricked and salted. We would go upstream a bit, lay a handful of roe on a flat stone and put another stone on top, so that the taste would drift down the stream. The trout would follow it up and we'd have a roe on a hook and just pull them out. Then we'd have a pod net, a big round net lying on the stones and we'd just flick it up, or you can use Domestos, it's like lime, you just pour it into the water and it takes the oxygen out of it.'

'So what were the river bailiff doing while all this was going on?' I said.

'Well, there were always plenty of bailiffs around,' he said, 'but one of them was very well in with a local man, he'd turn a blind eye. It was arranged between them that the local man would take salmon and flog them to the railwaymen down the Dale.'

'But didn't anyone ever get caught?'

'Oh aye. There's a few lads that have been caught for poaching over the years ... and a few that hasn't been. Years ago it was a bit of fun, but now the fun's gone out of everything.'

The fun involved everybody from the highest to the lowest. The Cumbrian poet Norman Nicholson once told me a tale of a salmon poacher who was complimented by a friend on his good fortune after the chairman of the local bench of magistrates had taken pity on his plight and paid the fine he had imposed from his own pocket. 'So he bloody well should,' the poacher said; 'it was him that got the salmon.'

William also told me another local legend, an essential part of the upper Dale apocrypha, about a winding, high-walled and very narrow lane in the town. Two of the local salmon poachers, fleeing from the long arm of the law, escaped by hurtling down the lane in their Mini. The pursuing police, normally based twenty miles away and lacking essential local knowledge, tried to pursue them in their patrol car and found themselves wedged between the walls, unable to go forward or back, or open the doors. The story was probably too good to be true; nonetheless, it provided a happy thought to speed the homeward journey.

If poaching was partly fun, however, it was often a matter of necessity as well. As we walked across the fields away from the river, rabbits scattered before us, prompting William to reminiscence about older, harder times. 'In the thirties and forties, farmers made the rent from rabbits; cattle and sheep were worth nowt. If it hadn't have been for rabbits we'd have hungered. Nineteen twenty-six, when the strike [the General Strike] was on, it was hell, there was nothing. We managed to get a few rabbits and hares and my mother used to jug them the old-fashioned way.

'By, they were good,' he added wistfully.

CHAPTER 13

Fried Sausages in the Nude

If the local horse fairs and agricultural hirings were truly ancient occasions, one of the other small towns a few miles from the Inn at the Top – the neighbouring town to William's – had for years played host to a far stranger and much more recent annual tradition: the Geordie homecoming from the Blackpool Illuminations – the spectacular seaside light show that has occurred every autumn since 1912. I had first encountered this extraordinary phenomenon a few years earlier, on a late-night drive home from Scotland. All good Cumbrians were normally safely tucked up in bed with a cup of malted milk and a digestive biscuit by half past ten, and I had seen scarcely a light since crossing the border, yet entering this obscure rural town at one in the morning, I was astonished to find it brightly lit, wide open and awash with people and traffic. I soon learned that for ten weeks every autumn, a cafe in the town was close to the proverbial licence to print money, and that the whole town stayed wide-eyed and occasionally legless until three in the morning, its plethora of cafes doing a roaring trade victualling the convoys of charabancs and coaches bringing tidal waves of tired and emotional Geordies home from the

Blackpool Illuminations.

The town owed its unexpected Midas touch purely to its geography. It was at about the half-way mark on the journey back to the North East and just about as far from Blackpool as men who had been downing a few pints in the town's pubs before setting off could be expected to sit still without demanding a comfort break, but the phenomenon was relatively shortlived. By the 1980s the town was beginning to slip back into a deep rural torpor. The coaches no longer stopped there, their occupants preferring fast food in a motorway service station to the uncertain reception of a town that was no longer sure it wanted them, for it was increasingly a place with inhabitants as old and greying as its buildings.

Many living there today would like to see a bypass take the remaining traffic for Blackpool and the Lakes away from the town altogether, leaving it to its farmers' auction mart and its strictly local trade, though the mausoleum air of its once-bustling neighbour might give them pause for thought: once thriving, it could scarcely be accused of setting the pulses racing these days. It had been an important staging post on a major road to the North since Roman times, and even a few years ago, you almost had to make an appointment to cross the road, so heavy was the flow of traffic. Now the vehicles hurtled along the new bypass with scarcely a backward glance, leaving the town high and dry, like flotsam left by a receding wave. Its inordinate number of pubs and, more tellingly, former pubs testified to its previous importance as a halt for travellers, but now it was a place where sleeping dogs might not only lie, but even do so in the middle of the main street, at little peril to themselves.

Had our own dog attempted to sleep in the middle of the road outside the Inn at the Top, she would have been run over within five minutes, for the inn had grown steadily busier and busier throughout the summer months. When we fell into bed at the end of some of the manic early summer days we had lain there saying to each other that we couldn't conceive how the inn could possibly get any busier than it already was, nor how we could conceivably work any harder than we already did, but the following week, and each subsequent one, it did and so did we.

None the less, when 'hay-timing' – getting in the hay crop – had begun in June, I arranged with Sue to take a day off from the pub and, as part of our 'community service', I set off to make my own modest contribution during one of the most important, demanding and sometimes fraught dates in the Dale's farming calendar. The hay meadows of the Dale were a wondrous sight in early summer, awash with flowers and wild herbs. Maintained virtually unaltered over centuries, their ecology was so rich and varied, and so precious, that much of the meadow land had protected status and there were restrictions on the use of fertilizers and even on the dates when the hay could be cut, to allow the flowers, herbs and grasses to 'set' seeds and thus preserve the beauty of the meadows for future generations.

Even in the most favourable conditions, it took

several days to cut the hay in all a farm's meadows, stir it two or three times to aid the drying process, allow the sun to cure the grass into hay, and then bale and gather it in to the barns where it was stored for winter feed. In hot, dry summers, though always hard work, hay-timing under clear blue skies could be a pleasure. As each meadow was cut and cleared and the hay gathered in, the stubble would be burned brown by the sun, and might stay that way for weeks, awaiting the rain that would bring the growth of new grass, 'the fog' as the farmers called it. But such summers are rare enough in Britain as a whole – and even more so in the Dale – and in many years the farmers were reduced to a gamble on a few fine days, and were often left racing to get in the hay while keeping a wary eye on gathering rain clouds. In some years the weather turned so bad after the hay was cut that the crop could not be gathered for weeks and became black and mildewed, and virtually useless as winter fodder.

So at hay-time every available person helped with getting in the crop and an extra pair of hands was always welcome, and I tried to do my bit by volunteering to help out on the farm of Clifford and Jenny, two friends and regulars at the inn. It was a blistering hot spell, so any worries about the weather were lessened, but it made warm work of trekking round the meadows, stacking the bales as the baler spat them out, loading them onto the trailer and then restacking them in the barn. I was on top of the stack when doing that and dripping with sweat in the furnace heat close under the roof. So much of the dust and pollen swirling in the air around me, stuck to my sweat-soaked skin, that I emerged looking like I'd been felted. The vast amounts of pollen that I'd inhaled also had more lasting effects; I'd never suffered from hay fever in my life until then, but I've succumbed to it every summer since.

After we'd finished getting in the last of the hay crop, we all staggered down to the river at the bottom of the fields and cooled off by jumping into the deep pool that the river had carved over centuries, just below the old stone bridge. The water was like snow-broth – only in the longest, hottest drought summers could it ever be described as warm – but it felt wonderful, setting my skin tingling, and after swimming and splashing around for a while, we came to rest on a rock shelf underneath a waterfall that gave us a power shower from above, while the water below bubbled like a natural jacuzzi. After towelling myself dry with my shirt, I left the other volunteers to eat their hay harvest supper and celebrate with a few drinks while I went back to my day job at the top of the hill.

Later that June, there was a particularly frenzied day when the inn was one of the way-stations on a celebrated vintage car 'Reliability Run'. It passed our front door at the same time every year, drawing an enormous crowd to watch, but Stan and Neville had neglected to mention this to us, so we neither had enough staff on duty, nor enough food and only just enough beer; we ran out that evening, though luckily a delivery was already booked for the next morning. Avoiding main roads as far as possible and passing through a series of dales by means of a succession of steep mountain passes, the Reliability Run would have thoroughly tested the most modern vehicle and was a punishing challenge for vintage cars. They arrived at the inn by way of the steepest route on the whole run, including a short but vicious 1 in 4 gradient that included a double bend, and many of the competing vintage cars pulled up outside the inn with their clutches slipping and their radiators boiling.

After a suitable pause to let both the vehicles and their drivers cool down and take on fluids, the route led on over an unmetalled road across the moors. We occasionally used it – it was a very rough track with a series of farm gates that had to be opened, but it shaved several miles off the journey to the town at the bottom of the moor to the north-east of us, though, so rough was the road surface, it was really only to be recommended to those with unshakeable confidence in their suspension or those driving someone else's car with a callous indifference to its welfare.

The vintage car owners were much less enamoured of it and one disgruntled driver complained to us that the road surface 'looked like it had been bombed by the RAF'. There had been heavy rain before that year's run and all the potholes were also brim full with water, making it impossible to discern – without stopping and probing each one with a stick – the difference between an innocuous, inch-deep puddle and a bottomless, axle-breaking pit. Only when the driver was irrevocably committed, could the latter be detected by the sickening thud and the noise of grinding metal as his car bottomed and did itself potentially terminal damage. Still, it's an ill wind and all that, and the farmer who lived at the midway point of the track and was untroubled by having to drive up and down it in his Land Rover or his tractor several times every day, may even have welcomed its disrepair. Each year when the Reliability Run was passing his door, he made a few extra quid by towing broken-down cars to the end of the track. The breakdown truck from the local garage refused to venture any further than there, the owner knowing full well what lay in wait further on.

Barely had the vintage cars moved on, than the thunder of motorbikes could be heard echoing around the fells, as a motorcycle club from the North East arrived for their annual jamboree. One hundred and fifty bikers, including the winningly and – as it turned out when I got downwind of him for a moment – correctly titled 'Smelly', descended on the inn en masse for a weekend of fun and frolics, though the sight of them frightened off at least that many other potential customers. All weekend we watched cars slowing to a crawl for a moment as they came over the brow of the hill and then, their drivers having taken in the massed ranks of bikes and bikers sprawled around the inn, accelerating away again at top speed.

The sight of them might have terrified some of our more genteel customers but, contrary to their outlaw image, the bikers and their 'molls' were as well behaved and trouble-free as a boy scout troop. Granted, they poured more Newcastle Brown and strange concoctions like 'Snakebite' and 'Pernod and Black' down themselves than should have been humanly possible, but they also policed themselves, placing a 'reception desk' outside the front door to screen out any undesirables, defused any ugly incidents before they got started and vacated the pub like lambs when we decided we'd had enough for the day. They even brought their own chemical toilets and cleaned up the pub and their camping ground before they left; if only all our allegedly more civilized customers had been as well behaved.

Among the many other clubs and societies who used the inn as the base for a members' weekend that summer, was a club with more prominent members than most: the British Naturist Society. After contacting us to seek reassurance that the sight of a couple of dozen naked men and women would neither cause us alarm nor frighten the horses – or, in this case, the sheep – the naturists duly arrived and set up their tents. A large contingent of farmers had also assembled to enjoy the free entertainment – I can't think who tipped them off about what was happening – but the naturists took it all in their stride. As one of them breezily remarked to me, 'Once you've fried sausages in the nude, nothing else can faze you.'

Unfortunately for naturists and spectators alike, the weather was pretty much par for the course on our lonely hilltop: freezing cold and pouring with rain, with the standard gale-force wind whipping over the moors. As a result, any farmers' wives or daughters who had turned out in the hope of a glimpse of full-frontal, exuberant

&/or protuberant manhood must have been disappointed, for they had reckoned without the cold-related shrinkage caused by the Inn at the Top's micro-climate. Even Errol Flynn would have struggled to make an impression while standing stark naked on one of the most wind-swept and frost-bitten plateaux in the land, and on the evidence of my own casual glance – and, it has to be said, on the basis of Sue's rather more prolonged scrutiny – there were no Errol Flynns in evidence, just a few Tiny Tims.

A few years later, connoisseurs of full-frontal nudity were able to enjoy an even more flagrant variety when a character christened 'The Naked Rambler', actually a forty-six-year-old former Royal Marine, passed through the area in 2005 and called at the inn. Wearing nothing but a smile, a rucksack and a pair of socks and hiking boots, the Naked Rambler, accompanied by his equally clothes-free girlfriend, was hiking the long-distance footpath that ran past the inn as part of an 874-mile trek from Land's End to John o' Groats, but kept falling foul of the forces of law and order, and the self-appointed public guardians of morality and decency that he encountered along the way.

He had actually completed the Land's End to John o' Groats walk solo the previous year, but was now doing it all over again with his girlfriend, albeit with less than crystal-clear motivation. He was repeating the marathon walk, he said, in response to a 'conscious urge' and because it was also 'a celebration of the human body and a campaign to enlighten the public that the freedom to go naked in public is a basic human right'. Anyone who felt moved to join the celebration/campaign/pilgrimage was free to join them and indeed several people did walk along with them at various stages of the journey, but the freedom not to suffer frostbite to your most precious and personal extremities was also an even more inalienable human right, in my opinion, so, even if I'd managed to overcome my innate modesty (aka cowardice) there was never the slightest chance of my following his example in the freezing climes ruling at the Inn at the Top.

The Naked Rambler and his girlfriend had already been arrested a few times by the police – or 'picked up by the fuzz', as one tabloid newspaper gleefully reported it – and they were then arrested again in one Dales village, after complaints from local residents. After a night in the cells, they were summoned to appear before the magistrates the next morning a few miles away in the thoroughly respectable town of Harrogate. Even though the Naked Rambler once more refused to wear any clothes for his appearance before the courts, the magistrates agreed to adjourn the case and free him on bail, but as soon as he emerged from the courtroom into the lobby, still wearing only his socks, boots and rucksack, he was immediately re-arrested for offending public decency.

After further representations by lawyers and realizing that they were only making themselves look ridiculous to the ever-swelling press contingent following the case, the police quietly returned the offending pair to the outskirts of the village where they'd first arrested them. They then issued a stern warning to the Naked Rambler and his companion, that if they turned back to the south, they would immediately be re-arrested, but if they set their faces – and everything else – to the north, the police would turn a Nelsonian blind eye to them – having already had considerably more than an eyeful during the process of arresting and charging them. With honour satisfied all round, the forces of law and order went back to the police station to compare notes, while the nude hikers continued on their merry way unmolested.

They stopped at the village shop a few miles from the inn to stock up on some essentials, but the shop owner, a doughty middle-aged woman who was a pillar of the Women's Institute, was completely unfazed, and indeed rather blasé about it. 'He was here a few years ago,' she said, 'but then he put his shorts on; he's obviously feeling braver this time. They came in just as we were closing so there weren't too many people about, but I did see people outside take a good look and there were a few giggles.'

They reached the Inn at the Top the following evening, downed a few drinks and then accepted a generous offer of free accommodation for the night; it would have taken a heart of stone to have made them sleep outside, they might have been dead from indecent exposure before morning. Most of the other customers were quite relaxed or possibly even quite excited by the sight of them, though one couple did walk out in protest.

It has to be said that customers of the inn occasionally had to deal with a lot worse than an eyeful of full frontal Naked Rambler. One owner of the inn, Tracy Daly, adopted a pet lamb, the runt of a litter of three. The hand-reared lamb, a male, took up residence in the inn and had the freedom of the bar, being petted by the customers and curling up in front of the fire on cold days. He and the landlady's dog, Sherbert, often chased a football around together, to the entertainment of the tourists and locals, and when the football World Cup was staged, the patriotic landlady even dyed its fleece in England colours and claimed her 'cloven-hoofed wonder-boy' was ready and waiting for a call from the England manager. 'He has a great left hoof that could solve our left-hand midfield problems,' she said, 'and he'll even keep the grass short, too.'

However, to prevent him from ever becoming a fully fledged ram – with all the potential butting and tupping hazards to customers that would imply – Tracy had asked a local farmer to place a strategic rubber ring around the pet lamb's prize assets, just as is the practice with all 'wether' (castrated male) lambs that aren't going to be used for breeding. It's claimed to be a relatively untraumatic process for the lamb, though most male customers of the inn had a reflex tendency to wince and cross their legs when discussing the topic.

In a couple of weeks, starved of their blood supply, the relevant portions of the formerly male lamb slowly atrophy and eventually drop off altogether. Unfortunately when the offending bits of the inn's pet lamb finally parted company from their owner, they did so in full view of customers eating their lunches, who then had to watch the pet dog, Sherbert, having spotted what appeared to be a couple of tasty dog treats, immediately scooping them up and wolfing them down.

Most farmers, abhorring waste above most things, would probably have approved of Sherbert's enterprise. Such self-reliance was one of the most prized virtues in the Dale and the uplands that surrounded it, and by now we prided ourselves on our own ability to deal with most things that were thrown at us, but some events were beyond the capacity of any individual to handle. Moorland fires were potentially disastrous. Although there had been cases of deliberate arson, almost all moor fires were caused by carelessness – a cigarette end tossed out of a car window, a hiker's campfire not properly extinguished before he moved on, or a piece of broken glass from a bottle smashed by some drunken moron magnifying the sun's rays enough to cause dry grasses to smoulder and then burst into flame. Driven by the wind, a fire could rapidly sweep across the fells, destroying the heather and grasses that fed the sheep and grouse – the two main engines of economic activity in the Dale.

In summer droughts the moors could be tinder dry and, hampered by a lack of available water and the difficulties of gaining access to the more remote parts of the moors, firefighters often struggled to bring such blazes under control. If a fire became well enough established to burn down into the peat-beds, which some farmers said were more than a hundred feet deep in places, it could remain a threat literally for years, apparently extinguished but still smouldering deep beneath the moor and bursting out with renewed vigour whenever conditions again became dry enough.

When a fire broke out on the moor near the inn one hot Sunday morning in high summer, therefore, it was the signal for instant alarm. We phoned the fire brigade as soon as we saw the smoke, and though we were not the ones responsible for starting the blaze, we couldn't escape the guilty feeling that the culprit had probably been a customer at the inn. By the time the fire engines had laboured up the long haul from their bases in the towns twelve miles away on either side of the moor, the fire was well established. Fanned by a stiff breeze, it had spread rapidly, burning the heather with a crackling noise that was audible from the inn, some distance from the fire-front.

While some fire-fighters played hoses – fed from water pumped from a moorland stream or the tanks on their fire engines – onto the flames, others, aided by the Fell Rescue teams who had turned out to offer their help, and other volunteers, including gamekeepers, shepherds and all the staff who could be spared from the inn, tried to control the lateral spread of the flames using beaters like enormous fly-swats to extinguish them. The fire-front was advancing too fast to risk that technique at the leading edge of the flames but fortunately the wind was driving the fire towards the road that bisected the moor. Using that as a starting point, other fire-fighters, helped by some of the farmers and gamekeepers, began a controlled burning to broaden the fire-break already provided by the road so that when the fires reached that point, they could make little further progress over ground that had already been burnt.

Over the next few hours, the firemen worked in relays to extinguish the remaining blazes and damp down the smouldering embers. While one group worked, the rest of their colleagues, safely out of range of the local fire-chief, cooled off from their labours with a few pints in the inn. They'd earned them; had they been less quick to respond or less effective at fighting the fire when they got there, the whole moor could have been ablaze with disastrous consequences for the farmers and the owners of the shooting rights.

The fast and willing response to that crisis was a further demonstration of the strength and mutual support the community in the Dale offered to each other, without hesitation. We took it as a sign of our growing acceptance into the wider community of the Dale, when Sue and I were asked to judge the children's fancy dress competition at the annual show of the village about ten miles away, at the midpoint of the upper Dale. It was a proper village show, with tents full of handicrafts, cakes and vegetables, and a fell race up and down the hill that loomed behind the village. It was a signal honour for 'offcomers' to be asked to be judges, but as we looked along the line of cute kids in fancy dress, surrounded by phalanxes of mums, dads, grandparents, aunts and uncles, it began to occur to us that it might also be something of a poisoned chalice. Perhaps the true reason we had been asked to officiate was because no one else would have been fool enough to have done it. By choosing the winner, we would be making one child and his or her family very happy, but we might also be earning the undying hatred of all the rest.

As I looked along the row of twenty or thirty cute kids in improvised fancy dress, I was tempted to follow the example set by a character in Spike Milligan's comic novel *Puckoon*. Faced with the task of choosing the winner of a fancy dress competition from a room full of people all dressed as King Farouk, he threw the prize in the air and let them fight over it. However, that seemed too much of a coward's way out, even for me, and after a prolonged and anxious scrutiny of the children, we chose a girl who appeared to be the youngest. Trying not to catch any of the other parents' eyes, we handed her the prize with positively indecent haste and then, breathing a collective sigh of relief, we merged back into the crowds and made a hasty escape.

CHAPTER 14

That Shouldn't Be There

The two men least likely to have been issued with, or to have accepted, an invitation to take part in any community event – the Inn at the Top's owners, those lovable rogues Stan and Neville – had been coming up to the inn every Saturday throughout the summer season. They did so ostensibly to give us the chance of a few hours off, though actually, we suspected, to pocket the takings from the busiest night of the week themselves and carry out a quick stock-check to make sure that their pub managers weren't cheating them. We weren't, but their entire system of values was based on the assumption that everyone was 'on the rob' and would steal everything from your hub caps and your false teeth to the pennies off a corpse's eyes, if given half a chance.

The fact that they could find no trace of evidence that we were cheating them merely seemed to convince them that we were operating some ultra-sophisticated new scam that even they hadn't heard of yet. Even though they told us a few times that they'd never made so much money from the pub, we could tell from their expressions that they trusted us no further than they would have trusted each other – and that, despite their lifetime's friendship, was no distance at all.

Counting the takings was certainly a disorganized business but it wasn't because of any dishonesty on our part, it was just because we were too damn busy to do it any other way. On busy weekends and Bank Holidays, whenever the till got too bulging to close, I simply took handfuls of banknotes and hurled them into the dark interior of the bulky steel safe that stood at the foot of the stairs. When things quietened down after the weekend, I'd transfer the contents of the safe to a bin-bag, dump them out in a mound on the kitchen table and Sue and I and any staff who could be spared would then grab handfuls of notes each and start sorting and counting them.

A previous landlord was even more slipshod. He never bothered to lock the doors when he was out and kept his entire takings – and he only went to the bank once a month – in a biscuit tin on the kitchen table, perhaps reasoning, just like the character in Edgar Allan Poe's *The Purloined Letter*, that no one would ever think of looking in such an obvious place. What would have happened if an intruder had fancied a biscuit was mercifully never put to the test. Another old-time landlord spent so much time sampling his own wares that would-be customers often had to shake him awake to get served; no doubt many more left him to sleep undisturbed and helped themselves either to his beer or his takings or both.

Stan and Neville's desperation to ensure that we weren't cheating them was matched only by their determination to ensure that they – and on their behalf, we – were fleecing everybody else, but one morning Stan phoned the pub in a state of total panic. 'Take the menus off the tables and hide the blackboard,' he said. 'We don't do food.'

'What do you mean we don't do food? We sold about 150 lunches and 100 suppers yesterday.'

'The VAT men are coming to inspect the pub today. If they ask, we don't do food.'

'For God's sake, Stan,' I said. 'We've got a kitchen full of catering equipment and Sue as a full-time chef.'

'Good point,' he said. 'Give her the day off. And if the VAT men ask...'

'I know,' I said. 'I get it. We don't do food.'

Being put on the spot like that and forced to lie through our teeth to the VAT men, whose cynical, suspicious expressions showed they didn't believe a word we said – and with good reason, since none of it was true – was just another reason for us to hate Stan and Neville's guts. We never heard from them whether the VAT inspection led to any further action, but the next morning the menus and blackboard were back in place and normal food service was resumed.

Our friends from the Dale still came up regularly and, by drafting in a stand-in barman for the night, we could even take up some of the invitations to their houses that we'd been unable to accept all summer because we were just too damn busy.

Our closest friends were Gavin and Ruth, a couple from the London area who had holidayed in the Dale every summer for twenty years before moving there permanently with their four children. Gavin was a fell runner and never happier than when pounding over the moors, up to his eyebrows in mud and peat. He regularly ran the uphill twelve-mile route across the moors from their house to the inn, while Ruth drove up with the kids.

Gavin entered quite a few of the local fell races held on Show Days at the villages of the surrounding dales, but he was blessed neither with the mountain goat-like uphill speed nor the near suicidal 'controlled falling' ability to come down a steep slippery, rock-strewn hillside flat out that marked out the winners from the also-rans. In compensation for his lack of blistering speed, what Gavin did have in spades was prodigious endurance; he could keep running all day and all night if necessary, which made him a natural for the fell-runners' marathons like the Vaux Mountain Trial, held on the mountains of the Lake District every year. However, in addition to endurance, the Mountain Trial also required participants to navigate their way between a series of fell-top checkpoints and that turned out to be another of Gavin's non-specialist subjects, something with which I could empathize wholeheartedly.

Once, striking off boldly in what seemed at the time an appropriate direction, but turned out to be diametrically opposed to the right one, he wandered lonely as a cloud in the mist for a couple of hours and then descended to the valley floor only to discover that, having already spent several exhausting hours on the tops, he now faced a further ascent and descent of one of the highest fells in the Lake District, or a fourteen-mile road run to get back to his starting point. He prudently chose the roads – after all they have signposts on those – but arrived back several hours after the winner to find a village that was largely deserted apart from Ruth, who'd been waiting for him in a state of mounting anxiety and was just about to call out the Fell Rescue team.

Undeterred, Gavin entered the Mountain Trial again the following year, but this time he had a Baldrick-style cunning plan. The runners started the race at one-minute intervals and, noting that a prominent Cumbrian fell-runner, who presumably could be relied upon to know his way around his native hills, was starting a few minutes after him, Gavin simply ran in circles for ten minutes and then dogged the Cumbrian runner's footsteps, following him for hours up hill and down dale until he was confident that he knew his way to the finishing line unaided. Gavin adopted a similar strategy in every subsequent year and though always having to follow someone meant that he was never going to actually win the race, he always finished in a respectably high placing and never got lost while doing so.

Gavin and Ruth were warm-hearted, outgoing types and very good friends to us. During the frenzy at the height of the tourist season we had to turn down several invitations to take a night off and go and have dinner with them, but when things began to quieten down in the autumn we spent several evenings with them. Not having to cook was a wonderful respite for Sue and not having to pour the drinks had a similarly beneficial effect on me, though seeing Gavin and Ruth and their kids in their beautiful house in a village at the foot of the fells was a slightly painful reminder of the family – and social – life we had forgone in return for chasing rainbows like the Inn at the Top.

While many of our friends in the Dale were 'offcomers' like us, others could trace their ancestry there back over generations, and it was a real mark of acceptance when we were invited into the farmhouse kitchen by them. Less welcome or more formal guests would be steered into the parlour, kept for 'best' and hardly ever used, but family and friends gathered around the kitchen table, and it was flattering and heartwarming to be made part of that charmed circle – perhaps a sign that they had decided that we weren't just another pair of get-rich-quick, rip-off merchants, ingratiating ourselves while we made some money and then moving on without a backward glance.

I couldn't claim much share of the credit for that. Beautiful, open and friendly, without a hint of 'side' to her character, Sue had charmed everyone in the Dale, young and old, men and women alike. Dick was far from the only local farmer who saw her as the living, breathing reincarnation of the legendary Susan Peacock – albeit a little less feisty – but she was also friendly with their wives, a wise counsellor to their sons and sometimes an agony aunt to their daughters.

As summer faded into autumn, we passed the last few milestones of the tourist season: August Bank holiday, the end of the grouse-shooting season, and then the school half-term holiday and the concurrent turning back of the clocks. We took a couple of weeks off in the autumn, while a friend looked after the pub for us, and it was a much-needed break; just about all we did for the entire fortnight was sleep. We went back to the inn with our batteries at least a little recharged and we were both really looking forward to the quiet time of the year.

As the nights drew in, we braced ourselves for the winter and started looking forward to Christmas at the inn. For the previous few years Stan and Neville had boarded up the inn at the end of the summer and left it closed until the following Easter. That seemed to us to be a miserable way to run a pub and a very poor reward to the locals for their loyalty, and we told Neville and Stan that we wanted to keep the pub open all winter for the first time in years. Even in a bad winter, we were sure that there would be enough trade to at least break even during those winter months and at times when the weather kept the customers away, we would be able to get on with some long overdue renovation and decoration, as well as catching up on some even more overdue and much-needed sleep.

Stan and Neville appeared to accept our arguments, but in private they had clearly decided that they didn't want us wasting money on inessentials like keeping warm over the winter. At the end of September, on what turned out to be their final visit of the year – though they didn't tell us that at the time – we returned from our time off to find Neville at work on the central heating boiler with his spanners and screwdrivers.

'What's up?' I said.

He gave me a shifty smile. 'The boiler's broken down.'

'That's funny – it was fine this morning.'

'It's only just happened. Things go like that sometimes.' He turned the part he had removed over in his hands and then clicked his tongue. 'As I thought,' he said. 'It's buggered. I'll have to take it away to get it fixed.'

'How long will that take?'

'Oh, not long. I should be able to bring it back next weekend.'

They disappeared down the road soon afterwards and that was the last we saw of the allegedly broken part – or Stan and Neville – until the following spring. We now had no central heating boiler but there was an open fire in the bar and in the early stages of winter we managed well enough without the heating, once we'd got used to getting dressed under the bedclothes and scraping the ice off the inside of the windows in the mornings. We were spared one winter worry, because we didn't have children. Previous landlords of the inn had had to board their children out for the winter with friends or relatives down the Dale, and farmers in the more remote farms around the head of the Dale had to do the same thing. If they did not, snow-blocked roads made it likely that their children would miss most, or even all, of their school lessons between Christmas and Easter.

The tourist hordes had now departed for the year, though there were still a few handfuls of hardy hikers and cyclists calling in during the week, including one of the inn's more dedicated customers, a gentleman in his fifties, who regularly cycled the 150-mile round trip from his home in Lancashire for a lunchtime drink, and in fact covered more miles on his bike in a year than most of us did in our cars. There was also an influx of car-borne visitors on any fine weekend, but otherwise, we were now more and more reliant on our locals for trade.

Keeping the inn open through the winter was not without its problems. In an attempt to boost winter trade, many pubs took part in darts and pool leagues, and organized trivia quiz nights or domino drives for other slow nights. Such was the obsessive concentration displayed by dominoes players of a certain age that World War III could have broken out without any disturbance to the measured clack of ivory laid on the table. I witnessed one game when the taproom door suddenly burst open and a man in a kilt, playing the bagpipes and leading a motley crew on their way to a fancy dress party, entered and circled the room. It was, to say the least, an arresting sight, not least since a few of the women in the party were dressed as limbo-dancers, but the only reaction to be heard from the doms table as the piper and his entourage disappeared back out of the door, was a plaintive voice asking 'Who played the double four?'

Despite the best efforts of the landlords to spice up their customers' lives, some of the Dale's pubs could still be echoingly empty on midweek nights in the long hard winter between the end of the autumn half-term and the start of Easter, when the first tourists of the season were almost as welcome a sight as the returning lapwings and curlews marking the onset of spring.

A darts team was a valuable as well as an enjoyable part of the winter trade for most country pubs, bringing in some welcome customers on a quiet weekday night as well as providing a good social evening. Unfortunately for us, although we did have both men's and women's darts teams – and disappointingly, I never saw any evidence that the Ladies' Darts League was the 'sea of unfaithfulness' that the local Methodist lay preacher had claimed – the inn's team had been through a few traumas in recent years, and eventually had been expelled from the local league, not because of anything we'd done, but as punishment for the misdeeds of our predecessors.

Two incidents in particular had been responsible for the trouble. On the first occasion the visiting team turned up on a freezing cold night to find that there was no fire lit. They bravely started to play in the icy taproom, but shortly afterwards, the generator failed, plunging the inn into darkness. Undeterred, they carried on playing by candlelight but, to round off a perfect evening, the pub then ran out of beer. Even this team were luckier than another who struggled through fog and a snowstorm to reach the inn, only to find that, unannounced, it had been shut down and boarded up for the winter.

Despite all our pledges, entreaties and promises that, come hell, high water, or ten-foot snowdrifts, we would be open for business every day that winter, the darts league refused to reinstate us. However, after I made a personal appearance and an impassioned plea for their support at their committee meeting, they did eventually concede that we could organize friendlies against any of the teams willing to take us on and, if all went well, they would then reinstate us the following year. We managed to play a few matches in the autumn and early winter which, assisted by a blazing fire and plentiful supplies of beer and sandwiches, went very well, but the deteriorating weather then made further games too risky to schedule until spring.

Our friends in the Dale were delighted that we weren't shutting the pub and cutting and running as the winter approached. They promised to look after us when the snows came but advised us to stock up with enough fuel and food to see us right through to spring. 'If it comes a big storm,' Dick warned us one night, 'you might be cut off and not see a living soul for weeks on end, but don't worry, we'll keep an eye out for you and make sure you're all right. You've a lot of friends here in the Dale and if anything does go wrong, we'll find a way to get help to you.'

The early winter was a wonderful time for us at the pub, mercifully free of tourist hordes and with clear, frosty skies instead of murk and rain, bone-hard ground instead of mud-patches and morasses, and the hills and dales empty of the summer armies of hikers. We couldn't both take time off together, for Neville and Stan would only pay staff wages in summer and there were now only the two of us to serve the customers, but it was quiet enough in midweek for us to take it in turns to have a day off. It was the perfect time to explore a bit more of the terrain surrounding our moorland kingdom, including 'The Nick', a spectacular fissure in the wall of the Pennines, giving wonderful views out over the valley far below. Like many of our most beautiful wild landscapes, it was also flanked by an army firing range and the footpaths leading from the village up to The Nick were often closed because of tank manoeuvres, strafing runs and gunnery practice.

If, like me, you preferred a circular walk, this presented a considerable obstacle, but if, again like me, you were stubborn to the point of mule-headedness, then the chances were that you would probably plough on regardless of the con-sequences. The Nick and I had not enjoyed a happy relationship in the past, for twice I had been driven back while attempting to reach it, once by natural forces and once by the armed forces. My first ascent ended in ignominious failure a few hundred yards from base camp. Sue had dropped me off at a fell-side village and gone to spend the day seeing a few friends, having arranged to collect me from the pub in another village after I had walked up to and around The Nick.

I waved her off on a sunny, windless morning, perfect for a stroll along the tops, and set off up the track in high spirits. After four hundred yards, I came to a juddering halt at a barrier across the track. A red flag fluttered from a pole and a notice warned me that the firing ranges were in use, entailing deadly peril if I went further. I defiled the morning with a torrent of imprecations against firing ranges, armies, guns, overgrown boy scouts and freelance journalists foolish enough to let their transport disappear without first obtaining a contact number. Then I beat a retreat, spending the day wandering among the fell-side villages, which was pleasant enough, but not quite what I had intended.

For my next attempt I took no chances, telephoning ahead to make sure the ranges would not be in use. Again Sue had dropped me off, this time with our dog and my friend Pete for company, and the three of us set off boldly for the hills. It was a close, overcast morning, with the clouds occasionally spitting a few drops of rain, but there seemed no great danger of any serious downpour, at least until we had climbed up past the ridge, when we looked up to see the sky darkening and heard the first faint grumbles of thunder beginning to sound over the hills to the north.

'What do you want to do?' Pete said.

'Let's go on.' I said. 'It probably won't be much of a storm. It might even pass us by altogether.'

We carried on, past the spoil heaps of the old mines at the foot of the upper slopes, intending to walk round by the tarns on the top of the moor, so that we would first see The Nick from its most impressive side, looking down the deep natural cleft towards the valley floor, far below. We were squelching our way across the moor when it began to rain, hard.

'Might as well carry on; even if we go back, we'll still get wet,' I said brightly, buttoning my coat.

We splashed on over the moor, enduring the reproachful looks from an already bedraggled dog. Thunder had been rolling around the edge of the hills for some time, but now the storm moved straight towards us. Its timing was perfect. We were at the furthest possible point from both our starting and end points, in the middle of a featureless moor without even a rock for shelter, exactly halfway between the tracks leading up and down from the moor.

Thunder was now roaring every few seconds, lightning forking into the fells around us and rain pummeling down on us. With characteristic understatement, an upland farmer would probably have described our situation as 'just fair', though we could have found far more explicit terms for it. The dog was doing her best to burrow into a streambed to get away from the noise, the lightning and the torrential rain, and I was sorely tempted to join her.

We abandoned any thoughts of reaching The Nick and beat a painfully slow retreat from the moor. So fierce was the rain that, long before we at last came down into our destination village, our wellington boots were literally overflowing and all three of us were soaked to the skin, the 'weather-proof' jackets that Pete and I were wearing proving to be no less permeable than the dog's fur.

To complete a memorable day, when we at last reached the streets of the village, we discovered that the torrential rain had caused the storm drains and then the sewers to overflow, forcing us to splash through water up to two feet deep, trying not to look too hard at the insanitary objects being carried past us on the flood.

Those who do not learn from their mistakes are doomed to repeat them. I set off once more on a bright early winter day, determined that, come storm, tempest or pub opening time, I would conquer The Nick without fail this time. The weather forecast was good and even though the army was once more in occupation of the ranges and the red danger flags were flying, I had worked out a route that would take me up past The Nick and high above the ranges along the shoulder of the hills, before coming safely back to earth on the far side of them. What could possibly go wrong?

I began the trek with a lovely walk through soft, undulating country, only slightly marred by the thuds, bangs and crashes from the ranges, and then followed the steep track up the fell-side and along the lip of The Nick to the very top. It was a spectacular sight, but I felt some slight sense of anticlimax after having finally achieved my goal. I paused a while to enjoy the view and eat an apple and then tracked on over the moor, applying a Nelsonian blind eye to the red danger signs warning me not to advance further. A stiff hour's walk past the grouse shooting butts established by local people but now largely pirated by the army for their own private use, according to my poaching correspondent, brought me back round close to the crest of the hills overlooking the valley.

As I climbed back on to the ridge, the cloud dropped without warning, shrouding the fell, blocking out my intended route and reducing visibility to a few yards. Within a few minutes I was, as usual, completely and utterly lost. Still, you don't spend a lifetime in and around the Pennines without picking up a trick or two. 'No problem to an old fell hand like me,' I thought, striding out purposefully through the mist. A few minutes later, my position on the ground did not seem to coincide with any feature marked on my map. 'No problem,' I thought. 'The wind is blowing up the face of the hills. All I have to do is keep the wind always in my face, drop below the cloud, get my bearings and then climb up again to rejoin my chosen route.' I set my face into the breeze and strode purposefully on.

Apart from an uncontrolled fifty-yard skid down a scree slope, all went well and I emerged from the clouds near some old mines. A quick study of the map showed me that I just had to follow the track down and pick up a stream flowing in from the east. Sadly, either the Ordnance Surveyor had for once erred, or, more likely, I had simply walked straight past the stream with my mind on higher things, like the opening hours of the nearest available pub.

Whatever the cause, the result was that I found myself only a mile or so from the village and losing altitude at a rate that would have terrified the pilot of a jumbo jet. A further study of the map ensued. 'Simple,' I said to myself. 'All I have to do is scramble over the hill and back up the fell-side to the ridge.' The guns had fallen silent long ago and I was quietly confident that even if my navigation proved to be as faulty as usual, the army had already finished work for the day.

I breasted the hill to find myself looking directly at an army observation tower about half a mile away. 'That shouldn't be there', I thought, reaching yet again for the map but then standing transfixed as the tanks on the ranges began firing again. There was a crash as a shell thudded into the hillside below me.

I am not a complete coward. I have faced a pub full of irate farmers, five seconds after I have called 'Time', a dressing room full of rugby league players five minutes after they have lost a Challenge Cup Final, and a living room full of an angry father, five hours after curfew time for his daughter, and lived to tell the tale. But the closest I had previously come to being under fire was while jogging half a mile from Lord Whitelaw on a grouse shoot. Nothing in my suddenly very precious life had prepared me for the moment when I found myself looking down the gun-barrel of a tank. In fact it was a country mile away and its shells were exploding on the hillside well below me, but this was scarcely a time for logic.

While my mind was still trying to come to terms with this new and fascinating experience, my legs were carrying me back over the hill and down the track to the village at prodigious speed. When I got there I decided that I had taken ample exercise and had quite sufficient excitement for one day, and I turned my back on The Nick, probably forever.

Such navigational inexactitude had been a regular feature of my life, but my belief in my innate sense of direction remained unshakeable, despite the ever-growing mountain of evidence to the contrary. Just as there are people who cannot board a northbound train at King's Cross without asking seven train company employees and fourteen passengers chosen at random 'Excuse me, is this the train to Leeds?', there are walkers who cannot get from one side of a field to the other without pausing to consult their Ordnance Survey map on at least half a dozen occasions.

Such pusillanimous prevarication was not for me, however. My approach to a walk was resolutely strategic rather than tactical. After a brief study of the map to capture the broad sweep of the landscape and the approximate direction of my ultimate goal, I was off, striding out manfully o'er hill and dale without so much as a momentary hesitation. The normal consequence of this was that within twenty minutes I would come to a juddering halt in a field from which the only exit was the gate by which I had entered and which turned out to lie at least several hundred yards off my chosen route.

A rather more prolonged study of the map then ensued, usually followed by an awkward and entirely unauthorized scramble over walls, barbed wire fences and – on tiptoe – through farmyards, trying to regain the sanctuary of the right of way without an altercation with an angry farmer, demanding to know what the hell I thought I was doing traipsing about on his land.

Years of such humiliations had not reduced by a fraction my unshakeable confidence in my innate navigational ability. Usually I had to bear the consequences alone, but there had been times when some other unfortunates had placed their destiny in my hands, with predictable consequences. On one occasion a friend from the south of England was making his first visit to Yorkshire and, obsessive as many Yorkshiremen are about the charms of their native county, I had dragged him off to the Dales for a few days muttering 'You've seen nowt like this in Dorking, tha knows'.

My uncle owned a holiday cottage in the Three Peaks and, as on many previous occasions, he had again allowed me to borrow it. As my friend and I wolfed down our breakfast, I announced the plan for the day. We would walk in to town to collect the groceries for our stay, taking in one half of the justly famous waterfalls walk on the way in and the other half on the way back. The circuit would be around fifteen miles and, allowing time for a break for a pint and a spot of lunch at the halfway mark, would see us back at the cottage in a few hours' time with a suitably healthy appetite for dinner.

I didn't take a map, for it would have been

completely superfluous. I had been staying at my uncle's cottage since I was a kid and knew the area like the back of my hand, or so I assured my mate, at any event. Part A of the plan went admirably well. We reached the town without mishap, did the shopping, which we loaded into our rucksacks, and enjoyed a pleasant interlude in the pub before beginning the return journey. We strode up the other half of the falls walk, 'oohing' and 'aahing' at the waterfalls, swollen by the previous night's heavy rain, and when we reached the halfway point, I led us unerringly off across the fells in the direction of the cottage.

The thought of a cold drink and a spell sitting in the shade of the trees around the cottage on our return was an enticing one, for it was a stiff walk and we had made a good pace. To enliven the last couple of miles of our journey, I was pointing out the wonders of the Dales landscape to my companion. 'It's amazing how different Whernside looks from this angle,' I said, pointing to the hill looming on our left. 'It's funny how your memory plays tricks on you though. I haven't done this walk in years, but I don't remember this hill on our right at all.'

We walked on for another mile, while I concealed my mounting unease behind a barrage of inconsequential and profoundly annoying chatter, before the horrible truth became too obvious even for me to ignore.

'Just one small problem,' I said, edging nervously out of reach of my friend. 'That isn't Whernside on our left. In fact, it seems to be on our right, so the cottage is the other side of it.'

My companion said nothing, but the look he directed at me conveyed more than a thousand words. In a silence as profound as it was total, we began the ascent of Whernside. We finally reached the cottage in a state of near-exhaustion and, strange to say, he has never been back to Yorkshire since; I can't understand why. Still, at the end of a fifteen-mile hike, there's really nothing that can compare with climbing the highest mountain in Yorkshire, carrying a rucksack full of groceries on your back. Try it some time, you'll see exactly what I mean.

CHAPTER 15

Excuse Me, My Face is Up Here

Back at the inn, Sue and I began making plans for our first Christmas there and, in a spirit of positively Santa-like generosity, I arranged to collect not just our own Christmas tree but several more as gifts for some of our local regulars. I could of course just have gone to the nearest town and bought a few, but in the spirit of pioneering, wild frontier self-reliance I was trying to cultivate, I decided to follow the 'Pick Your Own' example of strawberry farmers and, armed with a saw and plenty of stout rope, I set off for an enormous conifer plantation a few miles down the road from the inn. I parked in a disused quarry, extinguished the lights and tiptoed across the road and down the slope to the plantation.

I wasn't cut out for a criminal career and spent the hour I was there in a cold sweat of near blind panic, my heart beating out a rising tattoo at every hoot of an owl, or creak and rustle of the trees in the wind, and when a car passed along the road above me I practically gave birth. However, I – and my crimes – remained undiscovered and after an hour's sawing, sweating and staggering up and down the slope with a series of trees, I was back in our battered old Morris 1000. It was now so smothered with Christmas trees poking out through the back and passenger windows and lashed to the bumpers, roof, doors, boot and bonnet, that visibility was reduced to a six-inch square of windscreen. As I made my slow, perilous way back across the moorland roads to the inn, any bystander watching me pass must have thought that Tolkien's Ents were on the march or that Shakespeare's Birnam Wood was on its way to Dunsinane.

A few days later, with the rest of the trees distributed among our locals, our own newly decorated Christmas tree was taking pride of place in the bar, where one passing customer eyed it with more suspicion than admiration, then asked 'Where did you get that tree?'

Something about the way he posed the question made it clear that this was no time for George Washington-style true confessions. 'Erm, I bought it in town,' I said with a disarming smile, naming one a safe twenty miles away. 'A guy with a lorry-load was selling them at the side of the road. Why?'

'Because it isn't a Christmas tree,' he said. 'It's

a commercial forestry species grown for timber and it's probably been nicked from a plantation – maybe even from mine.' Blushing crimson, I tut-tutted with him at the shocking behaviour of unscrupulous tree-fellers for a few moments and then tiptoed away into the other bar, privately resolving that next year I'd be like everyone else and just buy our Christmas tree.

Aside from the potential risks involved in tree-rustling, our reliance on our locals for winter trade had one major drawback. We'd made some great friends while we were at the inn, but there were other regulars who we were less eager to know better. We'd already noticed that – to put it politely – some of our less interesting local customers used to time their visits to the pub to coincide with the least busy hours of the day: late lunchtime and early evening. It may have been just a coincidence, but we suspected that it was because they could then be certain of our undivided attention, a captive audience for their fascinating anecdotes and observations on life. The worst culprit of all was a shopkeeper from one of the nearby market towns. He was a lumpen, middle-aged man whose personal hygiene was on the less than perfect end of the spectrum – just one of the many reasons why he was still a bachelor – and his conversation was even less fresh and sparkling.

The term 'anorak' was yet to be applied to people in those innocent days, but it would have been entirely appropriate for him, since that was what he invariably wore. He owned a junk shop and had an unhealthy obsession with militaria, including Nazi memorabilia, and his conversation on each of his visits to the pub included a blow-by-blow recitation of what every single customer to his shop had said, done and bought; the mere sight of him approaching was enough to induce a sinking feeling in the pair of us. While eating, he talked with his mouth not only full but open as well, so that anyone within a couple of feet was at extreme risk of being pebble-dashed with bits of food.

His charmlessness also extended to his habit, when talking to Sue across the bar, of keeping his gaze permanently fixed on her breasts. She tried saying 'Excuse me, but my face is actually up here,' to him, but he just gave her a puzzled look and carried on scrutinizing her breasts. However, a customer was a customer, so we put up with his boorishness, smiling through gritted teeth at him, and Sue escaped whenever possible to serve another customer or carry out some unspecified and probably fictitious task in the kitchen or the cellar, just to get away from him for a while. She did get a measure of revenge by configuring the ingredients of his preferred dish – a gargantuan mixed grill – so that the chops, eggs, sausages, mushrooms, etc., formed a caricature of his porcine features, but if he ever noticed, he probably took it as a compliment.

His visits had become ever-more frequent as autumn shaded into winter and the numbers of other customers continued to dwindle, putting us even more in his thrall. Then one afternoon cloud like pewter began to mass over the moors. A wary stillness fell, broken only by the gabble of a grouse and the anxious bleat of a sheep. As the light faded, the snow started. The first few flakes drifted by in the wind, thin white flecks, dry on the skin, lodging for a second in a skein of grass, then drifting down to the frozen peat.

At first only a grey dust seemed to settle, but as the wind strengthened, the driven flecks coated and whitened the moor. Dusk was held back as light reflected from the snow, and the land now appeared fluid, shifting and changing as the snow flurries blurred and softened familiar landmarks. In less than an hour the moor was smothered in white, broken only by the thin, dark striations of rush stalks and a few black outcrops of rock. Even those features faded as the snow continued to fall.

It snowed all that night and the next morning and by the afternoon, we were completely cut off. A snow plough made a valiant try at breaking through to us late in the afternoon, but as the light faded, the driver abandoned the attempt a mile short of the pub. We watched from the top of the hill as he carried out the tricky manoeuvre of making a three-point turn in a snow plough on a single-tracked road, and then he rumbled off back down towards the Dale, leaving us alone, but blissfully happy; no customers – we could have the night off.

We opened a bottle of wine, put a casserole in the oven and while it was cooking, took the dog for a walk over the snow. As we looked down towards the track left by the snow plough, we saw the headlights of a car approaching. We looked at each other and said simultaneously 'It's him!' Our nemesis was on his way to pay us another visit, but this time he was in for a painful surprise. Barely able to stifle our gleeful chortles, we waited as the car moved along the ploughed channel with walls of snow to either side, and then came to a dead stop at the unbroken wall of snow blocking the way. We were still chuckling when the car's headlights were switched off and a moment later we saw a dark figure and the beam of a torch starting to move over the snow towards us, as he began to make his slow and unsteady way up to the inn on foot.

We hurried back and thought seriously about bolting the door and turning all the lights off, but reluctantly decided that even he did not deserve such cruelty after walking over a mile uphill through soft, new-fallen snow, so we sat and awaited our fate. Sometime later the door opened and in he came, stamping the snow from his boots. 'Bet you didn't expect any customers tonight!' he said. 'I'll have a pint and a mixed grill.'

We endured two of the most tedious hours of our lives, and when he glanced out of the window and said 'Snowing again. If I'm not careful, I'll be staying the night,' it was all Sue could do to stifle a scream of terror.

'Better not risk it,' I said, handing him his anorak. 'You've a shop to open in the morning. You don't want to disappoint those customers, now do you?'

With a feeling of indescribable relief we waved him off as he plodded back across the snow and, just in case he changed his mind, we had the door bolted and were in bed with the lights out inside five minutes. The snow continued to fall all night and by the next morning it had obliterated the snow ploughed track and left us isolated from even that persistent customer for a few days at least.

In summer the pub's isolation in the oceans of moorland that stretched away unbroken to every horizon had been rudely interrupted by a non-stop horde of walkers, trippers, tourists, hikers and bikers. There were times on hectic bank holidays, when the landlord's fancy turned to thoughts of blessed peace and quiet, snowed up alone in the depths of winter. The only problem with the dream was that, as usual, the reality turned out to be quite different.

It is hard for anyone who has not experienced them to appreciate the full force of the winter storms that rip across the fells around the Inn at the Top. In the lowlands, a winter storm is a matter of some inconvenience, disrupting the journey to work, perhaps freezing a few pipes, but rarely creating problems for more than a day or two. In the hills every winter is a disruption to daily life. It is impossible to plan any kind of social life when a sudden storm can arise which blocks the roads at terrifying speed. It was not unknown for people to enter the inn under clear skies early in the evening, and to emerge two or three hours later to find a blizzard raging and the snow lying thick on the ground.

One of our locals, a farmer's daughter and now a farmer's wife, could remember snowstorms so bad that her father and the other shepherds used to rope themselves together like mountaineers while out working on the tops looking for sheep, so they did not lose each other and would know if one of them succumbed to the cold. We were now getting a taste of what they had endured. High on the fells, a storm might rage unabated for several days. The wind was often so strong that it was as much as one could do to walk against it, even leaning forward at an angle of forty-five degrees, and several car drivers, incautious enough to let go of their door for a moment as they got out of their car, had seen it ripped off by the force of the wind and sent spinning down the road. The driven snow of the winter storms could also produce a complete white-out, when even ten yards from the front door, one could be completely lost. No landmark nor familiar perspective could be seen and even the wind often seemed to swing from quarter to quarter, preventing you taking a bearing from that.

On one occasion, taking the dog for a late-night walk, I became completely lost for a few frightening minutes in the swirling, blurring, driven snow. I was uncertain whether I had already crossed the snow-covered road in front of the inn or was still on the same side. Scarcely able to see or hear for the snow and the wind, I didn't know which way to turn, unsure whether I was heading back towards safety or out into the forbidding wilderness of the moor.

A minute ticked by and then another, as I stood there, irresolute. I couldn't follow our tracks back to the inn, because the snowstorm was so ferocious that I couldn't even see the ground at my feet. Even if I'd been able to do so, the wind-driven snow was filling and obliterating our footprints almost as fast as we made them. I looked expectantly at the dog; surely her keen nose and canine instincts would tell her which way to go? She gazed equally expectantly back at me: surely the creature with the opposable thumbs and the ability to use a tin-opener on the dog-food would know what to do in a crisis?

As we stared helplessly at each other, I remembered the chilling words of one of the farmers that autumn, when we had been talking about the winter storms to come. 'I've never been lost in a white-out,' he said. 'I've been on the moors often enough when it's been bad, but you still tend to find where you're at. You don't set off on those particular days when it's very bad, there is always a break when it eases off a bit, so we try to be out when the weather is kind of decent. If it comes on bad, I always preach to my own lads to be aiming for home regardless. You don't want to be stuck fast away out over those tops or you might never be seen again.'

It had come on bad that night, and like a fool, I had got myself lost. I could hardly see for the snow or hear for the shrieking gale and it was only by the greatest good luck that, after a few of the most anxious minutes of my life, a brief lull in the wind allowed me to hear the dull thud of the diesel engine of the generator behind me. I turned around and, with the dog at my heels, found my route back to the sanctuary of the inn. I had already walked right past it without realizing it and was some distance away and heading out towards the open fell.

In such snowstorms drifts piled up to astonishing heights, reaching to the first-floor windows and blocking the roads in as little as half an hour, often trapping unwary motorists at the inn for unexpected winter holidays. Even after the snow had stopped falling, the wind continued to scour the hillside, continually rearranging the drifts as it veered north or south of the cruel east wind – the 'lazy wind', as the locals called it, because it couldn't be bothered to go round you and went straight through you instead. The wind chill factor could reduce the temperature by several degrees more than the three degrees Celsius that the inn was always colder than sea level because of its altitude.

The strength of the wind forced fine powdery snow through every chink in the building. It found its way under the slates and roofing felt, and piled up in huge drifts in the loft, which had to be dug out before the thaw came or they would have brought down the ceiling and ruined the carpets and bedding. Drifts formed in every room from gaps round the windows or doors, cracks in the walls and even keyholes. In that terrible winter a narrow drift twelve feet long and four feet high even formed one night from the keyhole of the door in the end bar!

Although we had had a few snowstorms before Christmas, it really began to snow in earnest on 28 December. The blizzard continued non-stop for five days and even when the snow finally stopped falling, we were still unable to move or see out as the wind continually scoured and re-arranged it into fresh drifts. When the storm eventually abated enough to let us venture outside for more than a couple of seconds, the landscape had changed out of all recognition. Every familiar landmark had disappeared and no scale, perspective or distance could be judged; on all sides there was nothing but an eye-aching expanse of whiteness. For the first few days it was an exhilarating feeling, but it was a novelty that was soon to wear off.

In that harsh winter – which would prove to be the worst in twenty-five years – customers could often be counted on the fingers of no hands ... except, ironically, when fresh snow had fallen, when getting up there to see the snowdrifts became a near obsession for some people. Whenever we were snowed in, which was frequently, we almost always had a number of customers snowed in with us.

A succession of people would arrive, announcing that 'We've just come up to see the snowdrifts', and almost invariably they finished up seeing them from the inside as the drifting snow blocked their only escape route. Their initial joy at the drunkard's dream of being snowed up in a pub soon turned to disappointment at the realization of just how boring being stuck in the same place for days or weeks on end can be. Every snow cloud has a silver lining, however, and using their tractors, the local farmers had a nice little earner whenever the weather eased a little, towing out snowbound cars for a suitably inflated fee. We were doing less well, because our uninvited guests were eating us out of house and home, consuming all the precious stocks of food that were supposed to get us through the winter. We didn't feel that we could charge normal Bed and Breakfast rates to people who weren't staying with us from choice but from necessity, particularly as they weren't experiencing the warmth, comfort and full menus they would have expected in return, so we usually just asked them to make a token donation towards the costs of their food.

Not all those stuck in the snow were deserving of quite the same sympathy and some had only themselves to blame for their misfortunes. A few miles north of the inn, a dual-carriageway ran east – west over a high pass through the Pennines. It was a busy main route, much used by heavy traffic, but despite the best efforts of gritters, snow ploughs and motorway police running 'convoys' in bad weather, it was frequently closed by snow. If a busy dual-carriageway, without sharp bends and steep gradients, constantly patrolled by police and snow ploughs and crossing the Pennine chain at one of its lower points, was so readily blocked by snow, how much worse must the conditions have been on the tiny minor roads, including the one running past the inn, that crossed the Pennines at much higher altitudes?

Yet every time the main, dual-carriageway A-road over the Pennines was blocked by snow, a few intrepid spirits, or 'idiots' as one of the disgruntled Fell Rescue team members was wont to describe them, always thought it would be a good idea to try and make the crossing via the even higher, steeper, narrower and more twisting B, C and unclassified roads over the tops. Inevitably they would wind up either stranded at the inn, or worse, embedded in a snowdrift miles from anywhere, and would then have to be extricated by the Fell Rescue teams, who were sometimes putting their own lives at risk to reach them. Given those circumstances, 'idiots' seemed a pretty restrained description, though the local Fell Rescue team leader chose his words with rather more care when speaking for the record, remarking that the main dual carriageway had been 'closed for a good reason'. The back roads over the tops, he said, were 'dangerous roads and the trick is not to go out in those conditions. It's a different climate up there. What is winter in the valley is Arctic when you go driving in the snow over the fell tops.'

Each time the snow plough or blower broke through to the inn, it was often only long enough for one set of snowed-in customers to get away and the next lot to arrive. As soon as the snow blower went back down the road, the wind would begin to fill in the track it had made with loose snow. Those brief moments – sometimes as little as ten minutes after the blower had left, the road would again be impassable – were our only contact with the outside world, because buried under a thick coating of ice, the radio telephone had long given up the ghost.

During lulls in the storms, a few locals also managed to make it through the snow, one of them regaling us with the tale of one of his forebears who was said to have called at the inn during a particularly bad blizzard and to have requested 'Just a half, I've got the wife outside.'

'Ee, lad,' the landlord said, 'bring her in before she catches her death of cold.'

'She's already dead,' the farmer said, 'I'm just

taking her to the undertaker on the sledge.' No doubt the landlord was impressed by his customer's devotion to his swift half, no doubt the farmer's wife would have been rather less impressed had she been in any condition to notice.

Over the years, that farmer's wife was far from the only body to be delayed by bad weather on the way down to the nearest consecrated ground: 'the Cathedral of the Dales'- the parish church at the midpoint of the Dale. In medieval times, a 'Corpse Way' had been created along the Dale – a footpath running along the flanks of the fells, avoiding the often impassable tracks along the valley floor. It was still usable in our time and was still marked by the huge flat stone slabs, sited at regular intervals, that allowed the weary bearers to pause and rest their burden: the hazel or wicker basket, or winding sheets in which the remains were transported and buried. Baskets were used because, in the almost entirely treeless wastes of the upper Dale and the surrounding fells, wood for coffins was 'marvellous scarce'.

Snow was often a problem and on one twentieth-century occasion when the way through the Dale was completely blocked by mountainous drifts, a body was brought over the tops by way of the inn, accompanied by the road superintendent and a team of twenty-six men to haul the hay-sledge on which the body was carried and dig their way through the snowdrifts they encountered.

Our next involuntary guests soon arrived but proved to be rather less welcome than their predecessors. Two itinerant electrical engineers, who travelled from contract to contract around the North, had been staying at the inn while working on a microwave relay station – a sort of communications mast – that had been erected on the moors a few hundred yards from the inn. When the snow began to fall in earnest, the engineers found themselves not only unable to work but also unable to leave the inn. One was a genial enough character, a no-nonsense Yorkshireman, but his workmate, Peter, was undeniably strange. Taciturn, almost sullen, he spoke in a near-whisper and was given to long brooding silences and intense stares from under his bushy eyebrows. He had a wife or girlfriend, but when he spoke to her on the radio telephone, on the rare occasions it was working, once more he talked in whispers and every soft-spoken word he uttered seemed, at least to my fevered, hyperactive imagination, to be dripping with hidden menace.

With the snow falling harder and harder, it was clear that we would be spending quite some time in each other's company and it was not an enchanting prospect, even before I settled down to read the last newspaper the postman had delivered before the road was again blocked by snow. It was full of the latest news about the hunt for the Yorkshire Ripper, who was then still at large and terrorizing the North. As I read the latest summary of what the police thought they knew about the Ripper, I began to get a distinctly uneasy feeling. They were looking for someone from the North East, possibly with an engineering background, who knew West Yorkshire well but also travelled widely around the North as a whole. As I looked up from the article and caught our house guest's sullen stare from across the room, I tried to re-assure myself that it was probably just my paranoia.

Without saying anything to alert her to my fears, I walked into the kitchen and handed the news-paper to Sue. I watched her as she read the article and halfway down it, she froze, looked around to see if either of our guests were within earshot and then said 'My God, do you think it's him?' A paranoia shared is a paranoia doubled; that was it, we were now both thoroughly convinced that we were sharing our home with the Yorkshire Ripper. Even more terrifying, there was absolutely nothing we could do about it. We were separated from the outside world by impassable drifts of snow, the blizzard was still raging and our only means of communication – the radio telephone – was now again as dead as a Ripper victim.

The feeling of isolation when we were first cut off by the snow had been greatly lessened by the knowledge that the radio telephone would enable us to keep in touch with the neighbouring farms or call for help in an emergency. In the early stages of winter our neighbours and locals were constantly on the phone, checking if we were all right and asking us if we needed anything. Fol-lowing their advice we'd stocked up with food and fuel in preparation for winter and, despite the best efforts of our house guests, we hadn't yet run out, but just the knowledge that our locals and friends were thinking of us and were there to help if needed was a great psychological boost. However, the telephone had kept falling victim to the weather; the aerial was buried under a thick carapace of ice and no calls could be made, in or out of the inn.

During a whispered conversation in our bedroom that night, I tried to reassure Sue – and, if I'm honest, myself as well – that even if our mystery guest really was the Ripper, he would scarcely strike in a place from which he could not escape until the snow melted, and where he could be so readily identified by a string of witnesses, including his workmate, the postman and a series of customers who had seen him there during the previous week. He had also left his fingerprints in enough places to convict him a score of times. It all sounded perfectly logical but didn't really convince either of us. Since the Ripper was clearly insane, a logical approach was unlikely to loom large in his thoughts. If his internal voices or whatever he was responding to, told him to kill, that was probably what he was going to do. With that happy thought, and having double-locked the bedroom door, we fell into a distinctly uneasy sleep, jerking awake at the least sound from inside our darkened inn.

As the days dragged slowly by without prospect of release from our snowy captivity, we passed the time in a state of barely suppressed hysteria, faking false smiles whenever our eyes met his, watching him like hawks whenever we thought we could do so unobserved, and sleeping – still very uneasily – behind a locked door with a pickaxe handle next to the bed. Inevitably, everything he said or did, from wielding a tin-opener to digging frozen coal for the fire from the heap at the back of the building, merely served to fuel our terror and our conviction that he was the Ripper. His skill with the tin-opener must have been honed wielding the bloody tools of his nocturnal trade and his handiness with a shovel proved he was getting ready to bury his next victim. When he asked if we had an axe so he could split some logs from the stack, I gibbered 'No! I mean yes! At least, I'm not sure, I'll look in the cellar.' And then, when I saw that he was going to follow me, 'No, it's all right, you wait here, I'll go.'

The relief we felt when, after one of the longest fortnights of both our lives, we heard the first faint sounds of an engine in the distance and, running outside, saw the white plumes of snow against the leaden grey of the sky that showed a snow blower was cutting through the drifts towards us, was absolutely overwhelming. We remained outside, hearts in mouths, in case it started to snow again, until the bright red snow blower had arrived in the car park. We were desperate to pour out our fears to the driver, but with a wave of his hand and a thumbs-up, he turned around without even switching off his engine and began to make his way back down the hill.

With smiles that were even more fake than usual, we urged our terrifying guest and his workmate to make their escape before the wind blew the snow back into the track the blower had cut. Radiating insincerity, we shook their hands and waved them off as they drove away. We gave them ten minutes' start and then followed them down the road as far as the hamlet at the bottom of the hill where we used the pay-phone to contact the West Yorkshire police and report that we'd been playing host to the Yorkshire Ripper on his two-week winter holiday, just another of the hundreds of sightings that were being reported to them every day. It was to be almost two years before the Ripper was actually arrested and when we looked at the pictures published in the newspapers, we discovered that Peter Sutcliffe really was ... absolutely nothing like the man we had sheltered under our roof.

CHAPTER 16

The Winter of Discontent

After waving off those unwanted guests, the snow began to fall again and we went another fortnight without seeing a living soul. The 'Winter of Discontent' was now paralysing the rest of the country, with lorry drivers, railway workers, public sector workers and gravediggers on strike, bodies lying unburied and mountains of rubbish piling up in city streets. Our rubbish was piling up too but not because of strike action; we were completely cut off again from the world behind fresh barricades of drifting snow. We weren't alone in that – it even snowed in the Sahara Desert in February of that year, but there it only lasted half an hour; at the Inn at the Top it looked as if it was shaping up to last half a year.

We still had no heating other than the fire and

we now had no water either, because drifts from the winter snowstorms had buried the building up to the first floor windows and as the temperature plummeted, every drop of water in the place froze. Every time there was a thaw, some of the pipes burst. Each time, I jury-rigged repairs with the only materials to hand, lengths of hose-pipe and jubilee clips, and by the time spring came, the plumbing probably contained more hosepipe than copper pipe. It was so cold inside the pub that even the water in the lavatory bowls froze solid and the lack of running water led to some unusual improvisations. Although we could melt snow for drinking water, bodily functions required rather more ingenuity. Fortunately the kitchen stores included a large supply of freezer bags... After use, they could be sealed and placed outside, where the contents immediately froze solid and they could then be dropped in a bin-bag and safely left for more hygienic disposal when the weather at last relented.

The savage cold did not merely freeze the water; like previous landlords in harsh winters, we had to take hurried steps to protect our beer stocks, moving everything out of the barrel- and bottle-stores which were both now well below freezing, and keeping it all under and behind the bar. Even so, we weren't quick enough to save everything; the sound of detonations from the bottle store told us that a couple of bottles of frozen lemonade had exploded in the cold. Things could have been worse; in the winter of 1947 the cold was so intense that all the beer bottles behind the bar froze, pushing the crown corks two inches off the bottles on columns of frozen beer. As one contemporary observer remarked in disbelief, 'and this is England, not Alaska'. In 1963 the beer froze in the pumps, the whisky froze in the optics, tins of food split open and the snug had a foot of snow on the floor. The plight of the then landlords became so desperate that they lit a bonfire to summon help.

One of our locals still remembered that winter as if it was yesterday. 'It started snowing about Boxing Day,' he said, 'and it seemed to snow every day till about the middle of March. It froze every night till it was as solid as concrete. It's desperate weather when it's like that day in and day out, and it's the wind that does the havoc. There'll be a "Helm Wind" [named for the word for a knight in armour's helmet, the Helm Wind was marked by a cap of cloud sitting apparently immobile on the summit of the Pennines while a savage icy wind swept down the slopes]. And the snow fills up the road constantly when the Helm Wind's blowing.'

In theory the recurrence of the worst of those winter problems should have been prevented by the central heating; but in practice, as we had discovered courtesy of Stan and Neville, the dangers were just as great. In the bitterly cold easterly winds, even the diesel fuel for the generator would effectively freeze, with water and other impurities in the fuel forming crystals which made it 'waxy' and prevented it flowing. The only way of solving the problem was to warm the diesel – not the easiest thing to arrange when the fuel tank was outside and the drums containing spare fuel were frozen to the ground by several inches of ice.

Even if fuel could be fed to the generator, mechanical breakdowns in the cold and the wet were a high risk; our main generator had given up the ghost as soon as the cold weather arrived. When I finally managed to get somebody in to look at it the following spring, I discovered that generators are supposed to run on a very light engine oil. Those adorable tight-fists, Stan and Neville, had not only allowed the Start-a-matic – the battery operated system designed to start the generator whenever a switch was turned on inside the inn – to deteriorate from neglect to the point where it had ceased to function altogether, they had also refused to pay to have the generator serviced and were equally reluctant to waste money on such inessentials as the right kind of oil. Instead, they had obtained a drum of second-hand oil drained from lorry-engines in their native North East. No doubt it was extremely cheap, but it was also totally unsuitable for this purpose.

Despite the heavy oil, it had been possible – just – to start the generator in the milder days of early autumn, when the oil, being reasonably warm, was not too viscous, but as winter came on, the physical effort required to turn the crank-handle became greater and greater. I approached the generator shed each morning like a prisoner on his way to the condemned cell. If I could physically turn over the engine enough times by hand, the friction generated sufficient warmth to let the oil flow a little more easily and the engine might then start. Sobbing and cursing with effort, I would finally manage to get the generator firing and my ordeal was over for another twenty-four hours. That kept us going for another three or four weeks, but then as winter really started to bite, the generator proved absolutely impossible to start. The oil was so thick and viscous in the cold that even swinging with both hands on the handle, I could barely move it at all. Until the spring thaw raised the temperature again, the generator was effectively as dead as a hammer.

Fortunately, we had a small standby Honda generator, which unlike its big sister, was a breeze to start. Unfortunately it also proved temperamental and followed the example of its sibling by breaking down a few days later. Since by now the road was blocked by snow, there was no possibility of getting a mechanic out to it. My lack of mechanical skills is such that I would struggle to service a wheelbarrow and in normal circumstances I would not even have attempted to diagnose the problem and attempt a repair, but these were definitely not normal circumstances and it is amazing what you can achieve when truly desperate. Knowing that if I couldn't fix it myself we'd almost certainly be without light and power until spring, I dragged it into the garage, removed the casing and began stripping it down. Drawing on powers of deduction that I would never have dreamed I possessed, I managed to identify the source of the problem and then improvise a repair.

A couple of hours later, full of ridiculous pride at my achievement – one that virtually every farmer in the Dale could probably have managed with his eyes shut – I had the generator running once more. The only problem now was that the inn, on its isolated, wind-swept hilltop, was coming to resemble an icebound trawler on the Arctic Ocean. The temperature was permanently below freezing, and the cloud, mist and freezing rain streaming over the hill on the wind in the sub-zero temperatures produced icing similar to that formed by spray on the sub-zero metal surfaces on ships in the Arctic. Every single, super-cooled surface was rapidly encrusted with massive amounts of ice. Filling the coal bucket required a pickaxe as well as a shovel, because our entire supply, stored in a lean-to outside, had also frozen solid.

Opening and closing the door in the winter storms required several minutes' work, for as soon as the door was opened, driven snow would immediately pack the frame and drift across the jamb, making it difficult or even impossible to close it again. Sometimes the door could eventually be forced shut, but frequently the only solution was to jam it as far closed as it would go and then seal it by plastering snow around the edge. Rather more serious was the occasion when the door could not be opened. We had both gone outside to try to dig out some lumps of coal and logs from the frozen heaps at the rear of the inn and to try and free a drum of frozen diesel, but made the mistake, as it turned out, of closing the front door behind us. When we returned, twenty minutes later, we found that the door was completely frozen shut and no amount of pushing or hammering would move it. As fast as we chipped the ice from around the frame, it promptly refroze. Night was now falling, so was the temperature, and we were beginning to get frantic, but nothing we could do would shift that door.

We couldn't get in at the back door either, because it was bolted from the inside. In the end, in our desperation to get in out of the terrible cold, we were forced to break into the inn by smashing one of the side-windows and squeezing through the gap. I nailed a piece of plywood over the broken window and it remained like that for the rest of the winter, leaking a regular drift of snow from the chinks around the edge into the bar. It was two days before we managed to get the front door open again; not that it mattered, there weren't any customers for miles.

The standby generator also became a highly efficient ice-making machine. If I left it outside, within ten minutes the metal casing would be smothered in ice and the air intake so blocked by it that the generator would cough, splutter and finally expire. If I brought it inside the cellar where we normally kept the beer, it ran perfectly well, but the thick, black smoke from the exhaust seeped under the kitchen and bar doors and filled the entire pub.

The choice was having light and power and being slowly poisoned, or sitting in darkness and being able to breathe. We opted for the dark. From then on, for the rest of that desperate winter, whenever the weather turned ugly, preventing us from putting the small generator outside, we had no light. The final straw came when I was trying to move the generator to a more sheltered position. The wheels were iced to the ground but I kept heaving away, trying to shift it. In the end the only things that weren't frozen to the ground were my feet, and I slipped and broke my two front teeth in half on the casing of the generator. I couldn't get out to see a dentist for another fortnight and I was reduced to living on soup and bottles of Guinness drunk through a straw, and screaming every time cold air touched the stumps of my teeth.

Having given up on the generator, we made do with candles, and when they were running low, we decided to save the last few for emergencies and did without artificial light altogether, going to bed when the sun went down or just sitting in the firelight. Then one night, lying in bed in the pitch darkness, I heard the phone ring – the first sound we had heard from it in almost a month. It heralded what was for both of us undoubtedly the worst night of that whole terrible winter. After weeks of radio silence, it seemed like a miracle – perhaps a lump of ice had just fallen off the aerial and given us a momentary window on the world – but whatever the reason, I was determined to get there before the unknown caller rang off. I jumped out of bed and, not even waiting to light a candle – the generator was still dead – I groped my way along the landing by Braille. Unfortunately, confident of my position, I left the safety of the wall and struck out resolutely for what I thought was the head of the stairs. Instead, I was heading for the place where, had Neville and Stan bothered to install one, a banister or guard-rail would have been fitted to stop anyone from plunging head-first down the stairs. In its absence, there was nothing in the way but an empty night storage heater, left there by one of them either as some token protection or because they'd never got round to moving it. Had it still been full of firebricks, it would probably have stopped me with no worse injuries than a pair of barked shins, but Neville had removed the bricks and in their absence the storage heater was of no more use and little more solidity than a very large but very empty can of baked beans.

I toppled over the empty storage heater, landed first on my shoulder on about the fourth step down, bounced off headfirst onto the opposite wall and finally landed in a crumpled heap on the stone floor at the bottom of the stairs, very soon afterwards being joined both by the storage heater and by a fire extinguisher, which had been resting on a ledge halfway up the stairs. It fell on its end and immediately went off, blasting a jet of ice-cold water over me and the surrounding area, and bringing me temporarily to my senses. With admirable presence of mind in the circumstances, I picked up the phone and said, 'Sorry, I can't speak to you now,' put it down again, and then collapsed in a pool of blood and icy water.

When Sue eventually found a candle and came to see what had happened, she found me lying among the wreckage of the fixtures and fittings from the landing and stairs, soaking wet, concussed and with my face a mask of blood. When she lifted the phone to try and summon an air ambulance, she discovered that the line was once again dead. I couldn't get out to see a doctor, of course, but fortunately, though I was concussed and covered in cuts and bruises, my skull was intact – as far as I could tell – and I had no broken bones. Sue managed to suture the gash in my forehead with strips of Elastoplast and did it so skilfully that when it healed there was only the faintest trace of a scar to show for it. The shoulder, which had taken the brunt of the impact, has never been the same since – it was over a year before I could even raise my arm to shoulder level again – but the fact that any more serious injury could not have been treated until the storm abated made me realize just how close a call it had been.

Stan and Neville's indifference to the welfare of their employees and customers alike had, in part at least, caused me to lose my front teeth and also to fall headlong down the stairs, and Sue's fury and hatred of them now knew no bounds. 'I'll never, ever forgive them,' she said. 'And I'll never work for them again. As soon as the weather eases, we're quitting.' I was in full agreement with her.

I was very lucky to escape more serious injury that winter but there were others who were even more fortunate than me. Two pregnant women from farms in the upper Dale had to be taken to hospital by helicopter to give birth; they were fortunate that the storms had eased enough for the helicopters to fly, or they would have been giving birth at home with only the skills their husbands had learned at lambing time to help them out. A young woman also had cause to be very grateful that we had stayed open for the winter, rather than boarding up the inn as had happened for the previous ten years or so, for she collapsed exhausted after she and her boyfriend had set out to walk over the moors through the snow from a village in the Dale. Her boyfriend left her in an abandoned sheepfold and hurried on to summon help but the light was fading by the time he reached the inn.

The snow blowers had cut a track through to the inn that day so the road was at least open and while a couple of customers who had followed the snow blower up the hill went to summon help from the Fell Rescue team, we gave the man a hot drink and then set off at once back across the moors, following his footprints to reach his girlfriend. It was a long, exhausting struggle through the snow on the moor to the ruined sheepfold and when we got there, we found the young woman was so weak that she was unable to walk unaided. It was now pitch dark and too dangerous for us to try and move her, even with one of us supporting her on either side. She was also so cold that she was probably slipping into hypothermia, but we made her as warm as we could, then stayed with her, shouting and waving torches, until the Fell Rescue team spotted us. They hurried up to us, put her on a stretcher and carried her down to the road two miles away across the moor. A waiting ambulance then whisked her away to hospital. She suffered no lasting ill-effects and turned up at the inn a few days later to thank us personally for our help but it was a sobering thought that, had the inn been closed as usual that winter, she would almost certainly have died of exposure before help could have reached her.

To be out on the moors in such weather was to court disaster, as two young Dutchmen trapped in the snow could also testify. Attempting to drive over the Dale-head into the neighbouring valley, they became stuck in the snowdrifts in as wild and desolate a place as they could have found. They stayed in their car for a day and a night, but as the blizzard still raged and their car became completely buried in snow, they decided to set off on foot back the way they had come in search of help.

Some hours later, exhausted by their struggle with the snow, they came across a barn and were about to enter it when the snow eased for a second and they were spotted by one of our locals, Clifford, who had fought his way up through the drifts from his farm lower down the Dale to fodder his sheep. Leaving them in the barn while he finished his work, Clifford then returned to lead them the two and a half miles down to his farm, forcing them to keep going, battling through the snow, until they reached it. Both men were in a terrible state, one going into hypothermia, and it is certain that if they had not been spotted by him, they would have died. That they were found at all was a million-to-one chance, one made stranger by the fact that, for the first and only time in his life, Clifford had paused on his way out of the farm that morning and gone back to fill a hip flask with whisky to take up the Dale with him. By such threads can a life hang.

Although modest by comparison to such life or death struggles, the hardships of our own winter were increased still further when we became the thing that epitomizes despair: the pub with no beer. Although the brewery dray couldn't get through the snows to deliver to us, a number of hikers and walkers continued to do so, and as a result – admittedly helped by the landlord and landlady's personal consumption – our beer stocks dwindled almost to vanishing point, with only a few bottles of stout remaining when a brief lull in the storms allowed our latest lot of involuntary guests to escape. Then the snow closed in again, leaving us blocked in once more, but this time with only the dog and the bottles of stout for company.

With the weather forecast always uncertain, I didn't dare risk leaving the pub to have my injuries from the fall down the stairs checked or get my teeth fixed, in case a fresh storm left me unable to return to the inn, stranding Sue on her own. As we waited for the weather to improve, I was still existing on soup and bottles of stout, drunk though a straw. The stout supplies quickly shrank to a single bottle and I decided to save the last one to celebrate the arrival of the first snow blower of spring. Often I gazed fondly at the bottle as I passed the shelf, until one black morning when a local shepherd banged on the windows after battling his way up through the snowdrifts because he'd run out of cigarettes.

'Anything else?' I enquired brightly as we exchanged commiserations on the harshness of the winter, 'not that we've got much to offer.'

He scanned the denuded shelves behind the bar. 'Aye, I'll just have a Guinness before I head back.'

I couldn't pretend we didn't have any – the bottle was sitting in full view on the shelf – and I had to watch in silent horror, a slow tear trickling down my cheek, as the last drop of beer in the entire pub disappeared down his throat with a soft gurgle.

Salvation of an unexpected kind was at hand, however. As our food supplies also ran low, we gave thanks for the foresight of my uncle Olaf, a wise and practical, if somewhat unusual man. Interesting though the local characters were, none of them could hold a candle to my uncle. To call him merely eccentric was to denigrate him; he was the Leonardo da Vinci of eccentricity, always finding new, inventive and exciting ways to enliven our humdrum lives.

Knowing the harshness of the winters in the Dale, he had arrived in late autumn with a crate hermetically sealed in plastic. It contained what he said were 'survival rations': everything needed to survive an emergency, including dehydrated food, bandages, foil blankets, windproof matches, a torch and many other useful items. My uncle was also a gourmet, however, if not a gourmand, and when we opened the crate in our cold, dark, beer-less and nearly foodless pub, among the dehydrated food and essential supplies were nestling items of a far less essential, but even more welcome nature. Thus it was that in a pub with no heat, no light and worst of all, no beer, mine genial host and hostess and yet another snowed-in walker sat down to dine on pâté de foie gras and pheasant in red wine and cracked open a bottle of champagne, before rounding off the meal with Belgian chocolates and coffee freshly ground from the beans that had also been included in the 'survival' crate. Even the pain from my broken teeth couldn't spoil my enjoyment.

While we ate, Sue and I entertained each other

by recalling some of Olaf's more memorable exploits. A successful businessman of Scandinavian ancestry, he was not over-tall and, at eighteen stone, more than a little rotund. His Swedish roots were most in evidence in his complete lack of any of the normal British reticence and inhibitions, particularly about nudity. He had an unheated swimming pool behind his large detached house and it was Olaf's habit to take a cold water dip every morning. However, he chose to enter the water not by merely stepping or jumping in from the side but by means of the slide that ran down into it from the roof of the outbuildings surrounding the pool. So it was that every morning his next-door neighbours would open their curtains to be greeted by the sight of the barrel-shaped and completely naked Olaf appearing at the top of a ladder, striding along the flat roofs of the outbuilding, and disappearing down the slide into the pool with a splash that displaced most of the water, before he emerged dripping wet, like a large pink walrus. Whether the neighbours merely tolerated it, or actually took pleasure from Olaf's daily indecent exposure was never revealed, but no complaints were ever made and he continued to take his morning dip untroubled by any interruptions from the local police.

His eccentricities took a multitude of other forms. In the late 1950s, a leak of radioactive material from Calder Hall/Windscale/Sellafield (the Cumbrian nuclear power station/plutonium production facility/nuclear waste reprocessing and storage plant, that changes its name every time there's a nuclear accident in the hope that we won't realize it's still the same place) caused a brief scare about radioactivity levels in domestic milk supplies. Olaf promptly rushed out and spent several hundred pounds on a top-of-the-range Geiger counter. He ran it over the bottles on his doorstep for the next couple of days, but when it failed to register even a flicker of radio-activity, he lost interest at once and it joined a pile of other expensive and similarly discarded toys and gadgets in the attic.

Olaf also had a second home and a five thousand acre estate in the Yorkshire Dales – less grand than that sounds, because most of it was rough moor-land, and valued at only £1 an acre when he bought it in the 1950s. When travelling around his estate, Olaf had an unreasoning faith in his Land Rover's ability to get through bottomless seas of mud and water, and such journeys were almost invariably followed by a long walk back to his country cottage and a phone call to the neigh-bouring, long-suffering farmer who had to turn out with his tractor to tow the Land Rover out of its latest muddy resting-place. Olaf was also a keen naturalist and conservationist, planting thousands of trees on his land, stocking it with pheasants and guinea fowl, feeding them and other wild birds from scores of hoppers, and constructing a lake as a flighting pond for ducks and other waterfowl. If I owed him nothing else, I owed him a lifetime debt of gratitude for opening my eyes to the beauty of the British landscape and its wildlife.

He had been a keen shot when younger but now used his guns only on grey squirrels – which he called 'tree-rats' and hated with a passion for damaging his trees and driving out the native red squirrels – and, for reasons that were less readily apparent, wood-pigeons. Whenever a grey squirrel or a wood-pigeon was spotted within range of his cottage, Olaf would emerge from the back door, clutching his twelve-bore and clad from head to foot in Army surplus sniper-camouflage gear, including a netting mask over his face, and begin advancing stealthily on his prey. The rest of us, watching from the safety of the cottage windows, were reduced to hysterics at the sight of what appeared to be a short, fat, heavily camouflaged Hannibal Lecter stalking his latest victim, and when the inevitable gunshot followed, the squirrel or pigeon would almost invariably be seen making its escape, for Olaf was emphatically no marksman.

One day however, a pigeon fluttered down onto the roof of the barn next to the cottage and remained sitting motionless while Olaf donned his hunting gear, loaded his twelve-bore and emerged from the cottage. He tiptoed closer and closer to the unflappable bird and, ignoring our vocal protests about the clear breach of sporting etiquette in shooting a sitting target, Olaf took careful aim and fired. For once his aim was true and the pigeon fell to the ground in a flurry of feathers, but when Olaf came to claim his prize, he discovered that it had a ring on its leg. The unfortunate homing pigeon had chosen the wrong roof on which to rest from its labours for a few moments and would not now be completing its race. The ring was removed and posted to the address it contained, together with a note of apology and a cheque by way of compensation, and from then on, Olaf left his twelve-bore untouched on the gun-rack.

His ability to make snap decisions had served him well in his business career but it could have expensive ramifications on the domestic front. To give my aunt added peace of mind, he had installed an extensive burglar alarm system at their house, including a panic button in their bedroom, and one night, just as they were getting into bed, the alarm began sounding. It had a particularly strident note, sufficient to induce panic and flight in any intruder, but which was also deafening enough to unhinge the legitimate occupants if not switched off fairly promptly. Seizing a poker from the fireplace, Olaf searched the bedroom and every other part of the house without finding anything amiss and then went to the control box to silence and reset the alarm. Nothing happened. The control panel continued to insist that there was a burglar in the house and the alarm kept ringing despite his repeated attempts to key in the code and switch it off.

After twenty minutes, driven to distraction by the screeching alarm and unable to find any other way to silence it, Olaf put on his dressing gown, took a ladder and a sledgehammer from the garage, climbed up the outside wall and began belabouring the red alarm box. A few well-placed blows knocked it off the wall, but it had an emergency battery in case burglars cut the wires, and it continued to sound even while lying on its back in the bushes. Olaf was forced to descend the ladder again, track the alarm to its lair in the heart of the shrubbery and then pound the still-shrieking alarm with the sledgehammer until with a last defiant, dying screech, it finally fell silent. Having put the ladder away, Olaf checked the control panel, still showing an intruder in the house, and giving up in disgust, was just taking off his dressing-gown ready to get into bed when he noticed that, as he had got ready for bed earlier that evening, he'd accidentally pushed the bedside table against the panic button...

Apart from that tendency to over-hasty action, Olaf's only real vice was a weakness for alcohol. He was not an unpleasant drunk at all, far from it, indeed he became particularly friendly and affectionate, but it did increase his already strong eccentric traits to a sometimes extraordinary degree. He was obsessed with the human capacity for survival in adversity and, whenever too much drink had been taken, Olaf would announce to anyone within earshot that he could survive for months on end with nothing more than a hunting knife, living on nuts, berries and whatever fish and game he could catch. On several occasions he left the cottage intent on demonstrating this, having first of all strapped a knife to his hip and – rather more surprisingly – having removed all his clothes. In the thousands of acres of woods and moorland that surrounded the cottage, the chances of coming across any human beings other than the handful of sheep-farmers who were already well used to his eccentricities were sufficiently remote for us to leave him to it and, protected by his ample layers of fat, he would invariably return later that day or early the next morning, bleary-eyed, unshaven and somewhat goose-pimpled, but otherwise unharmed.

I often borrowed the cottage for weekends away with my friends, and on one occasion, while my girlfriend and I went back to work at the end of the weekend, I left behind two friends, an American ski instructor and his girlfriend, who were going to stay on at the cottage for a few more days. I'd barely settled at my desk forty miles away, when the phone rang. 'Neil,' said an American voice. 'A little fat guy just turned up here. He seems a bit strange.'

'Oh, that'll just be my uncle,' I said. 'He's a bit eccentric but perfectly harmless. Just tell him you're friends of mine and everything will be fine.'

A couple of hours later the phone rang again. 'Neil, we're getting a little worried. He's drinking an awful lot and he's started waving a knife around.'

'Ah, yes,' I said, trying to sound reassuring. 'He often does that when he's had a few drinks, but he'd be mortified if he thought he was frightening you. It's all part of his "I can survive in the wilderness" thing, but don't worry, he's completely harmless. He'll probably stick around a bit longer and then set off up the hillside to see if he can survive on bilberries and crushed cockroaches or something.' I was about to hang up when a further thought occurred to me. 'Oh and Chris? He does have a tendency to take his clothes off too, but don't worry; it's all perfectly normal, just part of the survival of the fittest thing?'

Chris's voice did not sound like that of a man who was wholly reassured as I said goodbye and broke the connection. All went quiet for a few hours and I was back at my flat that evening by the time the phone rang again. 'Neil, it's Chris,' the familiar voice said. 'He took all his clothes off, like you said.'

'See,' I said, 'I told you he was harmless.'

'Yeah, but you didn't tell us that he'd try to get into bed with us as well. We're leaving – NOW!' Strangely enough, it was the last conversation I ever had with him.

When the Cuban Missile Crisis was at its height, Olaf, convinced that a world war, a nuclear winter and a great famine were about to engulf us all, had purchased enough bottled water and tinned food to last his family for thirty years and stored it all in a specially constructed secret storeroom at his house. Much of it was still there decades later. He also put together fifty large packing crates of de-hydrated survival rations and other emergency supplies, stored some of them under the floor-boards of his cottage and buried the remainder at various places around his country estate. Unfortunately, a strategic thinker rather than a mere tactician, he neglected to record where the boxes were buried and soon forgot, with the result that most of them are still out there somewhere waiting to be unearthed in a few hundred years' time, to the probable bafflement of archaeologists who, based on the contents of the boxes, may form a very strange picture of what daily life in twentieth-century Britain was actually like.

CHAPTER 17

Gumming, Gurning and Toothless Gnashing

Our other visitors that winter were much less welcome than the unwanted guests who had been eating us out of house and home; the rats were back. Some tourists and especially some of the people who camped overnight by the pub in summer were not always the most civic-minded of individuals and, despite our efforts to clear the litter they left, there was enough waste food and debris pushed into cracks in the rocks or the dry-stone walls, or simply dumped in obscure corners, to feed a sizeable colony of rats. During the summer they were no bother to us, in fact we never even saw one. They kept themselves to themselves, except presumably in the hours of darkness, but as winter began to bite, the rats started looking for a warmer, safer refuge ... and what could be warmer or safer than a pub?

We were sitting in the bar one quiet evening, when we heard a strange noise, a rhythmic rasping sound, as if someone was filing a piece of wood. It turned out that something was. The noise was coming from the back door of the pub and when I opened it, I saw rats scuttling off into the darkness. When I looked at the bottom of the door, I found that they had been trying to gnaw their way through it. Even worse, it looked as if they were succeeding. Two minutes after I closed the door and returned to the bar, the noise resumed.

We were, as usual, snowed in, and I was dependent on what I could improvise from the supplies we had to hand, so I cut through a couple of empty baked bean tins with a pair of wire snips, beat them flat with a hammer and then nailed them to the bottom of the door. Even the rats couldn't gnaw their way through that, but it was only the opening skirmish in what was to prove a winter-long war.

They didn't give up easily and one enterprising rodent even attempted to force an entry by swimming past the U-bend in the Gents loo. Fortunately for us, if not the rat, the plunging temperatures had already left the water in the lavatory pan frozen solid and blocked off that means of approach. I spotted the rat under the ice the following morning, drowned and then deep-frozen but it was a few weeks before it thawed enough for me to be able to dispose of the corpse.

A few rats did manage to penetrate our defences by sneaking up a drain in the beer-cellar and pushing up the small steel drain cover. We realized they were in when the contents of the box of assorted fudge that we kept under the bar counter for sale to summer visitors, disappeared one night and we found the empty wrappers branded with the marks of rodent incisors. I tracked the rats' access route and blocked it off, then got my revenge on the intruders. I could have just kept feeding them fudge until they died a slow and agonizing death from tooth decay or Type-2 diabetes, but it seemed too long to wait, so instead I refilled all the empty fudge packets with Warfarin and left a stash of them inside the pub and another outside, shielded from the weather by a couple of old roofing slates. They were rapidly eaten and after a few days no more bait was taken, suggesting our problem was solved. We had no further rat-trouble that winter; any that still remained outside would probably have frozen to death anyway as the temperatures plunged to minus twenty degrees Celsius.

Our next visitor was a much more welcome one. After the most violent storm of the winter – known ever after in the Dale simply as 'That Thursday', when the ferocity of the weather surpassed anything even in that bitter winter – the sun eventually came out again and we came blinking into its light like moles emerging from underground. The first thing we saw, lying in the snow just outside the pub, was a mistle thrush. Normally thrushes would not have been found within miles of the inn, even in the warmest days of summer. On the barren moorland around the inn, there were no trees, no bushes and, except for a very brief period when the bilberries and crowberries were in fruit, nothing for them to eat. This one had obviously been driven before the gales all the way from her home territory in the lowlands and had finished up, spent, exhausted and near to death in the snow by the pub. She was still breathing though, and we picked her up, warmed her in our hands and carried her into the porch. We put her in a cardboard box on some shredded newspaper, put some water, some bread and milk, and a few stray bits of minced beef nearby and left her alone, not really expecting that she would live.

To our surprise, the next morning we discovered that she had not only survived the night, but recovered to such an extent that she was perching on the edge of one of my wellington boots. She had no fear of us when we went in, and over the next ten days, Thelma – as we had christened her – fed voraciously and began to regain her strength, flying a tight circuit around inside the porch and always coming to rest on her favourite perch on the rim of my wellington boot, which over the next ten days she managed to half-fill with birdlime. One fine day, not without a little reluctance, as we'd grown quite attached to her, we opened the outside door. She hopped outside and made a few test flights around outside the inn, but again returned to the porch to feed and roost on the wellies.

The weather then closed in again, but on the tenth day, the sun was once again shining and the wind was no more than a breeze. Once more we opened the front door and Thelma hopped out into the snow. She stood there for a couple of minutes, feeling the breeze ruffling her feathers, and then took wing. She circled the pub two or three times, getting her bearings, and then without even a goodbye or a thank you, she disappeared to the south, making for the more hospitable lowlands from whence she had come.

Taking my cue from Thelma, on the same morning that she flew away, with only the gentlest of breezes blowing and the weather looking set fair for the day, I decided to set off to get my broken teeth fixed and pick up some urgently-needed supplies. Towing a sledge behind me to load with food and other essentials, I walked the five miles through the snow to the edge of the moor – the road had been dug out to there, not by snow blowers but by JCBs, which were now the only things capable of moving the massive drifts of hard-packed, frozen snow. Some of the drifts were well over twenty feet deep, filling the stream-beds and gullies, and when I reached the lane near the edge of the moor I was walking level with the tops of the walls because the road was completely invisible, buried under the drifts.

One of our locals, a kindly gamekeeper who lived in a cottage just below the edge of the moor, gave me a lift to and from a dentist in the market town fifteen miles away, and having got a temporary repair to my teeth and bought as many groceries as I could fit on my sledge, I was dropped off back at the moor edge and began struggling back through the snow, dragging the laden sledge behind me. I arrived back at the inn, exhausted, just as the sun was going down. As I forced my leaden legs up the last climb to the inn, I kept reminding myself of the remarkable fortitude of a nurse the gamekeeper had told me about as we drove back: in the winter of 1947 she had made an eight-mile trek through the drifts to reach a snowbound lorry driver suffering from malaria.

That winter also saw the longest ever blockage by snow of the now-closed railway that ran near the head of the Dale. Snowstorms often blocked the line and in winter snow ploughs were kept in constant readiness, but there was little they could do on 3 February 1947 when a train became stuck in a cutting just west of the summit of the line.

Fortunately the last coach was retrievable and the passengers were returned to a nearby town for the night, but as the snowstorms continued to rage, the line became completely blocked. Once the storm had blown itself out, a force of railway navvies, augmented by troops from the army camp a few miles away, began attempts to clear the line, but neither soldiers with shovels nor flame-throwers proved effective. Lorry-loads of Italian prisoners-of-war were also brought in and put to work digging the snow, but one of our locals remembered seeing many of them throw their shovels away into the drifts to try and get out of the cold and escape the hopeless task.

Though snow continued to fall, most of the trouble was caused by the wind blowing it back into cuttings that had already been cleared. For the first week steady progress was made, but by 11 February, worsening weather conditions had pushed the clearers three miles further back than where they'd started. After trials in Devon, two rail-mounted Rolls-Royce jet engines were sent north to try to clear the blocked line. They began work on 1 March but, though they were success-ful in moving a thin covering of snow, they were completely ineffective on the packed snow and ice in the many cuttings. As the engines screamed and howled, the main effect of the jet-stream was simply to push the train away from the snow-face that it was trying to clear. Even more powerful jet engines were brought in but also failed to have any significant effect and when mechanical shovels and 'grabs' were tried, their machinery either froze or would not function in the intense cold.

Explosives were then used successfully to loosen the snow and ice, but it still had to be dug out and removed by hand.

By 7 March, the snow clearers working from east and west were only about one mile apart on either side of the almost buried station near the summit of the line – where Mick the log dealer now lived – but three days later, just as success was in sight, a fresh blizzard broke out, completely blocking the line once more, and forcing the digging to begin all over again. The line was not finally reopened until the end of March.

In our own horrific winter, after being blocked in for six straight weeks, a snow blower finally broke through to us. We had seen the graceful plume of snow it fired out as it cut through the drifts some distance away and at once ran outside to get our car ready. There was no garage of course, and exposed to the full force of the storms, the entire engine space of the car was filled with hard-packed snow. We scraped and brushed it out and wiped down every surface, then I took off the distributor cap, rotor arm and leads, removed the spark plugs, dried everything as well as I could on a cloth and then gave them to Sue to put in a low oven for a couple of minutes to dry off any remaining moisture. While she was doing that, I refilled the radiator – I kept it drained because even anti-freeze was not proof against the sort of freezing temperatures we could experience at the Inn at the Top. I reassembled the parts, said a silent prayer and then turned on the ignition and pressed the starter. It was touch and go – the battery was not far off flat – but after a few groans, clanks and wheezes, the engine fired and rumbled into life. I left it running to warm up while we waited for the snow blower to cover the last few hundred yards.

When it finally reached us, we had a quick chat with the driver and gave him a cup of tea, and as soon as he was ready to make the return journey, we jumped straight in the car – our old Morris Minor with four sacks of coal in the boot to improve the traction of the rear wheels on the snow – and followed him back down the road. It was an exhilarating ride. We couldn't go off the road because we were driving between two ten-foot walls of snow, so we were slaloming over the snow and ice and bouncing between the walls of hard-packed snow as if we were tobogganing on the Cresta Run. We put a couple of fresh dents in the bodywork along the way, but we already had a sizeable collection of those, so a couple more weren't really going to be a problem.

When we reached the small town twelve miles away in the bottom of the valley, we ran into the shop and pretty much cleared the shelves, filling the back-seat and the footwells of the car with groceries, fresh fruit and vegetables, and even fresh bread and milk – the first of either we'd seen in weeks. Then, always with an anxious eye on the lowering clouds, we set off straight back to the inn. The wind was already blowing the loose snow back into the track the snow blower had cut and we almost bottomed the car on a couple of the new drifts that were forming, but we slid and slithered through and just kept going, though our hearts were in our mouths until at last we saw the dark shape of the inn looming out of the mist and snow ahead of us. By the time we'd finished carrying our booty into the inn, our tyre tracks on the road were no longer visible and by nightfall we were once more cut off by snowdrifts.

When the weather at last eased enough for the brewer's dray and our locals to add us once more to their itineraries, my insistence on seeing a dentist to complete the repairs to my broken teeth by having two crowns fitted, was greeted with some bemusement by our regulars. Except in life-threatening emergencies, farmers in general and farmers from the Dale in particular tended to have no great use for doctors and dentists. If their livestock fell ill they would first try and dose them themselves and then, and only if that failed, send for the 'veterinary'. If their own health was suspect, the same rules applied and as for dentists, no self-respecting farmer in the Dale had time to waste on nonsense like six-monthly check-ups and preventative dentistry.

When self-medication ceased to work and the pain of toothache got too severe, the traditional local farmer would just have the offending tooth pulled out, and some even did that job themselves, with the help of a piece of baler twine and a slammed door. If that didn't work, they would reluctantly head for a dentist, pay cash and have the tooth extracted, fillings being another needless waste of time and money.

I'd had some experience of the consequences of that when I'd had toothache earlier in the year and gone to find a dentist to look at it. When I entered the surgery in the nearby market town and stated my problem, the receptionist just said

337

'It's £10 to have it pulled out.'

'I don't want it pulled out,' I said. 'I'd like a filling if possible.'

There was a stunned silence. I felt like a character in one of H. M. Bateman's 'The Man Who...' cartoons: 'The man who asked for a filling at the dentist's.'

'Just a minute,' she said and went to consult with the dentist. 'That'll be all right,' she said. 'Take a seat.'

When my turn came, the dentist took a look at my tooth and then shook his head. 'There's no point in putting another filling in it,' he said. 'It's too far gone for that. I'm afraid it'll have to come out.'

'Could you not root-fill it?'

He whipped round to stare at me. 'Who told you about root-fillings?' he said, as if I'd just revealed a state secret.

'My father was a dentist,' I said.

I got my root filling. According to a different dentist who subsequently redid it, the original one didn't make much of a job of it, but I could hardly blame him for that; he clearly didn't get much practice at anything except extractions.

As a result of their indifference to preventative and restorative dentistry, many of our older locals had gap-toothed, or even two- or one-toothed smiles, since few bothered to fill the gap left by extractions with anything other than a whistle. However, the younger and sometimes vainer farmers didn't want to damage their marriage prospects by gumless gurning at their prospective brides and, since crowns were both prohibitively expensive and almost unheard of in the Dale in those far off days, false teeth were the only option.

One of our younger regulars, Ernie, was a loud and somewhat chippy motor-mouth with a set of very bad teeth. He also had a few bad habits. I was changing a barrel in the beer-cellar one night when Sue put her head round the door. 'Ernie's on the pool table,' she said.

I gave her a puzzled look. 'Well he often is. He's the captain of the pool team.'

'No, I mean he's really on the pool table.'

When I got through to the back bar, 'Bat Out of Hell' was blasting out of the juke box at top volume and Ernie was indeed on the pool table – dancing on it in his work-boots, with his thumbs hooked into his belt, his eyes closed and a seraphic smile on his face. I switched off the jukebox, freeze-framing him in mid-stomp. 'Ernie,' I said. 'What do you think you're doing?'

'Dancing.'

I'd asked for that. 'Well, do you mind not doing it on top of the pool table?' I glanced down at his boots. 'Especially when you've been mucking out the cowsheds before coming up here.' He gave me a sheepish grin and clambered down.

When not stomping on the pool table, Ernie was often beset by toothaches that may not have been entirely unconnected with his excessive consumption of sugar, junk food and chocolate bars and his evident disinterest in the use of a toothbrush. By the time he was nineteen, the pain proved too much to bear and Ernie proudly announced his decision: he was going to have all his teeth – top and bottom sets, aching or not –

extracted and replaced with a glittering pearly-white set of false teeth.

He set off for the nearby market town one morning and showed up in the pub that night still groggy from the anaesthetic, pale of face and bereft of teeth. His bloody and swollen gums, he informed us, would need a couple of weeks to settle down before his 'falsies' could be fitted, and meanwhile he would be living on soup, crustless white bread and anything else his toothless jaws could cope with.

That first night his mouth was too sore to eat anything and he contented himself with a couple of pints, strictly against medical orders since the liquid sloshing around in his mouth was likely to set his gums bleeding again. By day two, he was teasing himself with a little sieved soup, and by day three he was up for solids. He tried potato crisps first, but the sharp edges hurt his gums and dunking them in his lager made both the beer and crisps unpalatable. We offered various alternatives, and while he was pondering his choices, his gaze was caught by a jar behind the bar and he favoured me with a toothless grin. 'I'll have a pickled egg.'

I had tried to get rid of the pickled eggs a few times in the past. The smell of malt vinegar whenever the jar was opened brought tears to my eyes, the eggs had the texture of parboiled squash balls and I couldn't imagine why anyone in their right minds would want to eat anything that hideous, but some of our locals loved them, so they had to stay. I fished one out of the jar with a spoon and placed it in one of the paper bun-cases we kept for the purpose. Grey-white in colour, the egg looked like a dead shark's eyeball and, for all I know, may have tasted like one too. I pushed it across the bar to Ernie, who picked it up, tried and failed to bite the rubbery egg in half with his toothless gums and then popped the whole thing into his mouth. Two minutes later he was still gumming away on the pickled egg, which, occasionally visible as he struggled for a better gum-grip, appeared to be resolutely unbroken.

I could see people nudging each other and heads turning around the bar, and the whole pub eventually fell silent as every eye watched Ernie's struggle. Finally, after almost five minutes of gumming, gurning and toothless gnashing, Ernie achieved a breakthrough and the crumbs of dingy yellow yolk spilling from the corners of his tooth-less mouth showed that he had at last chewed through the India rubber white. With a final gulp, helped by a mouthful of his beer, Ernie swallowed the last remnants. There was a poignant silence. 'That was grand,' he said. 'Give us another egg.'

For the next ten days, we endured the twice- or thrice-nightly ordeal of Ernie gumming a pickled egg to death and we were probably even more relieved than he was when the dentist at last fitted Ernie's new gnashers, allowing him to revert to his traditional pub fare of pork pie and plain crisps.

Even Ernie's gums would have been a welcome sight by the end of that shocking winter of 1979 – in the North at least, right up there with those of 1947 and 1963 as the worst of the century. In 1947 the first customer of the year had not appeared until 4 April, to be greeted with a cry of 'Happy New Year' from the landlord as the first living soul he had seen that year, and in 1963 the inn was cut off for fourteen weeks. Even with modern snow ploughs, snow blowers and JCBs to help with snow clearing, our first winter at the Inn at the Top saw us cut off for all but a handful of days between 28 December and the end of April.

Supplies of food were a continuing major headache. Like all Dale households, we had stocked up heavily with food and fuel in the autumn, but the length and severity of the winter and the unexpected numbers of stranded guests meant that, even with Uncle Olaf's emergency supplies and a very occasional top-up at the village shop when we could get out for a little while, our food supplies were constantly depleted. Even on the few days when the snow blowers broke through, it was impossible to go far in search of replacements, for even on a sunny day the wind would quickly blow snow back into the track cleared by the blowers, blocking the road again in an hour or so.

Most times our only way out was on foot, on fine days making the journey down towards the hamlet at the bottom of the hill, where our next-door neighbour – if that's an accurate description of someone who lived four miles away – left for us just inside the door of his outlying barn our un-delivered mail and newspapers and often the treat of some home-baked scones or cakes from his wife. On one occasion, I walked right down into the Dale to make sure a couple who had been snowed in with us for a week got there safely. It was a struggle for all of us, for the snowdrifts were enormous, and the new-fallen snow was as soft and powdery as talc, so that every footfall was an effort. Often we plunged waist- or even chest-deep into a drift and even had to roll around until we'd flattened the snow enough to give our boots purchase as we hauled ourselves out and struggled on.

Leaving them in the valley bottom, where they could continue their journey down the Dale to their home along roads that had been partially cleared by the snow blowers, I set off back towards the inn. Although relatively little snow was falling, the wind, the cold and the constant battling through drifts that were never less than waist-deep left me absolutely exhausted. Several times a voice in my head kept telling me to just stop, sit down and rest for a while, but I was frightened that if I did so, I would rapidly succumb to hypothermia and never get up, so I plodded on, dragging one foot after another until the inn at last came in sight. I was so shattered that, as soon as I got through the door, I lay down on the flagstone floor in the bar and Sue had to shake me awake to get me out of my wet clothes.

The landlord in the 1947 winter had an even greater struggle. He set out for a nearby town on the seventh of February, to visit his wife's parents and reassure them about their daughter, who had been unable to contact them for over a month. Leaving the inn at 11a.m., he and a local farmer trudged sixteen miles through the snow, encountering twenty-five-foot drifts on the way down to the Dale. Returning the next day, he was unable to walk further than the hamlet at the foot of the hill leading to the pub, where he stayed the night. He set off to complete his journey the next day, through a blizzard that reduced visibility to a couple of yards, but fought his way onwards and eventually reached the inn, having taken three hours to cover the last four miles.

On days such as those, with the wind lashing snow across the fells at terrifying speed and visibility dropping close to nil, only the most vital tasks would persuade anyone to leave the warmth and safety of their firesides. Yet every day, in all weathers, the farmers were out gathering and foddering their sheep, digging them out of drifts and often beating a path for them to follow down to the relative safety of the lower pastures.

One frigid day that winter, I set off to look for his sheep with Ben, one of our regulars. The snowstorm that had been raging for a couple of days had now blown itself out, leaving huge drifts piled up wherever a wall, a bluff or a drop in the ground had slackened the wind and caused part of its burden of snow to fall. Other exposed areas had been scoured clear by the force of the wind; dark, bare patches, almost shocking in their contrast to the aching expanses of white.

In a bad blizzard, the sheep often huddled together for warmth, like a flock of penguins in the Antarctic, but those on the windward side continually moved round to seek shelter in the lee of the others. As each rank was exposed, it also moved round to the other side and in that way, the whole flock could be driven for miles by the wind.

We were out on the fell early. A few small groups of sheep were visible, standing immobile, fleece-deep in snow, but many more were lost, buried in gills, behind walls and in a host of other places. They all had to be located and dug out, but first we started the long and arduous process of leading a group of sheep down to the foddering ground, a patch of moor swept clear of snow by the wind.

In deep snow the sheep either could not or would not move unaided and we first had to make a path, trampling a way through the snow for a few yards, then dragging one reluctant sheep along it. 'If the snow's that deep,' Ben said, 'usually you can't shift them until you have wandered a track through a big deep drift to set them off, but with sheep, if one goes, the rest will follow, they all go.'

Neither frost nor thaw had yet worked upon the new snow, which was so fine and soft it had the texture of flour. A drift would bear no weight at all, each footfall sank deep and there was no purchase to aid the next step. I dropped into a snow-filled gully and floundered helplessly for a minute, struggling to compress the snow enough to clamber out. Ben's keener eye had detected a difference in the snow over the gully and he had skirted it, pausing to watch my struggles with amusement.

Once the visible sheep had been moved and foddered, we began the search for the buried ewes. Struggling up the snow along a gill side, Ben's dog 'set' a buried sheep, her nose picking up the faint scent through the drift. She began scrabbling down through the snow, but Ben called her off and five minutes' digging with a shovel broke through to two bedraggled ewes, little the worse for their forty-eight hours beneath the snow.

I asked Ben about this uncanny gift some dogs have for finding sheep under the snow. 'Not many have it,' he said. 'We've been gare [very] fortunate that way, we always seem to have had one, but in my time, I've just had three out of near on a hundred dogs at one time and another with the knack.'

'How long would those sheep have lasted, if we hadn't found them?' I said.

He shrugged. 'If a sheep's buried under a drift, it could last a long time, unless it's thawed pretty fast and a big weight of snow has come down on it. It depends on the time of year; if it's January or February, when they're not too heavy with lamb, they could last up to a fortnight, but you try to find them within a week, if you know where to look, that's the point, like. They'll often get in gills, and follow them away down out of the wind and often enough, you'll find them at the back of walls, buried five or six foot deep. It's pretty good for a dog to sniff them out of those sort of places, you know, but you can imagine over a wide area, there are a lot of places where you can bury sheep; there are a lot of places where you can bury a man, like.'

We stayed out on the fell until night was falling, then Ben took a last look over his sheep, clustered around the hay he had scattered, and we headed for home, me to the pub and Ben to his farm at the foot of the moor. I watched him as he kick-started his three-wheeler, one of many recent changes in a shepherd's life on these fells. 'We got rid of our last horse a year ago,' he said. 'We've always used them for shepherding, but we use iron horses, three-wheelers and the like, now.' The engine kicked into life and he wheeled away down the fell, his dogs chasing behind, crossing and recrossing the tyre tracks through the snow.

Despite all the farmers' efforts and the sheep's strength and ability to endure hardship, many sheep buried under the drifts starved to death or suffocated in the unforgiving weather, and many others were to drown when the thaw at last came. Many of the survivors were so weakened that they lost their lambs or themselves died later in the spring, but sheep losses that winter of 1979 were nothing compared to 1947, when many farmers were virtually wiped out, with individual farmer's losses numbering several hundred sheep.

Ben had told me of one local farmer whose timing had been unfortunate enough for him to have moved on to a hill farm at the start of February 1947, just days before the snowstorms began. 'He took over a farm with 500 ewes,' Ben said, 'and finished up, three months later, with 170 ewes and twelve lambs. There would be chaps up this valley just about wiped out by the storms.' Back then farmers were unable to obtain or afford food for their sheep in the worst winter weather, and even if they were able to do so, there would have been little hope of transporting it to them.

While sympathizing with the misfortunes his peers had endured, Ben showed a farmer's brisk lack of sentiment about the animals they reared in his choice of the word 'stuff' to describe them. 'They wouldn't be fed the same as they are today,' he said. 'They would never really have had enough feed about and hay would be bad to get hold of. Well I suppose they soon starve to death, does stuff [livestock] if they don't get plenty to eat in what we call hungry weather, when the severe east winds are on. They're not getting much anywhere else if it's that bad and the ground's frozen up, they're just going to get what you give them. Now we give sheep the likes of sugar beet, which keeps them up, but in 1947 they would never get any other feed than hay. Well, it would be too long a storm, wouldn't it? And they wouldn't have had enough to eat. I would say that would be the top and bottom of it. They will only stand so much, will stuff, before they'll crack up.'

Farmers in 1979 were much better off. Their sheep entered winter in better condition and their diet of heather and moorland grasses was supplemented with hay, sugar beet and other feed. Nonetheless, many of our locals lost scores of sheep, together with an incalculable number of lambs to premature births, spontaneous abortions, or because their mothers were simply too weak to care for them.

Even when winter was apparently over it could still carry a terrible sting in its tail. In one year a bad, unexpected storm broke out at lambing time. 'It blew up drastic, out of the blue,' Ben said. 'I'd been out on the fells, gathering in sheep ready for lambing. It was a lovely, red-hot day. At night it was as quiet as it is now, but the next morning when we got up, it was snowing. It'd whitened all over, but that was nothing unusual for that time of year. You could often get a snow in the night but it'd usually have gone by dinner [lunch] time. This time it never did, it just kept snowing and snowing and by night it'd got quite a lot on. Then it got to blowing and there was a tremendous weight of snow, we'd forever of stuff buried under the snow. We were around the middle of lambing time. We lost about fifty lambs that would be born that day. As they were born, they were buried, they never got a chance to get up. I know we'd an awful lot, it kept us going doing nowt else but digging out sheep for days. At the end of it, we'd lost very few yows – adult sheep, as you might say – we lost a few hoggs that we'd not turned out on the moor so long, but on the whole we came off well with the situations as it was. With lambs you can't expect nowt else, they'd only be a week old or less and it just buried them wherever they were, there was that much snow in a short time and drifted too.'

Hard though the winter was for us at the Inn at the Top, we did not have to fight our way through the snow day after day and week after week to fodder sheep, nor did we risk losing our livelihood and perhaps even being bankrupted. We could only marvel at the fortitude of the farmers of the area, past and present, and at the tenacity of past landlords of the Inn at the Top, who, uncomplaining, survived the worst of winters with only tallow dips or oil lamps for light and an open fire for heat ... although, come to think of it, in that winter of 1978–9, that's all we had too!

Even up there on those cold, unforgiving 'tops', the weather eventually relented, and the snow began to thaw, though there were still decaying remnants of the giant drifts in north-facing gullies even in July. We had survived our first winter on that lonely, windswept hilltop. It would have been difficult in any circumstances, but Stan and Neville's tight-fistedness had caused us to spend one of the harshest winters of the century with no heat other than an open fire, no hot water, no light and no power and, had at least contributed to the loss of my front teeth and the fall down the stairs that could easily have fractured my skull instead of leaving me with concussion and a few scars. Coupled with their numerous other misdemeanours, we were disinclined to go on working for them any longer. We gave our notice to quit, but privately vowed to each other that if and when the pub ever came up for sale, we would somehow raise the money and come back there as owners.

Our departure from the pub was emotional, even tearful. We'd made a lot of good friends while we were there, many of whom turned out for the farewell party we threw on our last night and most of them were back again to say goodbye as we got ready to drive away the next morning. We promised them all that we'd stay in touch and that we'd come back and run the pub again one day, but they knew as well as we did that its fate was not in our hands.

We stopped at the moor edge and looked back at the inn, a dark speck in a wilderness of snow-streaked moorland, and there was an empty feeling inside both of us as we took a last look at what we still thought of as our home. 'We will be back one day, won't we?' Sue said.

I nodded, 'They'll have to sell it sooner or later, and when they do, we'll find the money to buy it somehow.' It was big talk from someone who now had no house, no job and no money at all, but as we drove on down into the Dale, I felt certain that, come what may, we'd be back at the Inn at the Top one day.

The publishers hope that this book has given you enjoyable reading. Large Print Books are especially designed to be as easy to see and hold as possible. If you wish a complete list of our books please ask at your local library or write directly to:

Magna Large Print Books
Magna House, Long Preston,
Skipton, North Yorkshire.
BD23 4ND

This Large Print Book for the partially sighted, who cannot read normal print, is published under the auspices of

THE ULVERSCROFT FOUNDATION